Auchinleck

Philip Warner, well known as a military historian and lecturer, joined the Army after graduating from Cambridge in 1939, and served throughout the war, mainly in the Far East. Among his works are *Panzer*, *The SAS*, *Alamein* and the *D-Day Landings*. Until recently he was a Senior Lecturer at the Royal Military Academy, Sandhurst.

Auchinleck
The Lonely Soldier
PHILIP WARNER

SPHERE BOOKS LIMITED
30-32 Gray's Inn Road, London WC1X 8JL

First published in Great Britain by
Buchan & Enright Ltd 1981
Copyright © Philip Warner 1981
Published by Sphere Books Ltd 1982

TRADE
MARK

Printed and bound in Great Britain by
Collins, Glasgow

CONTENTS

... I am become a name;
For always roaming with a hungry heart
Much have I seen and known; cities of men
And manners, climates, councils, governments,
Myself not least, but honour'd of them all;
And drunk delight of battle with my peers,
Far on the ringing plains of windy Troy.

From *Ulysses*, Alfred, Lord Tennyson

CHRONOLOGY

of the life and career of Field-Marshal Sir Claude Auchinleck

21 June 1884 Born at Aldershot

1896–1901 Wellington College

January–December 1902 RMA, Sandhurst

March 1903 Joins KSLI in India while awaiting posting in Indian army

April 1904 Joins 62nd Punjab Regiment

1906–7 Frontier duties at Gyantse, Tibet

1907 Commands 2nd Detachment, Sikkim

1908 Benares

1909 Captain and Adjutant

1912 Assistant Recruiting Officer, North Punjab

4 August 1914 Outbreak of First World War

28 October 62nd sail for France, but diverted to defend Suez Canal

3 February 1915 62nd drive off Turkish attack on Canal

12 July 62nd embark for Aden

21 July Sheikh Othman battle – Turks defeated
Operations against Turks and Arabs

31 December 62nd land at Basra for Mesopotamian campaign

7 January 1916 Join forces under Gen. Aylmer attempting to relieve Maj.-Gen. Townshend's division besieged in Kut-al-Amara

8 January 62nd in Sheikh Sa'ad battle

21 January Attack on Hanna Redoubt. 62nd suffer heavily. A. made Acting Adjutant

8 March Attack on Dujaila Redoubt. After heavy casualties and death of Lt-Col Commanding A. takes command of remaining 12 officers and 235 ORs

29 April Townshend surrenders Kut with 12,000 prisoners

August 1916–March 1917 62nd in operations (now under Gen. Maude) to recapture Kut. A. temporary Regimental Commander 8 February 1917. Fall of Baghdad 11 March 1917. Operations north of Baghdad

Summer 1917 A. Brigade Major to 52 Brigade

2 November 1918 Turkey signs Armistice

Summer 1919 GSO2 in Mosul

August 1919 GSO1 operations in Kurdistan

Late 1919 Promoted Brevet Lt-Col, sent to Staff College, Quetta on 1 year's course

Late 1920 1 year's home leave. Married Jessie Stewart of Kinloch Rannoch, Scotland, 1921

1921–5 DAA and QMG, Simla

1925–7 2 i/c 1/1st Punjabis (formerly 62nd Punjabis)

1927 1 year's course at Imperial Defence College, London

1929–30 CO 1/1st Punjabis. Promoted full Colonel

1930–3 Instructor, Staff College, Quetta

back to frontier. Beginning of 'Gazala Gallop'

20 June Tobruk cut off – Ritchie decides to fall back beyond frontier to Mersa Matruh

21 June Tobruk captured with loss of 33,000 Allied prisoners

25 June A. dismisses Ritchie and personally takes command of Eighth Army

25–9 June Holding action at Mersa Matruh (falls 29 June). Eighth Army falls back on El Alamein

1–27 July First Alamein. A. checks Rommel then counter-attacks, causing havoc, notably among Italians. British positions strengthened

27 July Eighth Army goes back on to defensive

3 August Churchill, Brooke, Smuts and Wavell arrive in Cairo to discuss Middle East command situation

5 August Churchill decides to replace A. with Gen Alexander as C-in-C, with Maj.-Gen. Gott in command of Eighth Army

7 August Gott killed, Montgomery chosen as Eighth Army commander

8 August A. notified, by letter, of his dismissal

12 August Montgomery arrives in Cairo. Takes over command of Eighth Army on next day, though official hand-over date fixed for 15th

15 August A. hands over officially to Alexander, and leaves for India

August 1942–June 1943 A. in India without formal position, having refused Iraq-Persia Command

30 August–1 July 1942 Second Alamein (Alam Halfa)

23 October–4 November Third Alamein

18 June 1943 A. appointed C-in-C India for the second time with effect from the 20th, with Wavell as Viceroy

24 August Formation of SE Asia Command, with Mountbatten as Supreme Commander. Indian Army operations in Burma and other theatres

8 May 1945 Unconditional surrender of Germany

June All-Party Conference in India. Jinnah proposes separate Pakistan

July General Election in Britain. New Labour government formed under Attlee

6 and 9 August A-bombs on Hiroshima and Nagasaki

14 August Unconditional surrender of Japan

November Start of trials in Delhi of former members of Indian National Army

1945–6 General elections in India confirm desire for independence

January–February 1946 Strikes at RAF stations in India. Mutiny of Royal Indian Navy at Bombay. Rioting in Calcutta in support of ex-INA soldiers

April British Cabinet Mission to India. Publishes proposals in May for transfer of power – rejected by Jinnah

1 June Auchinleck promoted Field-Marshal. Divorce from wife announced

16 August Muslim League's 'Direct Action Day'. Severe rioting in Calcutta and elsewhere. Visit of F-M Montgomery, now CIGS

20 February 1947 Announcement by British government for date for transfer of power – 'not later

INTRODUCTION

In 1884, when a son was born to Colonel John Auchin-leck, no one of military background expected the boy to become a general, still less a commander-in-chief. Anyone who thought that either he himself, or his son, might become a field-marshal would probably be considered to have been affected by the sun in one of the less attractive stations of his service. But Auchinleck's boy, christened Claude John Eyre, was destined to be just that, and more; three times a commander-in-chief, an honoured field-marshal, he would also be, in the eyes of many, the best general of the Second World War.

Yet the man who was to become so skilled at seeing and defeating his country's enemies would be sadly inept at perceiving and frustrating his own. His nature, however, would be such that he would bear neither resentment nor malice against fate and its instruments. He would be endowed with a magnanimity which would forgive, though not forget, and with a temperament which would exclude any form of self-pity; from his origins and his experience he would fashion a spirit at once humble yet self-sufficient, austere yet tolerant. An honest ambition to excel would bring him some of the richest rewards of service, and it would also bring him three blows each of which, singly, might have broken the spirit of a lesser man.

It might seem that a man who achieves the rank of field-marshal and lives to an advanced age in good health, admired and loved, has no cause for sorrow or regrets, and certainly Auchinleck displayed neither. But it cannot be easy to suffer the frustration of having one's achievements credited to another while being pushed oneself towards obscurity; to lose one's wife, after twenty-four years, to a friend and fellow commander; and then to be given the task of presiding over the destruction of an army to which one has given a lifetime. All these might seem ample reasons for bitterness, but there was none.

I have tried to show both the causes and the effects of Auchinleck's magnanimity. He was not a saint, and would have been horrified to have been thought so; for all his courage and skill he could be obstinate and, perhaps, over-fatalistic, and his kindness to others would lead to the sometimes well-founded charge that he 'could not pick his subordinates'. Those who hold that belief will cite his choice of Cunningham, Ritchie, Corbett, Dorman-Smith, perhaps forgetting that he also chose de Guingand, that Ritchie retrieved and convincingly won 'Crusader', and that under Auchinleck were formed or flourished the Long-Range Desert Group, the 'Jock Columns', the Special Air Service, and the Chindits – all of them well established among the legends of warfare.

In the end, Auchinleck was a soldier, an 'honest-to-God soldier'; in that, perhaps, lie the seeds of his loneliness. Superbly professional, his grasp of a battle, and his command of often ill-trained and ill-equipped – and sometimes demoralised – troops, were second to none; his eye for ground, his strategic planning and administration, and his ability to drive men on by his presence and example remain largely unrivalled. But he was no politician, having scant time or respect for that breed, in or out of the services, and his failure to learn the art of manipulation brought him humiliation at a time of considerable personal triumph. For that reason I have called him the 'lonely soldier'; not because he lacked friendship or popularity – indeed, few senior commanders can have been so well loved – but because he had schooled himself to face his setbacks alone and in the expectation that he would be treated as he treated others. And lonely, too, because his uncomplaining nature caused him to keep within himself, until dissipated, any reasons for anger or bitterness.

In writing this book I have received an enormous amount of help and encouragement from many sources, not least from those who knew or worked with the Field-Marshal. First I must thank the *Daily Telegraph*, which published my letter requesting first-hand information on Auchinleck's life and career. Secondly, I am very grateful to all those in the list below (which I hope is comprehensive) who have helped with this book and who have generously given me information, time and advice: Lt-Gen. Sir Terence Airey, KCMG, CB, CBE; Lt-Col. A. G. S. Alexander; Lt-Col. Clive Auchinleck; Mark Baker Esq.; Correlli Barnett Esq.; Mrs John Becher; Mrs Elizabeth Beecher; Col. Norman Berry, OBE, BSc; Brigadier Shelford Bidwell; Anthony Brett-James Esq.; Brigadier F. M. de Butts, CMG, OBE, DL; Roger Cary Esq.; Norman Clark Esq.; Leo Cooper Esq.; D. N. Cornock-Taylor Esq.; W. M. Cunningham Esq.; Captain A. J. Daldy; Brigadier M. Dauncey, DSO; David Dimbleby Esq.; Miss A. R. Dowe; Robert B. Dyer Esq.; Nicholas Eadon Esq.; Maj.-Gen. J. G. Elliott, CIE; Lt-Col. P. J. Emerson; I. H. Foulkes Esq.; Brigadier H. L. Graham, CBE, MC; Brigadier P. W. P. Green, CBE, DSO; Major A. A. Greenwood; A. Greville Young Esq.; A. R. Hall Esq.; DFC; Charles Harding Esq.; E. G. A. Hillesley Esq.; Mrs W. G. Hobson; Lt-Col. D. Holmes, DSO; Mrs Dorothy Hossack; Professor Michael Howard, MC; Sir David Hunt, KCMG, OBE; General Sir Peter Hunt, GCB, DSO, OBE; Mrs Cerise Jackson; the late Rear-Admiral Sir Rowland Jerram, KBE, DSO, DL; Geoffrey Keating Esq., MC; Mrs J. P. Lawford; Mrs R. B. Ledward, Ronald Lewin Esq.; Kenneth Lewis Esq., DL, MP; Captain D. Lynch, MBE, DCM; R. T. Macfarlane Esq.; Mrs P. MacGrath; A. MacKinnon Esq., MC; D. St J. Magnus Esq.; Mrs F. M. Marsh; G. Martin Esq.; Miss Glenise Matheson; Colonel B. A. E. Maude; C. F. G. Max-Muller Esq.; Mrs Anne Naylor; Lt-Col. R. C. Nicholas; Lt-Col. R. W. Niven; Michael Noakes Esq., PPROI, RP; Philip Oversby Esq.; Brigadier S. W. Packwood; Lady Peirse; the Rt Hon. Enoch Powell, MBE, MP; Major N. E. Price; Colonel W. K. Pryke; Neville Rayner Esq., JP; Mrs E. Rogers; Mrs Georgina Scott; Lt-Col. G. A. Shepperd, MBE; General Sir Frank Simpson, KBE, CB, DSO; G. P. Smart Esq.; Dr and Mrs Christopher St Johnston; T. C. Sutherland Esq.; Dr John Sweetman; Sir Ian Trethowan; Geoffrey Wansell Esq.;

Mrs B. Warren; the Rev. C. F. Warren; Miss S. Warren; Brigadier Peter Young, DSO, MC, MA.

I have received a great deal of help from the India Office Library, the Public Record Office, the Royal Military Academy, Sandhurst, Library, the John Rylands Library at the University of Manchester, and the Society of Antiquaries Library. And finally, I must express my thanks to Cassell Ltd which, at a sadly difficult time, permitted the script of this book to be released for publication.

The author and publishers are grateful to the following for permission to quote material which is copyright: the Estate of the late Field-Marshal Sir Claude Auchinleck, GCB, GCIE, CSI, DSO, OBD, LLD; Cassell Ltd for extracts from *The Second World War* by Sir Winston Churchill, and from *Auchinleck: A Critical Biography* by John Connell; the John Rylands Library at the University of Manchester, which holds the Auchinleck Papers. Transcripts of Crown Copyright material in the Public Record Office appear by permission of the Controller, Her Majesty's Stationery Office. All those whose conversations or letters are quoted appear in the list above, and their names also appear at the relevant points in the text.

ORIGINS

The world into which the future Field-Marshal Sir
Claude Auchinleck was born in 1884 was by no means as
stable and assured as it appears ninety-seven years later.
From the turmoil and uncertainties of the 1980s we look
back wistfully to the apparent balance, self-confidence
and orderliness of the Victorian era. Even its bad taste in
furniture, ornaments and architecture has a comforting
reassurance, even an exuberance. To the Victorians,
however, the outlook in 1884 may well have seemed
ominously gloomy. In the Officers' Club in Aldershot,
which since 1846 had been furnished in a way which made
it almost indistinguishable from any club from China to
the West Indies, the older members would read *The Times*
thoughtfully and ponder. Military experience had given
them the habit of making a mental summary of what they
had read. It was called – somewhat misleadingly – 'making
an appreciation'. It might have run something like this:

Russia was undoubtedly determined to expand, and
the lesson taught them in the Crimea had all too clearly
been forgotten. She was putting pressure on Finland,
was threatening Turkey and had just annexed Merv in
Afghanistan. Having got a foothold in Afghanistan what
would she be up to next? For some reason, the Russians
were persecuting and harrying their own Jews. They
couldn't even run the vast territories they already possessed, yet they seemed to be trying to acquire more.

Fortunately the Russians weren't in Africa, but the
Germans were which was as bad. When Gladstone had
been returned to power in 1880 everyone had hoped that
he would show some statesmanship. But almost at once
he had failed the country miserably in the Boer War of
1881. The Boers had declared themselves independent in
the Transvaal and had defeated a small force of ours at
Majuba Hill. Instead of sending in more troops he had left

the defeat unavenged and weakly given the Boers their independence. The folly of that was shown when rich gold deposits had been found on the Witwatersrand earlier in 1884. The Germans were encouraging the Boers and, unlike Britain's own dithering government, the Germans seemed to know what they were doing. Germany had occupied South-West Africa last April and they were going to do the same in Togoland and the Cameroons. Bismarck had organised a fourteen-nation conference on Africa in Berlin on the pretext of rooting out the remains of slavery and opening up the Congo river to free trade. Nearer home he had forged a link right down Europe by bringing Italy into the alliance the Germans already had with the Austrians; he would no doubt make a useful tool of this Triple Alliance.

The situation in Ireland looked as bad as ever. Only two years ago Lord Frederick Cavendish, the Secretary for Ireland, and his Under-Secretary, had been murdered in broad daylight in Phoenix Park by a group of fanatics who called themselves 'the Invincibles'. Gladstone would make the Irish situation worse than ever; you could depend on it. Instead of acting swiftly and firmly and then being generous afterwards he always tried to do it the other way round. Look at the Soudan. A Moslem fanatic who called himself the Mahdi had wiped out a British force under Hicks and had now penned up General Gordon in Khartoum. Gladstone still hadn't sent a relief force and God only knew what might happen to Gordon.

Of course, if you were a soldier some of this was quite good news, a chance of a scrap, decorations and promotion. But it would not be much fun if the odds were all wrong and Gladstone knuckled under at the first defeat. Nor if you were as heavily outnumbered as the 24th Foot had been at Isandhlwana in the Zulu War. There was a brighter note, however. An American called Maxim had settled in London and invented a reliable machine-gun which used the recoil to eject spent cartridges and reload. It would be very useful against large numbers, like these Soudanese fanatics perhaps, though of course it couldn't win a battle on its own. You would still need to go in with a bayonet and finish it – there was no other way. But

2

what a good thing Maxim was over here, working in London.

But all such thoughts, good or bad, would be far removed from the minds of those at 89 Victoria Road, Aldershot, on 21 June 1884. There Mary, wife of Lt-Col. J. C. A. Auchinleck, RHA, had just given birth to a son. A son was what every Army officer wished for, to follow him into the same regiment. This was wonderful news, for Mary was one of seven sisters and to have a son for their first-born was almost more than they had both dared hope for. Christened Claude John Eyre, he would go into the Army, of course, and the tradition of both sides of the family would be suitably carried on. They hoped he would do very well; and would command his regiment. Obviously some officers would go on and become generals but for the average Army family the height of ambition was to command the regiment. That achieved, life had few prizes to offer. To miss that appointment when it seemed within reach would be a devastating blow. Even the most unassuming and carefree young subaltern would have that particular ambition firmly fixed in the back of his mind.

From an examination of Auchinleck's heredity and early education it may be possible to discover the source, or sources, of his magnanimity. The Auchinlecks take their name from a village in Ayrshire (now Strathclyde) between Dumfries and Kilmarnock, about fifteen miles east of Ayr. The Gaelic name is 'Arch-ea-leuc' (sometimes given as 'Ach-an-leach'), meaning 'the field of the flat stone'. The district abounds in flat, shelving rock. The family appear to have been granted the lands, with a barony, under feudal tenure before the thirteenth century. The name appears on a 1292 Roll of those Scottish leaders who gave their allegiance to Edward I of England. At that period Anglo-Scottish relations were harmonious; soon after they deteriorated and remained bad for some 300 years. However, there were always bitter local feuds on either side of the border and these often continued when England and Scotland were at war; it is sometimes easier to hate a neighbour than an enemy of your nation. The Auchinlecks were related by marriage to the powerful Douglas family. In 1437 Elizabeth Douglas attempted to prevent the assassination of James I by putting her arm through the staples of a (missing) bar from the door. The younger sister of this intrepid woman married a James Auchinleck. There was more than one James Auchinleck at this time and one of them was killed in a feud with a Colville of Ochiltree Castle, which stands a bowshot from the original Auchinleck Castle. (There were two Auchinleck castles but both are now ruins.) James Auchinleck's death was promptly avenged by Earl Douglas who, in 1449, killed Colville and all his male retainers, and burnt Ochiltree Castle.

In 1499, when there was no direct heir, Sir John Auchinleck tried to settle the Auchinleck lands on William Cunningham, who had married Sir John's daughter. However, James IV of Scotland (later to be killed at Flodden in 1513) was extremely displeased at what he felt was a breach of feudal responsibility and confiscated the lands and the barony. He gave them to Thomas Boswell, who was also killed at Flodden, but the Boswells retained both subsequently. James Boswell, the biographer of Dr Samuel Johnson, came of this family.*

The Auchinlecks, therefore, having played a leading part in Scottish history for over 200 years, now found themselves without lands or title. When James VI of Scotland became James I of England he advised his Scottish chieftains to try their fortunes in Ireland, and the Auchinlecks took this advice.

Thus in the first years of the seventeenth century the Auchinlecks were Protestant settlers in Fermanagh, making no great impact but being comfortable in their lands. Several of them took Holy Orders, but in the early nineteenth century the two sons of the Reverend John Auchinleck chose to go into the Army. Both went into the Royal Artillery. The younger, William, had an uneventful career and became a colonel; he died at the age of sixty. The elder, John, went out to India, fought in the Mutiny in 1857 and in the Second Afghan War in 1878; he was

---

* The authorities for all these events are Chambers' *Caledonia*, and *Histories of Ayrshire* by Cranfield, Robertson and Paterson.

Claude Auchinleck's father. Officers in the Indian Army tended to marry late in life, possibly because their lives were too nomadic to make married life easy until they had reached a reasonable rank, and partly because there were not many opportunities for meeting suitable wives. Colonel John Auchinleck loved soldiering and he loved sport. The Gunners knew as much about horses as any regiment in the Army, and reckoned to be able to show the cavalry a thing or two when it came to sports involving horses; the cavalry might not always agree but sometimes found the Gunners' claim difficult to disprove.

John Auchinleck must have deemed himself especially lucky to have found a wife who was not only extremely beautiful but also as keen on horses and hunting as he was himself. Mary Eleanor Eyre was of old Anglo-Irish (Protestant) stock, daughter of John Eyre of Eyrecourt Castle, County Galway. She had six sisters, and they were known far and wide as 'the seven beautiful Misses Eyre'. At one time there had been a peerage in the family but it had lapsed when there was no direct heir. A more lasting influence was a very wild member of the family, Giles, who, a hundred years earlier, had brought them close to financial ruin. Another of her ancestors had founded the Galway Blazers, a hunt renowned for dash and daring in a country where the competition in such matters was exceptionally keen. She was fifteen years younger than he was. For ten years they had no children; then Claude was born. When he was a year old they went to India where Colonel Auchinleck commanded the Royal Horse Artillery batteries at Bangalore. There, Armar Leslie was born in 1887; then, back in England, came Cerise, always known as Cherry, and Ruth, known to many as Fay, but always called 'Goosey' by Auchinleck. Leslie, whose nickname was 'Tiny', had lost the sight of his right eye when he was hit by the lace of a football. He was therefore unable to take a commission in the Army, and instead went into the Colonial Service. He served in Northern Nigeria, but was on leave in Egypt when war was declared in 1914. He had originally been in the Cameronian 4th Special Reserve Battalion, and he now rejoined it. He was killed, two years later, on the Somme.

5

Those who knew both brothers thought that Tiny was potentially a more distinguished person than Claude, to whom he was a much-loved brother and constant companion. Their sister Cherry, now in her nineties, reports that as children Auchinleck and his brother fought endless campaigns and wars in the garden: Wellington's battles, Marlborough's battles, even Roman battles. There were no horses to ride, and only one bicycle in the family, and the Auchinleck children learnt to be self-reliant and to entertain themselves during the holidays. They often went to stay with their mother's family in Ireland in a large house with no amenities at all. The regime was very strict, too; Cherry remembers – though this could not have affected the children – that smoking inside the house at any time was strictly forbidden: anyone wishing to smoke after dinner, for instance, had to go out into the garden. The spartan atmosphere of this household probably helped in laying the foundations of Auchinleck's stoicism.

In 1890, two years before the last child was born, the Colonel retired from the Army. In the Third Burmese War in 1888 he had contracted some disease which left him with what was diagnosed as pernicious anaemia.

They went to live in a comfortable house in Langstone – near Havant in Hampshire – by the sea: it was thought that the iodine in the sea water would help to cure Colonel Auchinleck's anaemia. He lived for only another two years, however, dying in 1892 when his eldest child was eight, the second five, the third two and the youngest less than a year old.

There was very little money to add to Mary's widow's pension, although her late husband's brother often helped. She and the children moved to a smaller house in Warblington, not far from Langstone, and later to rooms. The outlook seemed bleak, but the wives of Indian Army officers became used to coping with unusual and sometimes terrifying situations. They learnt to put up with loneliness when their husbands were away on campaigns, and became accustomed to dealing with unexpected hazards such as snakes and scorpions. Mary Auchinleck wasted no time deploring her difficult predicament, but

6

tackled it with such resolution that she inspired her children to cope with whatever setbacks life might offer. She herself even went to work to supplement her pension of £90 a year; when her own family were away at school she helped to look after an invalid.

In 1974, when asked by David Dimbleby if his early life had been a struggle – 'Was it difficult for your family and yourself?' – Auchinleck's answer was: 'Oh, yes, because my mother was left a widow when I was quite young. Only about eight. And she had very little to live on except a widow's pension, which is not very much in the Army, really. But I was lucky because I was able to go to Wellington on a Foundation. Wellington is really a school founded for the sons of officers whose widows can't afford to send them to other schools. Otherwise I should never have gone to a public school. Quite impossible.'

It was during this period that Auchinleck's character and attitudes were formed. The Jesuit claim – 'Give me a child for his first seven years and he is mine for life' – has been proved often enough. Equally true is the fact that early influences and attitudes, perhaps from parents, perhaps from teachers, create a form of instinct. In Victorian times such attitudes were formed with a determination as strong as the Jesuits'; they came over in oft-repeated precepts and in the highly moral stories considered suitable reading or listening for children. As a young child Auchinleck probably had many such cautionary tales read to him; and when older he was an avid reader. He would have read of evil characters who were invariably defeated and killed, or would repent, sometimes on their deathbed. The evil-doers of Victorian days usually met – according to these stories – unpleasant though spectacular ends. Disobedience was enough to warrant such an end: disobey orders and go too near a cage, and get devoured by tigers; or wilful stupidity could suffice. The boy who cried 'Wolf!' because he liked to see the commotion his call created was eventually eaten by the wolf when his cries for help went unheeded. That there was good in everyone if patience was exercised; that evil doings brought their own reward; that compassion, truth and forgiveness were the greatest of virtues, were the themes

7

running through all the lessons which Claude Auchinleck absorbed, first at home, then at a small pre-preparatory school in Southsea, where he was a boarder.

Eight was quite a late age for becoming a boarder in Victorian times; children were often sent off to school much younger, particularly if their parents were abroad; many went at the age of five or six, and some began as early as two years old. At school the child had to rise early, and cope as best he could with awkward buttons and a starched Eton collar, which was agony to fix to a stud with fingers numb from washing in cold water. He learnt much by repetition on weekdays, and on Sunday experienced a day almost inconceivable in the present decade. Sunday meant best clothes, attendance at church, and no games of any kind; the only recreation permitted was the reading of books with a strong uplifting tone. Most children hated Sundays fervently, but felt guilty about doing so.

Such an upbringing might seem over-harsh to anyone nowadays, but it produced a child well-equipped for any setbacks life might offer. The virtues of hard work were stressed, but so was tolerance of the follies of others in the knowledge (or hope) that in time wisdom would prevail. Evil must not be allowed to triumph but great patience might be needed before it was defeated. The strong should help the weak. Aldous Huxley, product of a slightly later era, used to comment that from his uncle he had absorbed many ideas which he knew to be true, much which was nonsensical, but much, too, which influenced his thoughts without his ever being aware he had been taught it.

At the age of ten Auchinleck was sent to 'Mr Spurling's', a small preparatory school in the grounds of, and attached to, Wellington College, Berkshire. He did not, as had been surmised, go to Eagle House (then at Wimbledon) or to Crowthorne School. The school was run by the Reverend J. Spurling, who had been Assistant Master at Wellington under the first Headmaster, E. W. Benson, later Archbishop of Canterbury. Both Auchinleck and his friend Chenevix Baldwin recalled with concern their experiences at Mr Spurling's. The Spurlings were rigid disciplinarians, and the food was poor and inadequate. On

Sunday night a boy would have bread, butter and jam for supper if his weekly report was good. A moderate report meant no jam; a poor one meant no butter. The Spurlings stood at the dining-room door and informed each boy of his expectations. (Apparently the regime at this school was so harsh that some of the old boys considered taking some sort of action.)

When Auchinleck had measles, Mrs Spurling decided that healthy exercise would assist his convalescence. She produced croquet mallets and took him into the garden. Auchinleck, who had never played croquet, picked up a mallet and swung it like a golf club. Unfortunately, Mrs Spurling was just behind him and received a painful blow. From then on he was referred to as 'that evil boy Auchinleck who tried to kill the Headmaster's wife'.

In the summer term of 1896 Auchinleck left Mr Spurling's for Wellington College. Wellington had been founded in 1859 in honour of Arthur, first Duke of Wellington, for the education of the sons of deceased officers of the armies of England and India. Queen Victoria herself was the Visitor, the President was the Prince of Wales, and the Earl of Derby was Vice-President. Various suggestions had been made for a memorial to the Great Duke, and the endowment of Wellington was the most intelligent of them. The College was built and endowed from public subscription, and it provided for the education of Foundationers and Non-Foundationers. The former were the sons of deceased officers; they entered at the age of twelve at a cost of £10 per annum. However, it probably cost another £10 a year to keep the boy there, which Mrs Auchinleck was hard pressed to find. They had to pass an entrance examination in English, Arithmetic, Algebra, Euclid (Geometry), Latin and Greek. Subsequent education included Science, History, Geography, Divinity, French, German and Drawing. The aim of the course, from the beginning, had been for the boys to acquire a broad general education. Although somewhat austere both in appearance and setting, and with a strong military connection, Wellington has never been a 'philistine' school. On the contrary, the school has produced a number of boys who were later to rank high

9

in literary and cultural circles. Harold Nicolson was a contemporary of Auchinleck.

An advantage which a Wellington boy possessed over others in similar schools was to have a space he could call his own. This was because a boy entering Wellington became a member of a Dormitory, rather than a boy in a House as in other schools. Each Dormitory, containing thirty or so boys, had an equal number of partitioned cubicles. These contained a bed, a desk and a tin bath. This was a boy's own territory, where if he wished to withdraw and read he could; Auchinleck was an enthusiastic reader. There may be advantages in new boys sharing a common room at first and when more senior obtaining a study, but they are not too obvious to a quiet boy who finds the common room dominated by one or two large extroverts whose intellects have not taken them far enough up the school for them to qualify for a study. According to the Wellington archivist, Mr Mark Baker, Auchinleck joined the Beresford Dormitory (named after General Beresford of Napoleonic Wars fame)

and was given the school number of 348. His progress in the school appears to have been slow academically, in games and in the Rifle Volunteer Corps. In the Lent term of 1898 he was bottom of the Dormitory list. He went on to the Army side. In the Rifle Volunteer Corps he was promoted Lance-Corporal in May 1901 and Corporal in September. He played for his Dormitory XV as a forward in 1899, 1900 and 1901; this in itself does not mean a great deal as the Dormitories were then so small. However, his performance in the Michaelmas term 1900 was commended in the Dormitory book, he and another boy being the best among the forwards, who were a very good lot. But I can find no sign of his having played for the school.

In September 1901 the Beresford Dormitory was taken over by a new Tutor [housemaster] A. H. Fox Strangways, the distinguished musicologist.

He made Auchinleck a Dormitory Prefect, but he does not appear to have become a school prefect.

Conditions at Wellington between 1896 and 1902 were probably slightly more comfortable than in other public schools, for the buildings were newer than most, and were less cramped and inconvenient. Yet it was primitive by modern standards. Later, when Auchinleck showed complete indifference to personal comfort, particularly in the desert, memories of schooldays must have influenced his standards. He believed firmly in the virtues of the boarding school and at one stage mentioned that he did not see how a man could reach high rank without that experience. He was promptly contradicted by two other distinguished soldiers, Generals Montgomery and Simpson. Both had been day boys at public schools: the former at St Paul's, the second at Bedford.

But at home or at school a boy learnt to be self reliant. The two best known boys' magazines were the *Boy's Own Paper* and *Chums*. Both were full of rousing adventure stories, many set in distant and dangerous lands; the former was a little more careful of its moral tone but took care not to preach. Both contained a host of articles on how to keep any domestic pet, from spiders to donkeys, and both informed a boy how to make, with his own hands and cheaply, everything from a boat to an electric bell. The stories were written by authors who knew the countries and situations about which they wrote. Cold water seemed to be a universal panacea: schoolboys were advised to take cold baths (though usually they had no choice); one reader who complained of weak ankles was advised to pour cold water over them. In adventure stories near fatal wounds began to recover when washed in the nearest stream and bandaged up.

Among Auchinleck's friends at Mr Spurling's and Wellington were Chenevix Baldwin and Lewis Heath. Chenevix Baldwin – who later married Ruth Auchinleck – went on to command the 1st Gurkhas and was wounded in Mesopotamia. Heath (later Lt-Gen. Sir Lewis Heath) was recommended by Auchinleck to command III Indian Corps in Malaya, where Heath was forced to retreat down the peninsula to Singapore in 1942, there to be captured by the Japanese. In their days at school together. Auchinleck in his wildest dreams could not have visualised a situation in which he could recommend his friend to a command that would end in total disaster through circumstances well outside his control. Nor could he have imagined that his friend's predicament would, early in 1942, involve himself by taking away, as reinforcement, a division which was vital to his own needs.

Not a notably brilliant pupil at Wellington, Auchinleck did, however, achieve one distinction. He was joint winner of the Derby Gift. The Gift had been founded in 1865 by the Earl of Derby, then Prime Minister, and was financed from the royalties of his popular translation of Homer's *Iliad* into English blank verse. It was presented to the most deserving Foundationer of his year when he left the school – the qualities required were 'industry and good conduct' – and was intended to help the winner start his career. As it was originally worth £56, and was probably more at the end of the century, it must have seemed a small fortune to a boy living in the straitened circumstances of the average Foundationer. The terms of the Gift stated that it could be shared between two boys, which is what happened on this occasion: the other winner was Auchinleck's close friend Chenevix Baldwin, whose family circumstances were very similar to his own.

Where Auchinleck fell short was in mathematics, and, indeed, his lack of ability in that subject was a matter for concern as, to follow his father into the Gunners, Auchinleck would have needed to reach a certain standard of mathematics in order to try for the Royal Military Academy at Woolwich, which prepared cadets for commissions in the Royal Artillery and Royal Engineers. In the event it was to the Royal Military College, Sandhurst, which prepared for the infantry and cavalry, that Auchinleck went.

There were formidable problems at Sandhurst, however. Infantry and cavalry officers did not, and could not, live on their pay. Obviously, in the cavalry, with such expenses as horses, polo and elaborate uniforms, this might be expected; but it was unfortunately also true of the infantry, where even the most unassuming officers in line regiments had to keep up appearances. To live on his pay alone might have been possible for an officer who took no part in any activity or sport and wore his uniform the whole time – but nobody wanted an officer of that description. The ideal was a lively, sporting, well-turned-out, slightly reckless young man. The only hope for a man without private means was the Indian Army, where the pay was much higher and the cost of living, and sport, much less. Curiously enough, entry to the Indian Army was governed by the standard reached in the entrance examination to Sandhurst; a few years later this changed to the position on the order of merit on passing out. There were forty-five places allocated to the Indian Army on Auchinleck's intake and he took the forty-fifth. He was in, to everyone's surprise, not least his own. Six years later, when the system had been changed, Gentleman Cadet B. L. Montgomery passed out thirty-sixth. In that year thirty-five were taken for the Indian Army. It has been suggested that behind Montgomery's attitude to Auchinleck was the bitter disappointment of having failed, where, as he thought, a lesser man had succeeded. It seems unlikely. Montgomery was driven by a fierce and unscrupulous ambition which made him adopt some questionable tactics to achieve his ends, but it is doubtful that his attitude had such a petty motivation as having been rejected where Auchinleck had succeeded.

Sandhurst in those days was small. Today, now it has been amalgamated with the RMA Woolwich and takes in every candidate accepted for a commission on one course or another, long or short, its numbers fluctuate considerably but are never as low as the 360 of 1902. In Auchinleck's day the intake consisted of boys from public and, very occasionally, grammar schools. It was organised in companies and these were named by letters instead of after battles, as they are today. Auchinleck was posted to E Company, quartered in what is now known as the Old Building, which is the white Georgian edifice overlooking the King's Drive, Victoria Statue, and Lower Lake. Living conditions here were harder than they had been at Wellington. (In the nineteenth century life at Sandhurst had been so rigorous that at Wellington it was referred to as 'hell over the hill'.) A contemporary of Montgomery at Sandhurst said that the most fearsome part of Old College life was the lavatories which were out at the back of the building, and which he described as 'survivals from a former age'. (It was of course the custom then and much later to have lavatories outside.) Sandhurst made a great feature of riding but this did not have much appeal for Auchinleck. In spite of the enthusiasm for horses shown by both his parents, horsemanship had little interest for him. When he was Commander-in-Chief in India during the Second World War some magnificent horses were put at his disposal; he never rode once.

In December 1902 he passed out. His position is still confidential information, but it was much lower than the position at which he had entered. He was eighteen and a half, and the first stage of his career was over. After two months' leave, he sailed for India in March 1903.

So far, Auchinleck's achievements had been modest. At Wellington he had been moderately successful: he had worked hard, winning prizes in historical subjects, and his industry had received recognition in the form of the Derby Gift. He had played games with more enthusiasm than skill, but was a moderately good shot: his sister Cherry remembers him as not being attracted by team games, preferring to rely on his own skills in a contest, outdoor or indoor, rather than on those of a partner. At Sandhurst he appears to have coasted along gently, well aware that his next destination was assured provided he kept out of trouble. He had realised the first part of his ambition – for, from his earliest days soldiering had been his main interest – and if he had other ambitions he did not speak of them. Considering his circumstances he was probably wise not to seek to distinguish himself.

The greatest influence on him had undoubtedly been his mother, whose cheerfulness, courage and ability to see the humorous side of everything had enabled the family to be extremely happy in a situation that was far from easy. After many years observing his mother's refusal to be beaten or cast down by adversity, Auchinleck could never fall into the trap of self-pity.

INDIA

If a man could not enjoy himself when a subaltern (a second-lieutenant and lieutenant) he was unlikely ever to do so. Admittedly the euphoria of feeling that he had achieved a position of authority soon wore off and was replaced by an awareness of responsibility for which his seniors repeatedly pointed out he was quite unfitted. He might be regarded as promising material, but no one would give him any hint of it. For his first year in India Auchinleck was attached to the King's Shropshire Light Infantry to learn the ropes. This custom of attaching newly-commissioned Indian Army officers to British regiments was a sensible one, for they could learn from their mistakes without feeling too humiliated. There is general expectation that they will make mistakes and the regiments look forward to them with benign amusement. Warrant Officers and NCOs will tactfully proffer advice, and men will accept the discomfort caused by blunders as part of military life. Harmless jokes may be played on the inexperienced subaltern. Sometimes the humour becomes a little sharp and too many mistakes cause frayed tempers, but having been assured by contemporaries and seniors that they are absolutely useless, the worst product of Sandhurst they have ever seen, and so forth, the young subalterns soon learn, and in the course of that year often become quite efficient. The fact that all concerned know that this is what will happen perhaps makes it something of a ritual.

The KSLI (now part of the Light Infantry) gave Auchinleck two experiences which he remembered for a long time. The regiment was at Ranikhet up in the Himalayas when he arrived and an outbreak of cholera sent them into camp in the hills. This, combined with the fact that the KSLI was a somewhat dashing regiment, put him into immediate financial difficulties. It was much as if he had been posted to a regiment in Britain. There were basic costs for messing and a general charge to cover regimental entertainment. Auchinleck was not the first nor would he be the last officer to watch Mess guests downing drinks he had helped pay for but which he could not himself afford to drink, though he bore no resentment. At school and at Sandhurst he would have noted that some people always have more money than others and set a pace which is impossible for most of their contemporaries to follow; this he could cope with. What turned the scale was the obligatory (and totally unfair) charges of having to pay for a tent for himself and his batman, for a bed, haversack, water-bottle and even blankets (for it was cold in the hills). It was by no means unknown for officers to have to pay for accommodation and kit they were unable to use, to be sent on an expedition without tents but to be forced to pay for them just the same. Such charges were quite outside regimental control, being deducted by command paymasters. Many an enterprising officer went off on an expedition imagining that he was saving money while risking his life; his first pay slip on returning to civilisation told a different story.

This apparently senseless and inhuman practice was a survival from the old days of commission by purchase. The purchase of commissions had been abolished in the Cardwell Reforms of 1870. Up till then officers bought their commissions and promotion (except where gained on a campaign), equipped themselves, and were recompensed by a proportionate share of any booty or ransom acquired; it had been possible for an infant to hold the position of commanding officer of a regiment and thus take the major portion of any prize money. It was as good an investment as any. Unfortunately, for some time after Cardwell's reform pay was inadequate and officers were still as liable for equipment expenses as they had been under the former system.

The fact that Auchinleck was so hard pressed in those early times helped to make him extremely provident – although generous – for the rest of his life. It also left him unimpressed by officers who liked to take their comforts with them on a campaign, although such solaces were beyond the reach of those they were commanding. Austerity became a habit.

The Indian Army was just going through its most traumatic phase since the Mutiny of 1857 when Auchinleck joined in 1903. Kitchener had just arrived from his successes in South Africa and as Commander-in-Chief intended to put through what he felt were much-needed reforms. Curzon was Viceroy, and the stage was set for a considerable clash of wills. In Army matters, however, Kitchener had his way without check. Briefly, he reorganised the Army from a heterogeneous collection of regiments into a homogeneous, standardised army. There were still vast differences in the new organisation, but there was a reason for their continuing presence. By reducing the size of garrisons Kitchener had created nine divisions where four had existed, stationed five of them between Peshawar and Lucknow and the other four in the north-west, facing Afghanistan. With this, of course, went considerable regimental reorganisation. One of the reorganised regiments was the 2nd Madras Infantry, a unit with a fine fighting record. From October 1903 it was to be based at Fyzabad in Uttar Pradesh and retitled the 62nd Punjabis. This inspired move of blending into one loyal united regiment a number of different peoples who otherwise would have had no hesitation in cutting one another's throats, with or without a pretext, was to have a sad and bitter sequel just under half a century later.

The Commanding Officer of the 62nd Punjabis, Colonel Rainey Robinson, came from the Burma Infantry, and there were only three officers from the old 2nd Madras Infantry, but they and those newly transferred were all determined to make a success of this new regiment. In April 1904 Auchinleck joined it. It suited him so well that when, a year later, he was offered a place with the Gurkhas – an opportunity he would once have jumped at – he declined it. By that time he was mastering the different languages, and even dialects, which his men spoke. Although the British have a poor reputation as linguists in Europe, believing that English will always be understood if spoken loudly enough, it has always been a very different story in the East. There are 225 languages in India, excluding dialects, and it is impossible to know them all, but the person who takes the trouble to learn a few well finds that it brings its own reward. Hindustani, a dialect of Hindi, was at the time spoken by about sixty million people (out of some 400 million); Punjabi was spoken by only about twelve million. Auchinleck worked hard not only to speak several languages fluently but also to understand the customs and religions of the people who spoke them. People who encountered him in later life, when he was Commander-in-Chief in India, were astonished at his ability to go into villages and participate in village gossip. The effect of this man of exalted rank being able to move among Indians and understand all that they said and did was overwhelming.

His experience of seeing cholera at his first posting left its mark. Boys brought up in Victorian England were not unfamiliar with the occasional ravages of apparently incurable diseases such as typhoid, diphtheria and scarlet fever, but the speed and unpredictability of cholera put those into the shade. There were plenty of other killers in India too, of which he became quickly aware. Malaria accounted for thirty million Indians a year, and snakes and other wild creatures took a heavy toll, as did famine. But with an average of seven surviving children per Indian family, and every one of them married, fatalism and indifference were part of the Indian way of life. Auchinleck acquired some of their fatalism, but none of the indifference.

One great advantage he had at an early stage was the experience of commanding a substantial body of men. While an officer in a British regiment would have found himself responsible for some thirty men, Auchinleck found himself commanding a hundred (company strength) and occasionally two hundred (double company) when another officer was on leave or absent for some other reason. In 1906 he was commanding a detachment of the 62nd at Gyantse, 200 miles inside Tibet. In 1903, as a result of rumours about a secret treaty between Russia and Tibet, Curzon sent a mission to Lhasa commanded by Colonel Francis Younghusband. In 1904 Younghusband's forces, now reinforced, fought two actions against the Tibetans, killing some 600 of them, after which an Anglo-Tibetan convention was signed in order to settle the frontier problems. By 1906 the British had a representative in Tibet and the object of the British military presence was to note and frustrate any Russian attempts at incursion through that country; it was not the first time that the Indian sub-continent had been threatened with invasion from the north. Many would have found the station remote and dull, with no facilities for sport or spending money, but it suited Auchinleck well enough. Gyantse is 12,000 feet above sea level; the country, though rugged, is outstandingly beautiful, and Auchinleck was doing the job he had always wanted. Some idea of the sort of training which filled his day may be gained from the tactics manuals of the period. An outpost such as Auchinleck commanded sent out regular patrols to examine the surrounding countryside and to note any suspicious circumstance. In hilly country this requires a considerable degree of fitness. Detachments are continually sent to climb the hills ahead and on the flanks, while the main body passes through the valley (picqueting the heights), after which they descend and fall in at the rear. At best a march through hilly country will cover ten miles in a day. It is not, however, quite as simple as it may seem in theory. In practice one of the peaks may be impossible to scale, or may already be occupied by hostile forces. Even an apparently unoccupied hill-top should be treated with caution, for when the picquet is withdrawing it may be attacked by an enemy who has waited in concealment for this very moment and now falls first on the withdrawing picquet and secondly on the rear of the main body. An additional complication is that vital peaks may not be visible from the route of the main body, nor the main body visible from the peaks. Enemy encountered in such terrain would be experts at concealment, swift movement, marksmanship and surprise attack. Guarding a frontier such as that of India taught basic military lessons very quickly and thoroughly. Good luck might occasionally save a man from the effects of idleness or incompetence, but it was not likely to last for long. There were always hill tribesmen who resented the incursion of intruders and who saw fighting as the sole purpose of life.* In any encounter with the enemy, therefore, British and Indian regiments knew that there were no half measures; an opponent might be driven off or wounded, but unless you actually saw his dead body you could be sure he would be back.

The ultimate weapon as far as the infantryman was concerned was the bayonet; indeed there was a slogan 'the bayonet wins the battle'. This conviction lasted well into the First World War when men were taught that 'All the efforts of the other arms lead up to the first decisive moment when the infantry charge ahead with the bayonet – to get him with the cold steel'. Such basic military doctrines might seem to have little relevance to modern warfare but certain aspects of them have a continuing value. In any event they were taught to young officers long after the First World War had changed the entire weapon and communication systems, were used in training in the Second World War and are still used today to develop fieldcraft. The outcome of battles may no longer hinge on infantry getting him with the cold steel, but physical fitness, concealment, and the ability to make the best use of ground are still developed by assault courses and exercises.

After a year at Gyantse Auchinleck was moved to Sikkim, and in the following year to Benares. This last was a danger spot politically, and unhealthy as well. Auchinleck caught diphtheria almost at once; the CO died of cholera later. After recovery he went home on his first leave for six years – for eight months. He was delighted to be home again, but soon realised that this was not his real life, a feeling which many soldiers and adventurers have shared. The things which interest them are so totally removed from home life that conversation is difficult, and the only people who know the same places and conditions are not so much willing to converse as to unload their own experiences of several decades before. Apart from this he found himself homesick for India, something he had never felt for England.

By 1909 he was Adjutant and a captain. The duties of

* See Appendix A.

an adjutant are multifarious and it is said that many regiments are run by the Adjutant and the Regimental Sergeant-Major. The job of both is primarily regimental administration; in essentials it means that the Adjutant relays the CO's wishes and observes whether the officers are doing their jobs to the highest level of efficiency, and the RSM keeps a similar eye on the activities of Warrant Officers and NCOs. Adjutants, by the nature of their job, tend to be regarded with respect rather than liking, although indeed most of them are liked well enough.

Three years later, in 1912, he was home again and this time observed a large exercise taking place in East Anglia. It was, as might be expected, totally removed from the conditions he would experience later, in the First World War. It also showed the sharp contrast between his own life on almost continuous active service and the considerably less urgent approach of a home-based peacetime army.

On returning to India, he was made Assistant Recruiting Officer in the Northern Punjab. This was one of the happiest times in his life, and one from which he learnt much. In the villages were old soldiers, immensely proud of their regiments and former service; there, too, were the young boys who hoped to follow the same path. In other countries, especially in England, soldiers have been privately regarded as scum, treated as heroes in wartime and as a nuisance in peacetime (Kipling summed up this attitude as well as anyone), but in India it was different. Soldiering was a most honourable profession, and there was enormous pride in merely being a soldier, irrespective of the rank or distinction achieved. It is perhaps impossible today to understand the mutual respect and trust which existed in certain regiments, not only in the Indian Army but especially there. Discipline was strict but just, training was exacting. An Indian unit was an undemocratic hierarchy but every member of it, and anyone even remotely attached, seemed bound to it by an unshakable, almost absurd loyalty. Followers would travel after the regiment wherever it went, sometimes to other countries. Auchinleck found himself in harmony with all this – he too felt the bond of loyalty. His

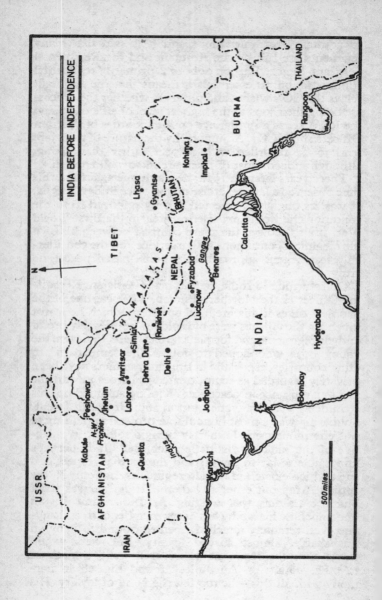

INDIA BEFORE INDEPENDENCE

understanding of the Indian mind made him outstandingly good at his job, though it was to make the task of breaking up that army on Partition in 1947 all the harder. Those who thought he turned down the offer of a peerage then out of pique at being displaced by Montgomery were totally mistaken. The peerage would have been in recognition of his services in India, but to him it was a mockery. As he saw it, the award would have been for destroying the army to which he had devoted his life.

In his nineties, when he was asked by David Dimbleby if he had at that early time thought that British India would go on for ever, or would one day come to an end, he replied: 'I don't think subalterns thought like that at all. They thought it was going on for ever. I think most British officers did. There was no question of India becoming independent or anything like that. There was a benign British rule which one thought would go on for ever.'

It was not surprising that the Army should have held this view; millions of others shared it. The British record in India, and elsewhere, was one of steady achievement. Famine had been countered by means of improved irrigation and better transport; medical services were better; security had been established. The continent was at peace. Why should it not continue on this path?

3

WAR-1914-1919

The declaration of war against Germany in August 1914 seemed at first so remote from India as to have little to do with it, but fuller realisation of what might be involved came when India offered four divisions to Britain for service overseas. Three were immediately available; the fourth was in reserve. The first was on its way to France by the end of August, and two others soon followed. The 62nd Punjabis were in the reserve division which was mobilised for service overseas on 28 October. That day, thirty-one officers – twelve British, one of them Captain Auchinleck, and nineteen Indian – and 808 other ranks sailed from Bombay. Although the division was earmarked for France, it was instead disembarked at Suez, the reason for the change in destination being Turkey's entry into the war. It had been hoped that Turkey would either remain neutral or, perhaps, join the Allies. The hopes were vain. Turkey felt that, with German help, the former Turkish Empire might be rebuilt and Russia and Britain be pushed out of what had once been Turkish territory.

The first Turkish move was to try to retake Egypt, now a British Protectorate. The Turks, blissfully unaware of the attitude of the Egyptians towards themselves, believed that if they could once put a Turkish force on Egyptian territory, the whole country would rise and overthrow the British government. Accordingly, in February 1915, a Turkish force of 20,000, with some artillery, struggled across the Sinai Desert, carrying with them steel pontoons to enable them to cross the Suez Canal when they reached it. The British view had been that the Turks would be unlikely to be able to cross the Sinai, but in case they did it would be as well to have a reception committee for them. Accordingly, 22 Indian Infantry Brigade, of which the 62nd Punjabis was a part, were deployed along the Timsah–Bitter Lake section of the Canal. There they dug in and awaited developments. The Turks soon appeared, and in greater numbers than had been anticipated. It began to dawn on some of the higher command, and would later dawn on others, that the Turks had been somewhat underestimated as fighting soldiers, a lesson made completely clear at the Dardanelles.

The action on the banks of the Canal gave Auchinleck his first taste of war. The attack began at 0330 hours on 1 February 1915. In his own words, when interviewed by David Dimbleby in 1974, 'That was only a very small battle, our first battle, when the Turks tried to cross the Canal. And we were on the west bank and they came over to the east bank and they actually got one boat across, and our men charged down the bank and put a bayonet into them and that was that. The next day we crossed and pushed them back. That was the first battle. That was most exciting.'

'Frightening?'

'Exciting.'

'Was it frightening?'

'Oh, yes. I was with the machine-guns. I had the machine-guns of the regiment. [There were only two.] I was across from the Turkish side of the canal in a sort of fort. And I remember going into action for the first time with them. And I remember the first bullet going over my head. Which made me duck damn quickly. But, after all, one got used to it very quickly.'

The battle was short. The pontoons were sunk and the Turks suffered heavy casualties. A second attack was launched but this was also held. Captain Auchinleck then led a counter-attack and took the Turkish forward trenches, though the Turks held on stubbornly. Just as the 62nd were about to launch their final attack the enemy decided to surrender; they had lost many men and there were only just over two hundred left. The 62nd had been by no means unscathed: seven men killed, two officers and eighteen other ranks wounded, but they were felt to have acquitted themselves well.

After their initial engagement the 62nd settled down to patrol activity and training. The essence of training is that it should be harder than war, and, if possible, more unpleasant. Thus there is general relief when the unit once more has orders to go into action. This applied less to Indian than to British regiments, for the Indians tended to enjoy their training considerably more than their British counterparts. In July 1915 another gap-plugging assignment fell to the 62nd, when the Turks overran Sheikh Othman, the main source of Aden's water supply. For this the 62nd were allotted to 28 Brigade and helped drive the Turks back. These actions were followed by what are now called search-and-destroy operations to the north of Aden, in an area populated by Turks and hostile Arabs. Later, two Turkish thrusts were held and pushed back, and although these were small-scale battles the results, had they been defeats, would have been anything but small.

By now, Auchinleck had missed both France and the Dardanelles campaign, to either of which he might have been sent, possibly to be killed, and he had engaged in fighting of a type for which he had had useful preparation. But the future would be less satisfactory. That December, the regiment was sent up to Basra in what was then known as Mesopotamia (since 1921 a part of Iraq).

By late 1915 the military situation in Mesopotamia had become precarious. In November 1914 16 Infantry Brigade, part of 6th Indian Division, had been sent to capture Basra and thus protect the Anglo-Persian oil installations from the Turks, who were in Mesopotamia, although not, at this stage, in great strength. The Brigade landed at the head of the Gulf, captured Basra after some opposition, and was reinforced by the rest of the Division. In April 1915 the Turks had counter-attacked but were decisively defeated at Shaiba, some twelve miles south-west of Basra. Nowadays the Battle of Shaiba is all but forgotten, but it had two different but momentous consequences: it stopped the Turks breaking through the defensive ring around the Persian oil fields, and it gave a false impression of Allied abilities in relation to the Turks. The defeated Turks were not the cream of their army, while the Indian Expeditionary Force (as 6th Indian

Division was known), excellent though it was, had serious limitations, deriving from the lack of reserve supplies in India. Equipping the first four divisions had exhausted resources in a country where the policy had always been 'if there's a shortage it can be remedied by local supplies'. The problems faced by units serving overseas in territory such as Mesopotamia need little imagination. But the Higher Command took an optimistic view, and decided to push for the capture of Baghdad, reinforcing the Indian Expeditionary Force for the purpose. What was not realised was that the small, ill-equipped Anglo-Indian force would soon be confronted by the resolute fighting qualities of Anatolian Turks. By using river steamers, Amara on the Tigris was captured on 3 June – the way must now surely be open for the capture of Baghdad. The success at Amara was followed by the capture of Nasiriya on the Euphrates on 25 July, and the next move was clearly to push on up the Tigris to Kut-al-Amara, duly captured by Maj.-Gen. Charles Townshend's column on 28 September. As the situation in the Dardanelles now looked like ending in stalemate, if not complete failure, further successes in Mesopotamia were clearly desirable. Townshend, with one poorly-equipped and somewhat weary division, the 6th, was told to press on and capture Baghdad itself.

On 22 November Townshend attacked the Turks holding Ctesiphon (most of whom had been permitted to escape from Kut), eighteen miles from Baghdad. A long-drawn battle followed, but it was obvious that Townshend's resources were quite insufficient for him to reach Baghdad; nor could he remain where he was. Accordingly, he fell back to Kut, his retirement greatly harassed by Turks and Arabs.

Eventually, on 3 December, the column reached Kut. Pressure from the Turks, who had been held by desperate rearguard actions, indicated only too clearly that Kut was itself vulnerable; however, there were valuable stores in the town and, after some hesitation, it was decided that the division, numbering some 10,000 men from British and Indian units, should stay there rather than fall back to a more defensible position downstream. The Turks,

27

two divisions of them, swept on round Kut, and Townshend was besieged.

Attempts to relieve Kut began almost as soon as the Turkish net closed around it, for it was understood that the town was close to starvation. It was full of civilians who had taken refuge there, and food was clearly going to be a problem; the British were unaware, however, that there were considerable stores of buried grain and the situation was by no means as serious as at first it appeared. Townshend believed that the position was so bad that he would have to surrender within days, and in consequence a force of two divisions hastily organised under Lt-Gen. Sir Fenton Aylmer began, on 3 January 1916, a series of urgent moves to relieve the town. The force encountered heavy Turkish resistance while still some thirty miles downstream of Kut.

Auchinleck's regiment had arrived at Basra in December 1915 with a strength of 942 all ranks. They were immediately sent upstream by steamer to join Aylmer's force at Hissah; from here, on 7 January, they went straight into action at Sheikh Sa'ad. It was the sort of situation which Auchinleck would encounter later; everything which could go wrong had either done so or was about to do so. The only consistent feature was the rain, which appeared to have begun on their arrival and which continued relentlessly day after day. It turned the whole area into a vast, sticky swamp. To add to everyone's misery the weather was bitterly cold with a northerly wind. Food was short because of the chaotic conditions, and fuel for fires almost non-existent. Aylmer's plan was to advance up both sides of the River Tigris simultaneously and then take one force across north of the town, but by 13 January his force had suffered some 6000 casualties. Crossing the river began to look more and more improbable as floods were now being accompanied by high winds, and there were no pontoons. An attempt to make a bridge of boats failed on 18 January when wind and flood water swept away the craft.

For Aylmer the only tactic possible now was the hazardous one of frontal attack on the prepared Turkish positions around Kut, which extended for some twenty miles downstream. Accordingly, on 21 January 1916 the British force attacked at Hanna, the main thrust being led by 35, 19 and 9 Indian Brigades; the 62nd was now part of the latter brigade. 35 Brigade led the attack at 0755 hours, but were met by concentrated and accurate fire from the entrenched Turks. Their casualties were so high that they fell back to their own lines, leaving 9 Brigade to continue the attack. This left the 62nd on the right and the Hampshires on the left; the Connaught Rangers were immediately behind. There was no cover and the 62nd had a reception similar to that which had devastated 35 Brigade. Casualties mounted rapidly as they pressed forward, and their commanding officer was killed. The Connaughts made a gallant attempt to back up the 62nd but a combination of pitiless rain and steady machine-gun fire from the Turks broke up their attacks. Men floundered around in the mud in increasing confusion. 21 January 1916 was a date they would long remember. An order for general withdrawal was sent out at 1530 hours but night had fallen before it reached the 62nd. By then the regiment had suffered 372 casualties. It was impossible to help the wounded, or even to collect up and rally the fit, in the morass which the rain had made of the battlefield. Many, even the unwounded, died of exposure. The 62nd's first large battle had been part of a costly failure. For the moment the regiment had ceased to be an effective fighting force; it was assigned to routine duties until it could be brought up to strength.

In March, though still under strength, the 62nd were back in action under their new CO, Lt-Col. H. H. Harrington of the 84th Punjabis. This time the attack on Hanna was to be concentrated on the southern side of the Tigris, at a point known as the Dujaila Redoubt. Following a night march the relieving force went into action at 0945 hours on 8 March, although by then surprise unfortunately had been lost and the Turkish positions were fully manned and ready. Here, as with other theatres in this war, the attempt to advance over open ground against machine-guns in strong trench positions proved disastrous. The 62nd were pinned down, Harrington was wounded, and Auchinleck took over command. The 62nd received the order to withdraw two miles to Ora. Their strength was now down to 247 men.

Incredible though it may seem, there were still 12,000 troops and plenty of guns at Basra. Unfortunately there was no easy means of getting them to a point where they could overwhelm the Turkish defences. On 11 March Aylmer was dismissed as a failure, but his replacement, Lt-Gen. Sir G. F. Gorringe, could do no better. Reinforcements available at Basra now totalled 30,000 troops with thirty-two guns, but there was still insufficient river transport to take them where they were needed. Gorringe continued to batter away during April, and the 62nd continued to lose more men. In repeated, costly attacks many of the Turkish positions around Kut were taken, but the relieving force was beaten back by a counter-attack on 22 April. On 29 April, with twenty men a day dying of starvation, Kut surrendered: Townshend had by then destroyed his guns, ammunition and stores. 9000 prisoners were taken, of whom 5000 disappeared without trace. Over 23,000 casualties had been sustained in the attempts to relieve the besieged garrison: the 62nd had lost more than half its original strength.

The fall of Kut left the Turks without any good reason to hold on to their exposed outposts in the coming hot season. They fell back into the town and allowed the British to occupy sites they had spilt their blood failing to reach a few months earlier. The 62nd were put in the Dujaila Redoubt, in tents. The temperature was 120° Fahrenheit, rations were short and fresh vegetables completely absent. Dust blew around in clouds and flies were a perpetual torment. There were no comforts, not even cigarettes, but everything which could crawl, bite or sting seemed to be present in those trenches. But gradually a leave rotation was established and Major Auchinleck was allotted a month in August. He went back to India and spent it in Simla. So far his health had stood up very well to the privations of the Mesopotamia campaign, but he needed that leave badly. Sadly, it was marred by the news of his brother's death on the Somme. He returned to a more cheerful scene.

The new C-in-C Mesopotamia was General Sir Stanley

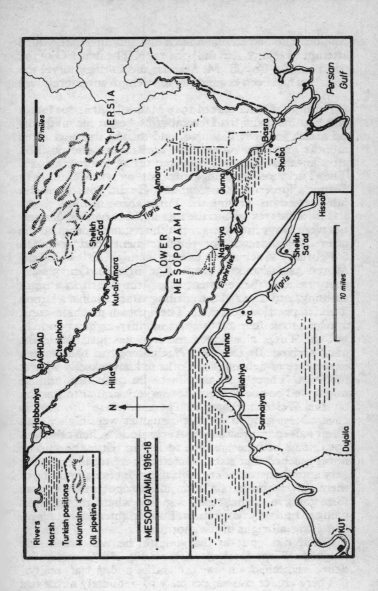

Rivers ⌇⌇⌇

Marsh ⫴⫴⫴

Turkish positions ⌇⌇⌇

Mountains ⩘⩘⩘

Oil pipeline ▬ ▬ ▬

MESOPOTAMIA 1916-18

N

50 miles

10 miles

PERSIA

Persian Gulf

Basra

Shaiba

Amara

Qurna

Sheikh Sa'ad

Tigris

LOWER MESOPOTAMIA

Kut-al-Amara

Nasiriya

Euphrates

Ctesiphon

BAGHDAD

Hilla

Habbaniya

Hissah

Sheikh Sa'ad

Tigris

Ora

Hanna

Fallahiya

Sannaiyat

Dujaila

KUT

Maude, who had commanded a division during the third attempt to relieve Kut in April 1916. The new CO of the 62nd was Lt-Col. G. M. Morris, and in the interval the battalion had been brought up to strength and morale was high.

During the latter part of 1916 Maude built up his forces and laid his plans. In December he began his methodical attack towards Baghdad, and during the next three months gradually ousted the Turks from one position after another; Kut was captured on 25 February 1917. The Turks resisted doggedly but by 11 March 1917 Maude's forces were in Baghdad. He did not stop there, but pressed on, driving the Turks ahead of him.

The 62nd was well to the fore in these battles. Casualties were heavy in February but the regiment declined the offer of withdrawal for reinforcements and refit. On 8 February Auchinleck became acting CO as Colonel Morris had taken command of 36 Brigade. On 23 February he took the regiment across the Tigris in a night crossing, and then led the ensuing attack against a strong Turkish position near Kut. The Turkish machine-guns, as usual, took their toll (eight dead, fifty-eight wounded), but the Turks abandoned the trenches just before the 62nd arrived. By this time Auchinleck had had enough experience of fighting the Turks to know exactly what it involved. There were certain to be casualties, and he might well be one of them. It was very similar to warfare on the Western Front, except that there the attacks covered less ground and the casualties were higher. But it left a deep impression on Auchinleck. When asked, in 1974, if he became immune to fear in battle, he said he never reached that state. Sometimes, he recalled, he felt very apprehensive indeed; this night, it seems, was one of them. 'I remember one night in Mesopotamia when we were going in the next morning, into what I thought was going to be a very nasty show. I was frightened that night. But I was all right in the morning.'

'What did you do that night?' he was asked. He laughed. 'Went to sleep. After a bit. But I remember being frightened – it was the end of a long war, really.'

There are, of course, people who genuinely never feel

fear, although they are a very small minority. In their case it is probably lack of imagination. A greater number are distinctly apprehensive and feel, in their apparent indifference, as if they are acting a part. There is yet another category, to which Auchinleck belongs, of those who are aware that danger exists but have become so inured to it that they can genuinely disregard it. Of course any of these reactions may be changed by wounds, extreme fatigue or heavy bombardment; the effects of these tend to be much greater on the once fearless than on the others. It has been said that 'Courage is like a bank', too many demands may exhaust it unless it is recharged by rest.

Although the Punjabis' task was now pursuit, casualties could and did still occur, and not only from enemy action. The main irritant was lice, which seem to appear from nowhere and make nights a misery; lice can also be the prelude to skin infection and other ills. The army was learning many lessons about field hygiene and the treatment of diseases which come from flies, mosquitoes and hot or wet conditions, but not learning them fast enough for many of the troops exposed to them. Nevertheless the army routine of scrupulous cleanliness of everything and everyone whenever conditions made that possible was now seen to be sound common sense.

The 62nd was in Baghdad for days before the official take-over of the town on 11 March; the Turks had already moved out. After a few days they moved on to Baguba, a station which, if not exactly flowing with milk and honey, at least had fresh food and clean water. Colonel Morris returned, and Auchinleck gave up his temporary appointment. The fact that he had done well, however, was noted and he was sent as Brigade Major to 52 Brigade. The Turks still held Mosul and Kirkuk, some 250 miles north of Baghdad, but they were already staggering under blows from Allenby in Palestine and were in no mood to launch counter-attacks. Equally the British forces were content to hold on to their gains without risking high casualties in an unnecessary campaign. They moved forward towards the two towns without any urgency. It was now mid-1918 and there was a reluctance to employ more experienced troops in the Middle East than was strictly necessary; it was felt they could be used to better effect in France.

In the event, however, the active part of Auchinleck's war in the Middle East was not quite over. After the Armistice with Turkey of 30 October 1918 he had various staff appointments in the Kurdistan area, one as GSO2 (Operations) in the 1919 campaign against the Kurdish rebels. He received a Mention in Despatches to follow the DSO and OBE gained in the earlier campaigns. Of Auchinleck's work in the 1919 campaign, Maj.-Gen. Theodore Fraser wrote:

> I wish to mention specially Major Auchinleck, DSO, OBE, my Chief Staff Officer, who has borne the whole burden of the 'G' work on his own back, and has proved himself a tower of strength. He has been most helpful to all my units as well as to myself, and the success of the operation is largely due to his vigorous personality, to his suggestive mind, and to his professional ability.

From his experiences in these campaigns Auchinleck had learnt much which would be useful later. Above all, he had learnt the folly of frontal attacks on heavily prepared positions. Even when successful they were inordinately costly in time and casualties, and he himself would never agree to men being sent into battle insufficiently prepared and equipped. In the end, he would pay a high price for that disagreement.

The importance of good food and adequate medical services was only too clear when they were lacking. On the way to Basra he experienced discomfort, danger, vermin, parasites and exhaustion. He would not forget these inevitable companions of the battlefield when he made his own plans in the future.

4

UNREST IN INDIA

In 1919 Auchinleck was given a vacancy at the Staff College, Quetta. He was thirty-five, a lieutenant-colonel, and considerably more experienced than many of his instructors. Attendance on a course of any type can often be a strain on the temper of an experienced officer. Much of the time he feels is being spent on outmoded doctrine, and the sheer tedium of being instructed day after day tempts the pupil to be a little cynical, if nothing more. There is a tendency for classes to behave like irresponsible schoolboys. Quetta, founded by Kitchener along the lines of Camberley Staff College, was a thoroughly efficient college, but there was a feeling that the course at Camberley must be nearer to the heart of things and probably more progressive. That view was not held by students at Camberley, which was going through a period of adjustment.

Auchinleck completed the year's course, and was now due for a year's home leave. He decided to give his mother and his sister Ruth a holiday in France, and the three of them went to Hyères, on the south coast, near Toulon. Staying there also was a widow, Mrs Alexander Stewart, and her daughter Jessie. Alexander Stewart had been a civil engineer, working in China and America, and the Stewarts were widely travelled. Jessie was a very attractive, lively twenty-one-year-old and Auchinleck fell in love with her at first sight; they married in London in 1921 before the end of his leave, apparently perfectly suited, although she was fifteen years younger than he (coincidentally, his parents had a fifteen-year gap between their ages). Mrs Auchinleck did not approve of Jessie's slight American accent, and thought that her son would have done better to marry a daughter of a serving Army officer. But her son never doubted that Jessie was the right person for him.

After their marriage, they sailed for India, where

Auchinleck took up his new post as DAA and QMG* at Simla. In 1923, Auchinleck was joined in Simla by Hastings Ismay who had arrived from Quetta to take up the post of DAQMG. They became firm friends; many years later, during the war, Ismay was to be Chief of Staff to Churchill.

After this period on the Staff Auchinleck returned to his regiment, which had been renumbered and had now become the 1st Battalion of the 1st Punjabis (1/1st Punjabis). Based at Peshawar, they undertook normal frontier duties. The fact that there was political unrest elsewhere in India did not affect the North-West Frontier, which during the early 1920s was unusually peaceful after the Third Afghan War of 1919 and the costly Waziristan campaign of 1919–20. For a short time Auchinleck left the regiment to serve as GSO2 on the staff of General Sir Robert Cassels, the Peshawar District Commander, whom he had first met in the fighting around Kut; Auchinleck was to take over from Cassels as Commander-in-Chief, India in 1941.

In 1927 Auchinleck, after a period of home leave, was on another course, this time at the Imperial Defence College in London (the IDC)† which had just opened and was striving to establish itself. Today it is well established and is now called the Royal College of Defence Studies. In the first intake were many names which would become more familiar, including the future Field-Marshal Lord Alanbrooke, the future Admiral of the Fleet Lord Tovey, Colonel (later General Sir) Eric de Burgh, and the future Air Chief Marshal Sir Richard Peirse. The Commandant was Admiral Sir Herbert Richmond, later Master of Downing College, Cambridge, and his second-in-command was the future Field-Marshal Sir John Dill, who became a good friend to Auchinleck. The aim of the course was to contemplate the problems of all three services, thereby facilitating mutual co-operation. This had

---

* Deputy Assistant Adjutant and Quartermaster-General, a grandiose-sounding appointment usually held by a major who keeps an eye on unit numbers, reinforcements and equipment. The title dates back to the Napoleonic Wars, when the post provided a man who could co-ordinate the equipment needs with the personnel available. It is nowadays usually abbreviated to 'DQ'.
† See Appendix B.

not been of enormous importance in the past but was to become so.

At the end of the course which Auchinleck found, as had been hoped, both broadening and stimulating, he returned to the regiment, now quartered at Jhelum, near the Kashmir Mountains. Here, in 1928, he was appointed to command the battalion, a post which he had held temporarily in wartime, nearly twelve years ago. This, of course, was the summit of most officers' ambition. But, pleased and proud as he was to have attained this ambition, Auchinleck realised that he would soon have to go from it. After two years, in 1930, he was posted again, this time to the Staff College at Quetta, with the administrative post (plus some teaching) of GSO1, and the rank of full colonel – ten years after he had been there himself as a somewhat over-age student.

Auchinleck had derived enormous pleasure and satisfaction from commanding his regiment, but he enjoyed his new post too. When he had been a student many of his contemporaries had known as much, if not more, than the DS (Directing Staff), as the instructors at service colleges are called. The situation was now very different. None of the students was old enough to have fought in the First World War; but even among the DS, Auchinleck stood out. Students listened intently to him, not because he was a full colonel, but because he was so clearly master of his job, and equipped with the ability to pass his knowledge on. His own understanding had been gained by experience rather than textbook and classroom, and he could always produce a suitable inference, or reference, from the North-West Frontier, or Aden, or Mesopotamia, if needed. Tact is required, however, if the instructor is not to build up resentment in those never likely to experience the same opportunities and dangers; but Auchinleck had no such problems, though others did.

The Staff College course aims at producing clarity of mind – and in Auchinleck it had a very clear-minded instructor. Every activity is given a reason, and the aim is clearly stated. At the end of the course the findings are summarised, and problems isolated and discussed. Lucid speech and writing are emphasised to a degree that many students feel is petty. As with all army courses, the student who arrives with a good idea of his own knowledge and importance is quickly reduced to matchwood; he is then rebuilt on lines which will make him a better member of a staff team. It is testing for the student, but it is also testing for the DS, and no doubt Auchinleck found it a bit trying at times.

From childhood, as has been mentioned, he had little interest in sports, especially team sports, and this feature of Auchinleck's character now became more noticeable; although he could, and did, take his part in the social round, he did not, as many did, regard social activities as the be-all and end-all of existence. Pig-sticking, for instance, was a popular pastime, but it was not one that appealed to Auchinleck who preferred gardening or walking. His years in the barren parts of Mesopotamia had instilled in him an instinct to make the desert bloom. Early experience of responsibility in a lonely place in Tibet, followed by campaigning in the land of biblical history – Mosul, where he had been stationed, was ancient Assyria, Hilla adjoins what was once Babylon, and Qurna, where the Tigris and Euphrates meet, was said to be the site of the Garden of Eden – had made Auchinleck more than usually thoughtful and self-contained. He knew his own mind and reach, but he was tolerant of the requirements and foibles of others. A number of people with experience similar to his tend to be irascible or withdrawn, or even unbalanced. It is interesting that, however severely Auchinleck was tested – and in later years the strain on him as a commander-in-chief was at times immense – he never broke down. He was not an ascetic, but ease and luxury meant little to him.

After his tour of duty at Quetta followed another home leave; then, in 1933, he received command of the Peshawar Brigade, based near the North-West Frontier. Soon the Brigade was engaged in pacifying a number of Afghans, who were only too ready to join in any fighting available. For his part in quelling the disturbance, Auchinleck was Mentioned in Despatches and received the CB. This period of trouble was comparatively short, but two years later, in 1935, it broke out on a much larger scale, again at the hands of the Mohmand tribesmen.

So far, the Army had managed to steer clear of politics, even though at times it was called in to restore order or to clear up the results of agitation. During the First World War Indian troops had fought in France, Mesopotamia and German East Africa, but the Indian National Congress (the chief political party, founded in 1885) had neither criticised nor used the opportunity of Britain's difficulties to make trouble. In 1917 the Montagu Declaration had affirmed that it was Britain's intention to assist India to full responsible government, but the Rowlatt Acts of 1919 – which gave the Government special powers to suppress sedition – made this look unlikely to Indian eyes. Differences between Hindus and Muslims in 1918, and the non-cooperation movement led by Ghandi, exacerbated Indian resentment, which came to a head in 1919 with the Amritsar massacre, when Brig.-Gen. Reginald Dyer gave orders to fire on a crowd of Indians in that city who refused to disperse. More than 2000 were killed or wounded and, even though a Government of India Act was passed that year, in accordance with the Montagu Declaration and implementing many of its reforms, Anglo-Indian relations were embittered. From 1930 onwards there had been a series of Round Table Conferences, the results of which enabled a further Government of India Act to be drafted in 1935. Independence was obviously coming, but thoughtful people were only too aware that it would not be a panacea for India's troubles, which stemmed from so many problems. While India was passing through a period of exceptional restlessness in 1935, the outlook elsewhere seemed equally gloomy, with Hitler's rantings in Germany, pacifism in Britain, and the Suez route to India threatened by Mussolini's belligerence in the Mediterranean.

So far, Auchinleck had been able to contemplate such distant events with detachment, but the time was rapidly approaching when his own life and career would be affected by them. For the moment he had more immediate concerns. The North-West Frontier had been stirred to rebellion by the Haji of Turangzai, and as the tribesmen were now making frequent forays from the hills it was necessary to put an end to the nuisance. Since his District Commander was on leave, Auchinleck, by now a brigadier, took over his duties. (A fellow brigadier was the Hon. H. R. L. G. Alexander, a man with a much wealthier and more aristocratic background than Auchinleck's, but a similar personality. 'Alex' was of Irish ancestry, and was as admired and liked by his soldiers as Auchinleck was by his. The two men became firm friends.)

The Mohmand operation of 1935, directed by Auchinleck, was arduous but interesting, and in it tanks were used for the first time in India. These were Vickers Mark IIBs, which had a 47-mm gun and a machine-gun, weighed eight tons and had a top speed of 22 mph. Curiously enough, these versatile tanks were sold to and used by many other countries but found little favour with Britain. A weakness was that their armour was thin, though that was no problem against the opposition encountered on the Frontier. Even with three brigades and modern weapons, progress was slow, and communication was made more difficult since all radios had just been withdrawn for their annual overhaul! The operation was brought to a successful conclusion before the year was out, but not before 5/12th Frontier Force Regiment had been ambushed by tribesmen and sustained heavy casualties.

At about that time he met Colonel B. L. Montgomery, then an instructor at Quetta Staff College, who was on a tour of the North-West Frontier. Montgomery afterwards remarked to Lieutenant P. B. I. O. Burge, 'The best man was a chap called Auchinleck.' He, however, could not have left much of an impression on Auchinleck. When, a couple of years later, Montgomery left Quetta to take command of a brigade in Britain, a favourable report on him was sent to Whitehall, to which was appended a note of commendation from the Chief of General Staff, India. Auchinleck, as Deputy Chief of General Staff, was also invited to add a few words – but his only response was: 'I do not know Colonel Montgomery well enough to be able to report on him.'

For his skill in handling the campaign Auchinleck was awarded the CSI and received another Mention in Despatches; a year later, in 1936, his promotion to major-general was gazetted. He and his wife spent much of the ensuing leave at her family home at Kinloch Rannoch in Scotland.

Auchinleck's next appointment was to be Deputy Chief of the General Staff, India, succeeding a friend from IDC days, General Eric de Burgh, which took him to Simla once more.

5

APPALLING OUTLOOK 1938–1940

Auchinleck was well aware that he would have many problems in his new post. India's internal troubles were clearly becoming worse rather than better, war was impending in Europe, and the political situation in Japan made it unlikely that any news from that quarter would be favourable. Nevertheless, it seemed that moderate optimism was justified, both in India and elsewhere. For himself, he knew that the period of simple, straightforward decision-making was over and that now, for most of the time, he would be dealing with committees and policy-makers whose motives and outlook might be different from his own. In his wildest imaginings he never contemplated that he would rise so high nor fall with such speed, nor that his simple integrity would make him so vulnerable.

As Deputy Chief of the General Staff he found himself working under an old friend: the C-in-C India, was General Sir Robert Cassels. The Chief of General Staff was General W. H. Bartholomew (to be replaced by General de Burgh in 1939). Auchinleck's tasks were numerous and varied, being designed to contribute to the effective modernisation and training of the army, a brief that appears considerably simpler in theory than it was to prove in practice. Political considerations made the 'Indianisation of the Army' – the replacement of British officers – desirable, but this could not be done rapidly. British officers would have to be 'phased out' and Indian replacements of similar standard found; it would be easier to get rid of the former than to find adequate replacements, and to achieve the task without dislocation would take years.

Another problem was that of equipment. As the European situation deteriorated there was less and less to spare for India, which still relied heavily on the United Kingdom for almost everything. Later, India would become an arsenal, but such a possibility could not be foreseen in 1936. Moreover, there was, in India, a strong political feeling that the Indian Army should not be used overseas, but reserved for home defence.

Immediately after taking up his appointment Auchinleck was able to assess that army in a not inconsiderable operation. Waziristan had a long history of turbulence and in 1937 the general ferment of Indian politics now reached and stirred up the region once more. The centre of the trouble in Waziristan was the Fakir of Ipi, a skilful organiser, a bold campaigner with a fine sense of timing, and a man whose sexual aberrations impressed even the most unshockable. After a year's campaign in which 40,000 troops were engaged the district was calmed, but the Fakir and his henchmen remained uncaught. (He bided his time and emerged again in the middle of the Second World War, when there was even less time to spare for him.) It appeared that there would be no more trouble in the immediate future from that quarter.

In 1938 Colonel Eric Dorman-Smith was appointed Director of Military Training and in that capacity worked closely with Auchinleck. They became good friends. Opinions about the abilities of Dorman-Smith differed widely, as we shall see later. His brother, Reginald, was a Minister in the Chamberlain government and subsequently became Governor of Burma during the war.

Committee work soon began. First was an internal committee appointed by General Cassels. Auchinleck was made Chairman and its members were the Director of Staff Duties, the Director of Military Operations and Intelligence, and the Director of Military Training. It dealt with the obvious subjects such as guarding the North-West Frontier, maintaining internal security, organising coastal defence (of which there was little) and establishing a general reserve for all contingencies. It was a small efficient committee of people with the same aim and a thorough knowledge of their own fields. It tackled a huge agenda and produced a comprehensive, intelligible report, which was accepted by the C-in-C without amendment. But, as so often happens, another, larger, committee was being formed before the ink was dry on this report.

This was the Chatfield Committee of 1938. Back in London it had been decided that events in Europe, after Munich, required a joint Service review of the problems and resources of India. The basis of it, according to a letter written by the Secretary of State for India, Lord Zetland, to Auchinleck, was the need to examine the cost of modernising the Indian armed forces in relation to the vast cost of modern armaments. The committee, styled 'The Expert Committee on the Defence of India 1938–9', was chaired by Admiral of the Fleet Lord Chatfield, and consisted of Sir Ernest Strohmenger, Lt-Gen. Sir B. N. Sergison-Brooke, Air Marshal C. L. Courtney, Maj.-Gen. C. J. E. Auchinleck, Messrs S. K. Brown, A. J. Newling and M. J. Dean, Paymaster-Captain R. C. Jerram*, and Major P. R. Antrobus – all experts in their various fields. It held seventy-eight meetings and consulted sixty-three witnesses, before its members left for London in January 1939 to complete their findings.

It might seem that an obsolete report of this nature, some forty years out of date, would be a dry-as-dust affair. Curiously enough, it is a model of clarity, foresight and restraint. Its findings remained secret for many years, for it was felt that if its frank account of India's shortcomings in defence at that time had become known it would have been as dangerous politically as it was militarily. The outcome was that more money, though, needless to say, not enough, was allotted by the British government for the purposes of Indian defence.

The Auchinlecks, reunited in England, managed one more leave before war broke out, spending it partly in Scotland and partly in America. On 3 September 1939, the day on which war was declared, he was ordered to report for duty in Edinburgh. There he received further orders to sail back to India on the *Duchess of Bedford*. The Auchinlecks sailed in a blacked-out convoy, one of many voyages the *Duchess of Bedford* would make in that guise during the war. In India Auchinleck was given command of 3rd Indian Division, with headquarters at Dehra Dun; his brief was to prepare the division for modern war. Lack of equipment made this an exercise in improvisation.

---

* The late Rear-Admiral Sir Rowland Jerram, KBE, DSO, DL.

For many units in India and elsewhere the process of mechanisation was described as having their horses taken away with nothing being put in place of them.

It was a frustrating time for Auchinleck. Except at sea, where unrestricted hostilities had begun on the first day, there was a widespread belief that the war would never come to anything. After a time Hitler's bluff would have been called and everyone would go home. Nowhere was this felt more than in the East, and particularly in India. One division had gone from India to the Middle East, but that seemed the end of the matter. Social life was completely unaffected. There was no black-out in India to cause inconvenience and remind people that they had just entered on what might well turn out to be the biggest war in history. There were no shortages, except of military equipment. The motto was 'business and pleasure as usual', but particularly pleasure. Auchinleck found the atmosphere of blissful indifference somewhat sickening, and avoided social occasions as much as possible. But in January 1940 he received news more cheering to him. He had been appointed a corps commander in Britain, with the rank of lieutenant-general, and was to return immediately. There was no military aircraft to fly him there, so he travelled alone in a civilian aircraft.

His new assignment was command of IV Corps which, it was thought then, would be ready to take up position in France in June, six months later. Although he could hardly be expected to have been in close touch with officers in the United Kingdom, Auchinleck had no illusions about this being an easy assignment, and in this assessment he certainly did not err. The attitude to 'the phoney war' (or 'the Great Bore War', as the Americans termed it) was nearly as carefree in Britain as it had been in India. Poland had fallen, admittedly, and the Russians had made some sinister moves both there and against Finland, but in Britain, apart from there being large numbers of volunteers and conscripts training with obsolete weapons in large camps, there was little to show in the way of national effort. Even Churchill, he noted, who had been predicting the war for the last few years and stressing Britain's unpreparedness for it, was merely First Lord of the Admiralty; Chamberlain, who had made such a fool of himself over Munich, was still Prime Minister and Hore-Belisha, who had been for three years Secretary of State for War, had been pushed out again, though he had been a man who left his mark, whether it was in the form of traffic-beacons or battledress. General Lord Gort was C-in-C of the British Expeditionary Force in France and General Sir Edmund Ironside Chief of the Imperial General Staff at the War Office. (The 'Imperial' has now been dropped from this resounding title, which now reflects more accurately the appointment of C-in-C of the British Army. In the distant past the holder of that appointment also commanded the forces in the British territories overseas.)

Ironically, Auchinleck's first headquarters was in the Staff College at Camberley, but he was soon moved to Alresford in Hampshire. One of the IV Corps divisions was in Dorset, another in Peeblesshire, the rest were scattered over southern England. He had arrived back in Britain to one of the severest winters for many years, which made travelling around more than usually difficult. Conditions during that winter were verging on the bizarre. The National Service Acts had called up thousands of men who had now been joined by Territorials, Reservists and volunteers. Holiday camps, racecourses, cricket grounds, schools, even garages had been hastily requisitioned for accommodation and training purposes. Recruits were drilling on roads, on playing fields and on seaside promenades. Proper training areas were being built as fast as possible, but there was a desperate shortage of all suitable materials, particularly wood. Many of the 'camps' lacked any form of heating; recruits were either in flimsy chalet-type buildings which had been designed for warm summer weather, or in tents on to which the rain froze.

Regulations and restrictions poured out of the new bureaucratic ministries by the hundred. Thousands of people were invested with authority over others but lacked the sense of responsibility required. Many took a delight in refusing any request accompanying it with the words 'Don't you know there's a war on?' As Shakespeare put it:

But man, proud man,
Drest in a little brief authority,
Most ignorant of what he's most assur'd,
His glassy essence, like an angry ape,
Plays such fantastic tricks before high heaven
As makes the angels weep ...
(*Measure for Measure*, Act II, Scene ii)

The services were not exempt from this phenomenon. Out of retirement came many officers and NCOs glad to be back in a position of authority; they were joined by others rapidly promoted but almost totally without experience. The phase passed, but at the time that Auchinleck was trying to put IV Corps on a war footing muddle was widespread, and not alleviated by the black-out which made night travel arduous and confusing, since car lights were reduced to a small unblacked-out cross on each headlamp. In the cramped, cold, stuffy atmosphere of blacked-out barrack rooms influenza and other ailments spread rapidly.

February 1940 produced exceptionally unpleasant weather. The Corps he commanded was a mixture of Regular and Territorial Army units, and both were supplemented by young officers and soldiers as they completed their initial training. The fact that the corps commander came from the Indian Army could not fail to make him an object of suspicion to anyone who did not know him. The stereotype of the Indian Army officer, purple and corpulent from whisky and curry, was a standard stage joke, and although most people realised that this was an exaggeration, anyone from the Indian Army had to overcome at least some prejudice before he was accepted. Very quickly, the realisation that Auchinleck was quite unlike the caricature penetrated through the Corps, and it dawned on them that they were lucky to have him. One of his most surprising qualities was his total lack of prejudice or preconceived ideas, disconcerting though this could be at times. He did not find his Territorial units inexperienced and undertrained in relation to the Regulars; he found each as unready as the other. This was a sharp shock to those who believed that

47

Regular units were inherently better than the TA. Auchin-leck's response to such a claim was 'If it's true, prove it. I shall judge for myself.' The result was a rapid stimulus to efficiency, each element trying to outdo the other. It was not, it might be added, entirely the fault of the Regular Army that it was in a low state of readiness. For years pacifist movements had mocked at army recruiting, defence estimates had been parsimonious, hampered by the 'No War for Ten Years' Rule, and in 1939 all that could be spared in the way of men and material had been sent overseas.

IV Corps was assigned to take over the Lille District in France, and in April Auchinleck flew over to inspect the area. It looked placid, and theoretically there would be time to raise the Corps' efficiency to a reasonable standard before settling in two months later. But the Intelligence summaries Auchinleck was receiving told a somewhat different story.

6

'THIS RAMSHACKLE CAMPAIGN'
NORWAY 1940

On 9 April the Germans, who had a non-aggression treaty with Denmark, invaded that country. The Danes, whose army numbered some 14,000 men, capitulated within hours. On the same day, in spite of sustaining casualties from the Royal Navy and the Norwegians, the Germans had seized Oslo, Stavanger, Bergen, Trondheim and Narvik. The Norwegians, with greater resources than the Danes, were able to put up more resistance, but even they could do little except delay a substantial German force, which included airborne troops. Norway, up till this point, had been neutral. Britain, not suspecting that this invasion was a dangerous prelude to a wider war, responded half-heartedly.

The Norwegian situation was, in fact, considerably more complicated than was generally realised at the time, or for long afterwards. The country is three times as large as Britain but the population numbered, in those days, three million (now four million). Those three million were not evenly distributed – unsurprisingly, since half the land is over 3000 feet and only 30 per cent of the total area is cultivated. As may be expected, railways were few, airfields difficult to construct and maintain, and roads dangerous and rough. The winter is severe, but the spring can produce even greater hazards for anyone depending on mobility, and the problems of digging trenches in rocky, frozen, or flooded ground may be imagined all too easily. Bodø and Narvik, which figure conspicuously in the account which follows, are both within the Arctic Circle; on the other hand the southern tip of the country is on the same latitude as northern Scotland. Narvik owes its importance to the fact that in 1902 a railway was built (through nineteen tunnels) to link the port with the Swedish frontier and enable iron ore mined at Kiruna, in

Sweden, to be transported to the Norwegian port for export.

In 1939 there were good reasons for wishing Norway to be neutral yet friendly. After Britain and France had failed to stop the Germans marching into Austria, Czechoslovakia and Poland, countries like Denmark, Norway and Sweden clung tenaciously to their neutral status, feeling that overt sympathy with the Allies might bring down upon them the wrath of their large and powerful neighbour. Britain, for her part, was not anxious to stretch her existing commitments and weaken what she felt would be the main front in France. In late 1939, however, the Ministry of Economic Warfare informed the War Cabinet that if Germany were to be deprived of Swedish iron ore, which was shipped from Narvik, she would not be able to wage war for more than twelve months. Of Germany's normal twenty-two million tons of iron ore imports, nine million came from Sweden, and a further nine and a half million had come from sources which had already been cut off by the Allies. Clearly the import of Swedish ore was of great value to Germany and the sooner it could be stopped the better; in the last resort this might entail the occupation of Narvik. It was thought, however, that less extreme measures might produce the same result. One such measure would be an attempt to induce the Scandinavians to lessen the export to a trickle by normal trade agreements; if that failed, the second expedient would be to mine the route by which the ships carried the ore to Germany.

These ships sailed southwards from Narvik through the Leads, sheltered sea routes that lie between the mainland of Norway and the many islands off its western coast, and it was felt that if British forces had to enter Norwegian territorial waters for military purposes the Norwegians could hardly object, since by early 1940 the Germans were already operating submarines there with impunity, and occasionally torpedoing British ships. Accordingly, permission to mine the Leads was requested, but it was promptly refused by the Norwegian government who, naturally enough, felt that this would merely be asking for real trouble from Germany. The *Altmark* incident, however, when a German ship full of British prisoners taken from vessels sunk by the *Graf von Spee* was intercepted in Norwegian territorial waters by a British destroyer, HMS *Cossack* on 16 February 1940, showed that the Norwegian attempts to be neutral were becoming less and less successful. Scandinavian reaction to this incident was vociferous, however, and was to hamper later Allied plans.

Further complications arose from the Russian attack on Finland on 30 November 1939. The Allies hoped this would persuade the Norwegians and Swedes to allow an expeditionary force to cross their territory and aid the Finns against their large neighbour. But, quite apart from the military dangers to which this might expose them, the Norwegians and Swedes had a suspicion that both the British and the French – particularly the latter – were planning a new front against Germany and her Russian ally which would take attention away from France; the French were prepared to go to some trouble to prevent their country being a battleground once more. The RAF did, however, manage to send the Finns 150 aircraft from their own very limited resources, though these were mostly of obsolescent types.

February arrived before the idea of an Allied intervention force was approved by the British government. This scheme, known as Plan R4, sought to establish some 150,000 men in Scandinavia, accompanied by six and a half squadrons of aircraft, in order to help Finland. The *Altmark* incident alone was enough to prevent Norway and Sweden from accepting the plan.

In the meantime, Hitler had been misled by a Norwegian Nazi-sympathiser named Vidkun Quisling. Quisling, whose name is now given to any traitor from within who supports an enemy from without, told Hitler that Norway would welcome occupation, and that this could occur without bloodshed. Large numbers of Germans already knew Norway well from adventure-holidaying there, and there was a formidable network of German spies and agents in consulates and business firms.

Although Hitler moved first, British plans for the mining of the Leads were, by April 1940, so far advanced that there was little margin between the intervention of the two countries in Norway. Unfortunately, confusion among the Allies was already rife. When the Finns had signed a peace treaty with the Russians on 12 March, ceding them certain territories, Plan R4, designed to help Finland, had naturally to be abandoned. Its component parts – those forces ordered to stand by for service in Scandinavia – were then dispersed. Regrettably, one was an unusual unit described as 'the 5th Battalion, the Scots Guards'. The battalion had been specially recruited from the Brigade of Guards and included a number of veterans of the 1935 Everest expedition, and 150 officers who had laid aside their commissions to serve in the ranks of this highly qualified special unit. Its existence and constitution are worth remembering in view of the fate which later overtook another battalion of the Scots Guards in Norway, and one cannot but wonder whether Auchinleck's expectations of that other battalion were not partly based on what was known of the constitution of the 5th Scots Guards.

The presence of German troops in Norway before the Allies would make a considerable difference to subsequent events. Very swiftly after the invasion the Germans had been able to capture every usable airfield. In a country like Norway, where the iron in the mountains helped to make radio communications difficult but where aircraft could appear without warning over troops in valleys and ships in fjords, the possession of the available airfields was likely to be decisive.

Meanwhile it was the turn of the Royal Navy, though the RAF carried out a number of bombing raids on airfields and other targets. From 9 April German ships in the Skagerrak were attacked by British submarines, though unfortunately it was not possible to sink all of them. The aim was to sink as many German ships as could be found in Norwegian waters, but British efforts were hampered by an Arctic storm which made visibility poor and high-speed chase extremely difficult. On the evening of 9 April aircraft of the Fleet Air Arm attacked German shipping at Bergen and sank the light cruiser *Königsberg*. And at Narvik on 10 April the five ships of the 2nd Destroyer

Flotilla, led by the gallant Captain Warburton-Lee, having travelled through a continuous snowstorm for fifty miles, took on twice their own number of larger ships. The story of that fight is one of the epics of naval history; it was entirely successful, and had the rest of the Norwegian campaign been conducted in a similar spirit it might perhaps have had a different outcome. The British lost two destroyers sunk and a third seriously damaged, but they had sunk two of the much larger German destroyers, and damaged or seriously damaged five more, as well as sinking or damaging a number of supply ships. Captain Warburton-Lee died of wounds and was awarded a posthumous VC.

Meanwhile, the Allies strove to put into effect a hurriedly conceived counter-attack. Between 14 and 19 April three invasion forces were landed in Norway; the two largest at Andalsnes and Namsos, to the south and north of the port of Trondheim in Central Norway, occupied by the Germans on 9 April. The Germans now had some 24,000 well-equipped troops in Norway, backed by powerful air support and a strong naval presence. To oust them the Allies had approximately 14,000 men (though the French thought they might be able to raise a further 6000 Alpine-trained men later), with very little air cover, and much of that involving obsolescent aircraft operating under appallingly difficult conditions. Only the Royal Navy seemed able decisively to influence events in Norway. The two forces near Trondheim met with little success in their attempts to relieve the town by a pincer operation, and by 3 May all Allied troops from the two landings had been evacuated by the Royal Navy. The third Allied landing, near Narvik in Northern Norway, met with greater success. This expedition was under the command of Admiral of the Fleet Lord Cork and Orrery (a very senior man for a force of this size) with Maj.-Gen. P. J. Mackesy as commander of the land forces, and under the overall direction from London of Lt-Gen. H. R. S. Massy, the Deputy Chief of the Imperial General Staff.

Lord Cork's forces arrived at Harstad, an island some fifteen miles from Narvik, on 14 April 1940, and here

Mackesy's troops disembarked. Harstad was not, in fact, a proper port at all but a landing point, and each ship's arrival made the congestion worse; the fact that it was an island also meant that further transport was needed to ferry troops to the mainland. In addition, it soon became apparent that the two commanders were not seeing eye to eye. The Admiral was decisive and forceful; the General felt that impulsive or even swift moves were more likely to lead to disaster than to victory, and he could not be prevailed upon to launch an immediate attack on Narvik. With hindsight it is easy to appreciate both viewpoints. Lord Cork felt that speed was essential and that boldness should be the keynote; Mackesy felt that the troops at his disposal, although excellent, had been so disorganised, as well as being separated from much vital equipment, that a cautious policy was essential.

Mackesy held at his disposal 24 Guards Brigade (1st Scots Guards, 1st Irish Guards, 2nd South Wales Borderers with ancillary troops), 146 Brigade (1/4th Royal Lincolnshire Regiment, 1/4th King's Own Yorkshire Light Infantry, the Hallamshire Battalion of the York and Lancaster Regiment), 5 Demi-Brigade Chasseurs Alpins and, to follow, 1/5th Royal Leicestershire Regiment and 1/8th Sherwood Foresters. Most of these units had suffered from being hastily assembled, then embarked and disembarked. They lacked signals equipment, artillery, and anti-aircraft guns. To make up for this, each man had an issue of Arctic equipment which it took three kitbags to carry – but no transport for them. Had they worn the full complement they would have been completely immobilised.

In addition to these regular troops, Mackesy had at his disposal a contingent known as 'Scissor Force', consisting of five Independent Companies and an HQ under Colonel C. McV. Gubbins. Each Company, comprising nearly 300 officers and men, was issued with Arctic equipment, a month's normal ration and pemmican for a further five days, small arms ammunition, and a large amount of money in British and Norwegian currency. Each component of 'Scissor Force' was expected to live off the land, striking at German forces in order to delay them as the opportunity arose, though they were hampered by the problems of finding and carrying heavy reserves of ammunition and food. The men were all volunteers, but had received no special training.

In a letter to Dill later, Auchinleck expressed his doubts about the value of the Independent Companies, which seem to have been intended to operate as a sort of guerrilla force. He felt that guerrillas could only work inside their own countries, which they would know better than an invading enemy; guerrillas in a foreign country, however, even with the support of the local population, were likely to be hazardous rather than productive. In the event, the Independent Companies proved their worth during the staged withdrawal north to Bodø, but here they were operating as conventional infantry using accepted defensive tactics. Interestingly, twenty officers from the Indian Army were attached to 'Scissor Force' as advisers, on the grounds that their knowledge of mountain fighting would prove invaluable. The mountains of the Frontier are, however, a far cry from those of Northern Norway.

In London there was a strong conviction that Narvik must be taken and held at all costs, not merely as a matter of prestige but as a major factor in winning the entire war. This consideration overrode any idea of aiding the Norwegians who, until the evacuation of Allied forces from around Trondheim, had made a gallant fight of it in Southern and Central Norway against overwhelming odds, and continued to do so further north. In fact, anyone who knew the terrain might well have concluded that the central Norwegian battle was ultimately more important than simply occupying Narvik. Indeed, when the Germans had first been reported as being in Narvik Chamberlain had informed the House that it was probably a mistake for Larvik!

In order to make any sense of the situation in which Auchinleck found himself a short time later, it is necessary to set out the problems involved. Churchill, in his history of the war, described Norway as 'this ramshackle campaign', a fair description of the higher level planning, but somewhat ungrateful to the sailors, soldiers and airmen who did their utmost to make the best of a near-impossible situation.

While the plans for Narvik were being considered by the Chiefs of Staff on 10 April, the importance of Trondheim had been given due thought, since this was strategically the more valuable, though the Narvik force was approved. By the time Mackesy's troops had landed, Trondheim had once again been deemed essential to Allied plans. Orders and counter-orders had begun to produce chaos in what was already a confused command situation. By the third week in April, however, not long before the evacuation of Allied troops from around Trondheim, the War Cabinet had reached the conclusion that Narvik, after all, was the vital objective. Its capture was to be combined with the occupation of certain strategic areas down the coast to the south.

Mackesy's plan for the recapture of Narvik, in which Lord Cork had been forced to concur, depended upon a gradual wearing down of German forces to the north, east and south of the town. The Germans were isolated from their countrymen advancing from the south, and were short of supplies; in addition, they were engaged at several points by Norwegian and French troops. As has been said, Mackesy would not risk a direct seaborne assault on Narvik from Harstad, and he considered the conditions, chiefly the very deep snow, to be a major handicap to his troops. Accordingly, he used detachments of his forces to contain the Germans north and south of the town, and aimed to take Bjerkvik to the north, in order to permit the fjords to be used as highways for a direct assault. On 7 May the Foreign Legion landed at Bjerkvik, pushing east and north, while Polish forces advanced to join them from the west and the Norwegian and other French troops continued to push from the north and east. Landings at Bjerkvik continued for several days, and by 14 May (by which time Auchinleck had taken over) the area north and west of Narvik was securely in Allied hands.

The other strategic areas which concerned Mackesy were well to the south of Narvik. If he could contain the German advance from the Namsos area he could make Northern Norway a secure base from which the Germans could be driven back. To aid the Norwegians, he sent French and British troops to Mosjøen on 30 April, having previously secured Bodø as a base. The evacuation from Central Norway allowed the Germans to advance from Namsos, however, and Mackesy therefore decided to hold Mo, to which British and Norwegians began to withdraw (the Independent Companies had been sent to Mosjøen on 8 May). On 12 May Mackesy sent the Scots Guards to Mo, and continued to hold Bodø, supported by the Navy. The Allied forces were continually subject to heavy bombing, and the small, ill-equipped RAF contingent could do little to halt this.

By the third week in April, however, the Chiefs of Staff had decided to remove Mackesy, who did not get on with Lord Cork and whose health was far from good, and replace him with Lt-Gen. Auchinleck. On 28 April a message arrived at IV Corps HQ at Alresford while Auchinleck was having his supper; he was to report to the War Office and see the CIGS, General Ironside, at once. There he was informed that, together with certain members of his staff, he was to be sent to Norway as military commander of the Allied forces. His instructions, signed by Oliver Stanley, the Secretary of State for War, and dated 5 May 1940, are remarkable in that they show the muddle and uncertainty which prevailed in the War Cabinet at the time. Some of the uncertainty was due to poor Intelligence; as it was difficult to know what was happening in Norway itself, it must have been almost impossible for those in England to form a proper opinion. At this date Ultra – the code-name given to German signals gathered and decoded by Enigma machines in Britain – was too new to be contributing anything of value; in fact, it would not be an effective instrument for some time yet. And it is obvious that the Cabinet appeared to have taken scant notice of the persistence with which the Norwegian army was continuing to fight, against the most discouraging difficulties. Narvik had once more become the prime objective, though there were other areas where Norway's forces were resisting with some success.

*

The instructions to Auchinleck read:

1. The object of His Majesty's Government in northern Norway is to secure and maintain a base in northern Norway from which we can:–
    a) Deny iron ore supplies to Germany via Narvik.
    b) Interfere as far as may be possible with iron ore supplies to Germany via Lulea.
    c) Preserve a part of Norway as a seat of Government for the Norwegian King and people.

2. As a first stage in the achievement of this object, operations are now in progress for the capture of Narvik. The present forces assembled for this purpose are under the command of Admiral of the Fleet Lord Cork and Orrery; the Military Commander Major-General Mackesy being subordinate to him. A list of the Anglo-French troops at present under Major-General Mackesy is given in Annexure '1'.

3. It is the intention of His Majesty's Government that there should be no interference with the existing plans of Lord Cork and Orrery until they have either achieved success or been abandoned. At some future date, however, it will be necessary to revert to the normal system of command.

4. You are appointed GOC-in-C Designate of the Anglo-French Military Forces and the British Air Component in this area. His Majesty's Government will decide when the present system of unified command shall terminate. Thereafter you will be in independent command of the Anglo-French Military Forces and the British Air Component and will act in close co-operation with the Senior Naval Officer in the Narvik area.

5. You will proceed to the Narvik area with an officer detailed by the Chief of the Air Staff, and, in conjunction with Admiral of the Fleet Lord Cork and Orrery, report for the information of the Chiefs of Staff the forces required to attain the object in paragraph 1 above and the area which you recommend should be occupied. You should also take into account the necessity for making arrangements to enable any iron ore now at Narvik to be despatched to

the United Kingdom, and, if the situation permits, for resuming the supply of iron ore from the Swedish iron mines at Gallivare.

Your report should include recommendations as to the practicability and desirability of repairing the railway from Narvik to the Swedish frontier.

Scale of Enemy Attack up to November 1940

Naval

6. The scale of naval attack that may be expected against Narvik is:—
   a) Raids by capital ships or cruisers which, although not very likely, are a possibility.
   b) A heavy scale of submarine attack by both torpedo and mine.
   c) Light craft and MTB attack. Germany will probably take full advantage of such measure of control as she may be able to obtain over Norwegian waters to secure the approach of attacking light craft.

Land

The scale of land attack that may be expected is:—
   a) Raids or attempted landings by parties carried in coastal vessels.
   b) Sabotage, especially of the railway.
   c) Parachute landings.
   d) A German advance from Sweden following invasion of that country.

Air

The Narvik area is within reach of German bombers based on or re-fuelled in Southern or Central Norway. A daily weight of attack of 40 tons is possible from these bases from now onwards.

To this must be added a light scale of attack from seaplanes operating from fjords. The scale and frequency of these attacks would be very seriously increased if the Germans succeed in establishing air bases in Sweden such as Boden (near Lulea) and Ostersund, or further north in Norway.

To meet this scale the Chiefs of Staff estimate that two or three fighter squadrons, one bomber servicing unit and some Army co-operation aircraft are required.

7. When you have taken over command it is intended to withdraw Major-General Mackesy and the Staff of 49th Divisional Headquarters less such personnel as you may wish to retain.

8. The forces operating in Norway south of the Narvik area, at present under the command of Lieutenant-General Massy, may at an early date be placed under your command. The policy as regard operations in the area is described in the attached telegram which is being dispatched to Lord Cork and is at Annexure '2'.

9. Should you become a casualty or otherwise be prevented from exercising command of your force, command of the Anglo-French land and air forces will pass to a British officer to be nominated by you until another British officer can be appointed. This officer will be given the acting rank of Lieutenant-General.

10. You will act in co-operation with the Norwegian Commander-in-Chief.

11. You will maintain constant communication with the War Office.

(signed) Oliver Stanley.

One might wonder, in a situation as desperate as that in Norway, how anyone could be expected to organise the dispatch of iron ore and the reopening of railway lines. Instructions like 'maintain constant communication with the War Office' would at best be difficult and, at times, as, for example, when no cipher officer was provided on the vessel out, absurd. But, looked at from the point of view of the War Cabinet, if the gamble came off and Auchinleck's force could manage to retake Narvik the boost to national morale would be tremendous. It would not be the last time that Auchinleck would be asked to do something strategically unsound and tactically very difficult for the sake of someone's political face, in this case that of the Chamberlain government. Holding Tobruk unnecessarily would prove to be another such request; being pressed to attack in the desert before being reinforced yet another.

Auchinleck had set out his military needs as follows:

1. A light tank regiment.
2. A squadron (or more) of armoured cars.
3. A battalion of lorried infantry.
4. Five battalions of field artillery.
5. A howitzer battery.
6. Four companies of Field Engineers.
7. Twelve infantry battalions.
8. One machine-gun battalion.

This was a minimum shopping list; among other things, Auchinleck assumed that adequate air cover would be provided. It was one way of saying that the assignment was unnecessary and impossible, for he must have known very well that this balanced force was not available. Churchill who, as First Lord of the Admiralty, was anxious to prevent the Germans threatening our sea lanes from new bases in Norway, and who saw the restoration of national prestige as vital, backed the idea of the expeditionary force strongly. He found Auchlineck's calm deliberation irritating – the first time the two men brushed up against each other.

On 4 May another message had been sent to Lord Cork and Mackesy informing them that Auchinleck had been appointed to command the Anglo-French forces in Norway, but that their own plans for capturing Narvik and other strategic points should in no way be affected. Typical of the muddle prevailing, Auchinleck's staff had no official French interpreter and, as the French commander did not speak English nor Auchinleck French, the task of conveying technical information on arrival in Norway fell to Auchinleck's Staff Captain, C. F. G. Max-Muller, whose schoolboy French had not included such refinements; somehow he managed to achieve Anglo-French understanding. As has been mentioned, there was no cipher officer with the party and any message had to be decoded by a staff officer detailed for the purpose. The opportunities for error here were impressively large, for a cipher message replaces each letter of the original with another, or with a figure, but not necessarily in sequence. A minor error in transmission can make the message meaningless, and it would have to be referred back to the originator. Confusion reigned in the matter of supplies, too. One of the requirements on which Auchinleck had insisted was a number of 3.7-inch anti-aircraft guns. These were duly provided, but the ammunition for them was put on a different ship – which was sunk on the voyage.

After being equipped with what looked like almost totally unsuitable clothing for any form of mobile activity, Auchinleck's party embarked on a Polish liner, the *Chrobry*, on 7 May. The journey to Norway took four days. There was no means of replying to messages which came in by lamp. Anyone who has tried to read a lamp winking out its message in bad weather will appreciate that the chance of error is very large indeed. At times the lamp may be completely obscured by spray without either the sender or receiver realising it.

Among the messages, however, was one which riveted the attention of all on the *Chrobry*: on 10 May, one day before Auchinleck's party docked at Harstad, the Germans had launched a major attack through the Low Countries towards France. The principal theatre of war had now become Belgium, Holland and France. The new military commander for Norway was in transit, however, and could do little except wonder what effects the attack would have on his theatre of operations.

Military cynics firmly believe that if you are issued with winter clothing it is a sure sign that you are designated for the tropics (or vice-versa) – the over-clothed force stepped ashore at Harstad to a mild spring day.

Auchinleck and Mackesy were old acquaintances, having been at the Staff College, Quetta, together. Mackesy's plan for the recapture of Narvik seemed sound to Auchinleck when they met, and he now set off to discuss the situation with Lord Cork on his flagship, which entailed a journey by launch through stormy fjords. Lord Cork was well known for being somewhat volatile, but he and Auchinleck got on well from the start. He gave Auchinleck his appreciation of the position. He felt that the Allies could hold a substantial piece of Norwegian territory around the Vest, Ofot and Rombaks Fjords, that Bodø could be held and the area probably extended, but that the Swedish frontier could need watching. Narvik might perhaps be recaptured from the Germans now, but the operation would at best be hazardous and uncertain. Had an attempt been made earlier, Lord Cork felt, then the town would have fallen with considerably less risk and effort.

Auchinleck pondered on this. What he alone knew was that the War Office's intention, stated to him in a secret personal directive from General Sir John Dill, the Vice-Chief of the Imperial General Staff, was that he should take over control from Mackesy at the earliest possible opportunity and assume full responsibility as commander of the joint force. This was in sharp contrast to his stated orders, which had appointed him C-in-C Designate of the Anglo-French Military Forces and the British Air Component, but with the rider that Lord Cork's plans – and thus those of Mackesy – should not be altered. Mackesy, who had been unwell earlier, was now ill again. It was obviously necessary to replace him, in view of his differences with Lord Cork, and this recurrence of ill-health made Auchinleck's position somewhat easier. He therefore relieved Mackesy of his command but made it clear to the War Office that the latter's appreciation had been of the greatest tactical value. Privately he thought he had been over-cautious and too slow. The only painless way of relieving Mackesy was to have him recalled to London for consultation; Auchinleck proceeded to arrange this by a signal to the War Office, and officially took over command on 13 May. On the 12th he had watched French troops land at Bjerkvik under cover of a British naval bombardment, but the situation elsewhere seemed to be progressing less well.

The position to the south of Narvik was rapidly deteriorating in the face of the steady German advance, and, realising the desperateness of the situation, Auchinleck sent 24 Guards Brigade south on the 13th. Allied and

Norwegian forces had fallen back on Mo by 17 May, but this too had to be abandoned by the afternoon of the 18th. The Germans were attacking with greater persistence, and the Allies suffered heavy casualties from air raids. Auchinleck had written to Dill on the 17th that further reinforcements were essential if the position was to be held; the minimum infantry requirement was seventeen battalions.

It has been suggested that Auchinleck had little confidence in the Allies' ability to hold a position as far south as Mo, the proof being that he sent the Irish Guards to Bodø, rather than using them to strengthen the other forces around Mo. In the event, the Irish Guards were temporarily put out of action by a salvo of bombs which hit the *Chrobry*, on which they were travelling. The survivors were taken back to Harstad, bombed all the way but behaving with exemplary courage and discipline, but on their arrival it was found that there were not enough reserve stocks to re-equip them. Eventually they were taken to Bodø, and then marched south to Pothus to cover the withdrawal of the 1st Scots Guards from Mo. The latter battalion had already been under tremendous pressure, dive-bombed, machine-gunned and constantly attacked on the road north. Their casualties were now the equivalent of an entire company. After leaving Mo on the 18th, the Scots Guards were ordered to make a stand at Krokstrand, which they reached on 19 May. Auchinleck's command was 'You have reached a good position for defence. Essential to stand and fight. I rely on the Scots Guards to stop the enemy', and this order was influenced by instructions to Lord Cork from London that Bodø and the Saltfjord area must be held at all costs. The Krokstrand position had been chosen from the map, but Auchinleck had not been able to examine it personally. Had he been able to do so he would undoubtedly have seen that a firm stand there for any time was impossible in the existing circumstances.

The CO of the 1st Scots Guards, Lt-Col. Thomas Trappes-Lomax, had already achieved miracles with a force which had arrived in Norway short of the equipment necessary for that terrain; in any case, unlike the

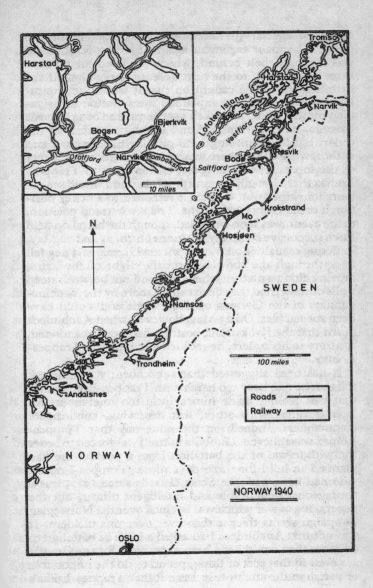

Harstad

Bogen   Bjerkvik

Ofotfjord   Narvik Rombaksfjord

10 miles

Tromsö

Harstad

Lofoten Islands

Narvik

Vestfjord

Bodö   Rösvik

Saltfjord

Krokstrand

Mo

Mosjöen

SWEDEN

Namsös

Trondheim

100 miles

N

| Roads | ——— |
| Railway | —·—·— |

NORWAY

NORWAY 1940

OSLO

dispersed 'special' 5th Battalion, it was quite untrained to use it. The main argument against holding Krokstrand was the snow belt behind, which extended for twenty-three miles north to the next defensible position. If the battalion should be caught on that it would be annihilated. Trappes-Lomax explained the situation to Brigadier Gubbins, who had taken over command of 24 Guards Brigade, on the telephone and Gubbins confirmed the order, lightly modifying it to one for hitting hard and withdrawing only if there was serious danger to the safety of the force. It was, however, all too clear to Trappes-Lomax that a last-ditch stand at Krokstrand would see the battalion wiped out, while if it retreated to a better position it could carry on the fight. The Krokstrand position, in the event, was soon enfiladed, though the battalion held three successive company positions on 20, 21 and 22 May, inflicting casualties on the advancing Germans. They fell back through the snow belt on the night of the 22nd, moving along a plateau where the road ran between steep walls of snow; had they been caught there by the machine-gunners of the German air force their end would have been spectacular. On 23 May, however, when Auchinleck heard that the Krokstrand position had been abandoned, contrary to his orders, he recalled and replaced Trappes-Lomax.

It has been suggested that subsequently Auchinleck felt that he had been too harsh with Trappes-Lomax, and that this feeling made him a little too tolerant in his later dealings with other, less deserving, subordinate commanders. Indeed, on the same day that Trappes-Lomax was relieved, Gubbins himself was forced to order the withdrawal of the battalion from a position he had planned to hold for three days more. Trappes-Lomax, who had been with the Scots Guards since 1917, was a courageous, honourable and intelligent officer, but the general fog of war which was so thick over the Norwegian campaign seems thicker than ever over this incident. It was not that Auchinleck had asked a Guards battalion to do more than could have been expected – for the Guards are used to that sort of thing, proud to do the impossible or perish in the attempt. It was not that Trappes-Lomax felt he knew better than the general from the Indian Army; it was simply a matter of mistaking a firm order for a flexible one, and no doubt Trappes-Lomax, when the campaign was over, would have seen it in that light. (In the event, it had no lasting effect upon his career, and he was promoted Brigadier two years later.) But it was a situation totally foreign to the thinking of both those concerned, and Auchinleck undoubtedly would have realised later that the affair was unlikely to have occurred if he himself had known the state of the ground. The characteristic of all his later battles is that he knew the ground as well, if not better, than the subordinate commanders who fought on it. He was always well up forward with his troops, enduring the discomfort and dangers they underwent, and that too is perhaps related to his experience of the Norway campaign.

Meanwhile, preparations for taking Narvik went on. Since the bulk of the British troops were to the south, delaying the Germans and falling back on Bodø, the attack on Narvik would be made mostly by French and Polish troops, under the command of Général de Brigade Béthouart. Auchinleck liked Béthouart and thought that his officers seemed to know their jobs; he was further impressed by the quality of the French troops.

On 18 May Lord Cork, who had received notice from London that the evacuation of Northern Norway might be a possibility, had sent a signal to the Chiefs of Staff. It struck a realistic note:

a. Narvik is not yet in our hands. No precise date can be given for its occupation. In any case Narvik by itself can have no value as a base for some time for the reasons given.
b. Narvik cannot be considered apart from the whole area which has to be defended.

Six other points followed, amplifying those above, and he added:

i. An appreciation of the situation created by your telegram under reference will shortly be forwarded by General Auchinleck and myself based on these facts which it is hoped, in the meantime, may receive the most earnest consideration of the Chiefs of Staff.

On 22 May Auchinleck followed this with another signal which requested:

> ... Three field batteries, 25-pounder or 4·5-inch howitzers, two 6-inch howitzers, some kind of mobile units for patrolling, one machine-gun battalion ...
>
> Forty-eight heavy and sixty light anti-aircraft guns can, of course, be distributed to give some apparent protection in vital areas but this is unlikely to be effective should enemy put in heavy air attack on bases and aerodromes, as appears possible.
>
> I cannot agree that there is reasonable prospect of my being able to achieve my tasks if less than half my considered demand for anti-aircraft artillery is to be provided which itself is only two-thirds of the original estimates prepared by the General Staff and the War Office before my departure from London.

A similar survey of air force requirements followed. He then added:

> The inevitability of the evacuation of Northern Norway in the circumstances envisaged in your telegram is, in my opinion, entirely dependent on the enemy's will to avail himself of his undoubted ability to attack ... If ... larger considerations lead His Majesty's Government to decide that Northern Norway must continue to be held with the diminished resources laid down by them I cannot answer for the consequences but you may rest assured every effort will be made to do what is possible with the resources at my disposal.

As early as 21 May, Churchill had told the Cabinet that the forces in the Narvik area might have to be withdrawn, and on 22 May the Chiefs of Staff concurred with this view. The situation in France had become desperate, with the Allied armies defeated everywhere and pushed back towards the northern coast. On 24 May Lord Cork received the following telegram from the War Cabinet:

HMG has decided your forces are to be evacuated Northern Norway at the earliest possible moment. Reason for this is that the troops, ships and certain equipment are urgently needed for defence of the United Kingdom.

We understand from military point of view operation of evacuation will be facilitated if enemy forces are largely destroyed or captured. Moreover destruction of railway and Narvik port facilities make its capture highly desirable.

Norwegian Government have not repeat not been informed and greatest secrecy should be observed.

Lord Cork sent for Auchinleck on 25 May, and the two then called in Béthouart. The news of the decision to abandon Norway was worse for the French general, since his own country desperately needed those troops which would now be involved in the temporary capture of Narvik. But he did not complain.

The attack on Narvik began on the night of 27–28 May. Under cover of a naval bombardment, French and Polish troops, with some Norwegians, stormed ashore and drove the Germans from the town, with a cost of only thirty killed and eighty wounded. Auchinleck observed the joy of the 6000 Norwegian inhabitants with sorrowful concern; like any honest man he hated deceiving those who trusted him, even for the wider good. But security demanded that the Norwegians should not be told of the forthcoming evacuation, since a panic among the Norwegian troops would have jeopardised the chances of getting Allied forces away safely – a singularly unworthy view, as it proved.

In the meantime, the forces to the south, Norwegian and Allied, continued to withdraw in the face of the German advance. The British reached Bodø on 27 May, while the Norwegians, now separated from their allies, fought a most effective rearguard action at Røsvik on the 31st. That same day, the British and other Allied forces were successfully evacuated from Bodø to Harstad, despite heavy German bombing.

On 3 June, at the same time as the end of the Dunkirk

evacuation, 25,000 Allied troops began to be evacuated from Norway, and by 7 June the evacuation was completed. The Norwegian Royal Family and many prominent Norwegians sailed with them, together with a large part of Norway's merchant fleet and navy. Two days after the safe evacuation of their allies, the Norwegian forces surrendered.

The Germans attacked the convoy all the way back, finally managing to sink the carrier *Glorious*, loaded with aircraft and pilots from the campaign in addition to her own complement. It was the end of a sad episode, but not the end of the war. Auchinleck landed at Greenock on 12 June, having been in Norway less than a month, and took the train to London. He was ready for his next assignment.

7

THE DEFENCE OF ENGLAND

The Norway campaign had been a disaster, but nevertheless it had provided some useful lessons. One was that
effective planning is impossible unless you have good, up-
to-date maps, preferably supported by aerial photo-
graphs. Britain is particularly fortunate in having had for
many years an excellent supply of Ordnance Survey
maps; this facility has been misleading in the past, however, as planners have often assumed that maps of similar
quality exist for other countries. This is far from being
true – in the First World War troops were sometimes sent
to capture features, such as hills, which did not even
appear on their own maps. The briefing for Norway had
been the best available, but it had been backed with the
issue of thirty-year-old maps to some units and even less
satisfactory material compiled from railway timetables,
tourist publications, and picture postcards. The fact that
much of the information was out of date had only been
discovered when it was too late to supplement it. But even
the best of maps could not have warned the troops of some
of the conditions they would encounter: a troop leader in
the Royal Lincolnshire Regiment related how his patrol
suddenly broke through the thin crust of snow and found
itself waist-deep in slush. The experience was, alas, not
uncommon, and the only way to cross such a treacherous
surface was to roll over it. Indeed, when Lord Cork had
gone with Mackesy to take a look at the Narvik defences
he too had sunk waist-deep into the snow, an occurrence
which made him more sympathetic towards Mackesy's
refusal to attack at once.

Auchinleck had been able to note the danger of having
too many small independent units in the field. In Norway
'Scissor Force' had consisted of five Independent Companies, each approximately 300 strong: the proportion of
officers, twenty per company, was high. They were keen,

they were courageous, but they were inexperienced and they were operating in unknown and extremely difficult country. It was a stupid waste of resources. On later occasions when Auchinleck was asked to sanction independent raiding units he did not do so until he was fully satisfied that they were trained and properly briefed for their task.

National confidence had been badly shaken by the defeats in Norway and France, and the Chamberlain government had fallen; fortunately Churchill, now Prime Minister, was in a position to rebuild Britain's faith in the future. It was a daunting task, and he accomplished it by matchless oratory. He looked like an old bulldog, and he symbolised all that was best in British determination and courage. But for those working close to him, unless they were his personal friends, he could be very difficult indeed, a fact which Auchinleck would know only too well later. For the moment, however, there could be nothing but unqualified praise and admiration for Churchill. His response to the threat of invasion had been the speech which included those memorable words: 'We shall fight on the beaches, we shall fight on the landing grounds, we shall fight in the fields and in the streets, we shall fight in the hills, we shall never surrender.'

Auchinleck had returned just before the Germans entered Paris on 14 June, but France was still resisting and did not conclude the Armistice with Germany until the 22nd. Nevertheless it was obvious that Britain's Continental allies were now out of the war and that a dramatically changed situation must be faced. The dull but secure days of the phoney war were over; instead Britain was fighting for her life. Auchinleck's first task was to complete a report on the Norwegian campaign. He commented on the lack of training and experience among British troops, using words like 'callow' and 'effeminate' to describe them, and comparing them unfavourably with the French, whom he called 'real soldiers'; but he blamed not so much the men themselves as the spirit of the 1930s. The report was ill received in the War Cabinet and he himself was criticised for its forthrightness. It was suggested that his long period of service in India had given him a wrong perspective. There were plenty who knew that he was right, however, and training methods from then on became increasingly rigorous. It would have been interesting to have had his view of the troops waiting to invade on D-Day some four years later, after a very different sort of training from that of the unfortunates of Norway.

On 14 June, the day after he got to London, he was told that, immediately after completing his report, he was to form V Corps, Southern Command, using the staff he had taken with him to Norway from IV Corps. His headquarters were to be in the nostalgically named Bhurtpore Barracks, Tidworth. It was probably the most vital command of the war, for if the Germans had invaded it would have fallen to V Corps to repel them. (A corps can be as small as thirty men but equally can include hundreds of thousands: a normal-sized corps, however, consists of three divisions, that is 45,000–50,000 men. The difficulty of giving precise figures for any organisation comes from the administrative needs of a fighting formation; thus if the entire supporting elements of a division is taken into the total – the divisional 'slice' – it may reach 41,000 men. However, for normal purposes a division is reckoned as about 16,000 men.)

V Corps included 4th and 50th Divisions, with 48th to come later. There was just enough intact equipment in England to equip two divisions – the material losses in France had been vast. In terms of manpower there were twenty-four other divisions in the country, but half of them were recently evacuated from Norway and France and the others were not yet trained. General Sir Alan Brooke was GOC, Southern Command, and Anthony Eden was now Secretary of State for War. These appointments were a ray of light in an otherwise gloomy picture. It was certainly needed. Even after Dunkirk there was a mood of bewilderment and apathy in many units.

Auchinleck set out to change this by some brisk orders.

There is no question of being on or off duty. All ranks are permanently on duty and will be ready to act against the enemy at a moment's notice. Permission to leave the immediate vicinity of quarters, except on duty, will be granted only in exceptional circumstances – this applies particularly to officers. Working parties while at work will have their weapons under armed guard (at least two sentries) placed ready for instant use in their immediate vicinity. Guards and sentries will be tactically sited and protected wherever they may be. No compliments [saluting] will be paid to anyone by guards and sentries. Sentries, who will invariably be posted in pairs, will make themselves as inconspicuous as possible and will not slope arms [carry them on the shoulder] but will carry them ready for instant use. The two sentries of a pair will always be disposed so as to cover each other and never so that both can be disposed of at once by an enemy.

There were many other practical hard-hitting provisions in these orders. Those receiving them would have no doubt about the attitude of the originator, nor the actions required of them. The last paragraph stated:

It is the duty of every commander down to platoon and equivalent commanders to impress on all under their command that they are now in a forward area which may at any time become a battle zone without notice and that their duty as soldiers comes before any other considerations and must always be in their thoughts.

Clearly an attack, perhaps at dawn, by a parachute division and a landing on a wide front from the sea were envisaged. This, of course, was flexible, modern warfare, but it drew lessons from Auchinleck's experience on the Frontier where a sentry who gave away his position would soon be picked off, and where, when danger threatened, an attack could come from any direction, usually the least expected. Auchinleck's father had fought in the Indian Mutiny, which started with an attack on a church parade, since it was known by the sepoys that troops would not be carrying arms.

However, the immediate transition from casual static forces into a mobile, highly motivated fighting force was not going to be easy, good orders or not. Recruits had been trained to stand upright, look to their own height, swing their arms and take even paces; now they were to behave more like Boy Scouts or Red Indians. Soldiers with experience of France or Norway saw the point of it quickly enough, but even the imminent threat of invasion could hardly break through the innate conservatism of others, including that of many officers. Civilians were treated with suspicion because of the exaggerated fear of spies and saboteurs. But as Auchinleck said in a letter on 29 June to the Vice-Chief of the General Staff (General Haining), 'I am ... making bricks without much straw. Two divisions on a hundred-mile front!' He went on, however, with the more optimistic view that the enemy might be stopped without too much difficulty on the coast. He was less sanguine about Britain's chances if the Germans were ever allowed to get their 'heavy stuff' (tanks, guns, transport, bridging equipment) ashore. Like many others at the time, he realised that everything depended upon the ability of the Navy and Air Force to hamper such traffic on the way over. In the same letter he expressed his dismay at the rumour that there might be an issue of a 'Dunkirk Medal'. 'We do not want to perpetuate the memory of that episode, surely?'

He emphasised one point very strongly:

People are still persisting in perpetuating and stressing the difference between Regular and Territorial Divisions. This, to my mind, is lamentable. If the Regulars are so much better than the Territorials (which is not *generally* true in my opinion) then they should be used to leaven the Territorials and not be kept as a corps d'élite in separate divisions. We shall not win this war as long as we cling to worn-out shibboleths and snobberies. I am sure of this. Cobwebs want removing at once.

Some people found such ideas upsetting; others found them stimulating and sensible. Montgomery, as Nigel Hamilton suggests in his recently published biography, must surely have been one of the latter – but apparently he would not express agreement with Auchinleck's theories. At his corps conference Auchinleck stressed another vital point: 'All resources, civil and military, to be co-ordinated. Army, LDV [Local Defence Volunteers, later the Home Guard], Police, ARP, must co-operate with a spirit of give and take.' (ARP was the civilian name for Air Raid Precautions; in the army those dealing with such matters, which included everything from tackling incendiary bombs to taking anti-gas precautions, were described as being engaged on Passive Air Defence.)

The summer of 1940 was tense, but had an air of unreality about it. Those who had believed that the German Army would follow the Dunkirk survivors across the Channel were surprised when they did not, and decided that the Royal Navy had once again demonstrated the invincibility of these islands. In fact, the reason for the lull in the onslaught was that Hitler thought that Britain would now be ready to sue for peace. As those hopes were shown to be unfounded, he directed the Luftwaffe to prepared for the invasion, preparations which meant bombing British ports and communications wherever possible. But the Germans had plenty of problems to solve before they could contemplate the implementing of Directive 16 – the plan for the invasion of Britain – which was issued at the end of July. The Directive named the period between 19 and 26 September as the only possible time when wind, tide and weather would permit an invasion. It did not, however, give details of how sufficient landing-craft could be assembled in time, nor how air superiority could be established, nor how the five battle-ships, eleven cruisers and many ships of the Home Fleet could be satisfactorily eliminated. The initial landings were to take place somewhere between Ramsgate and the Isle of Wight; subsequent landings were to be further north and further west.

On the British side of the Channel the problems of the Germans seemed considerably less formidable than Britain's difficulties over defining the most likely landing area. Invaders have the advantage of complete mobility while at sea, and, provided they have any control over the waters they are traversing, can pose a very worrying problem for the defenders. Once ashore, however, they are ill equipped to deal with resistance and counter-attack, for they are in an exposed position and armed with light weapons. Even if tanks are available they must be below a certain size if they are to be landed on open beaches rather than through ports.

Auchinleck had to keep all this in mind, but the major task that summer in Britain was to instil a sense of urgency into everyone and every action. If the invasion came before the country was ready – and the British did not know of Hitler's choice of dates – the defence could crumble at once. Beaches had to be mined and wired, gunpits and blockhouses built, communications established, mobility facilitated so that units could act as military fire brigades.

In view of the importance of high morale, great stress was laid on dealing promptly with defeatist attitudes. Woe betide the soldier, of any rank, who uttered defeatist sentiments. He was to be arrested and, if necessary, court martialled. Clearly the Corps Commander had his ear close to the ground. After Dunkirk most people, against all odds, looked forward somehow to an ultimate victory, but there were a few who believed Britain stood no chance. Their views were based on the statements of German invincibility brought back from Dunkirk by those who felt some explanation was needed of the collapse of France.

Auchinleck was not destined to stay a corps commander for long. On 19 July he learnt that he was promoted GOC, Southern Command, in place of Alan Brooke, who became C-in-C, Home Forces on the retirement of General Ironside, who was promoted Field-Marshal and given a peerage. Auchinleck's own command, on which he had only just started, was given to Lt-Gen. B. L. Montgomery, until now a Major-General commanding 3rd Division in Eastern Command. In his new role Auchinleck travelled extensively, examining defences such as flame-throwers; supervising training, and on one occasion arranging a demonstration for Queen Mary. He found the morale of the Home Guard impressive; a large number of them were veterans of the First World War, and they had not forgotten many of the lessons, even if their bones now creaked a little.

Throughout this period Auchinleck was having some trouble with one of his subordinates: as GOC, Auchinleck was Montgomery's boss – which could not have pleased Montgomery greatly, as he had conceived a dislike for his superior officer. He had taken over command of V Corps from Auchinleck on 22 July, sweeping into Auchinleck's just-vacated HQ early in the morning and immediately issuing new orders and countermanding others. Without reference to Auchinleck, he gave out a new policy; work on beach defence was to stop at once, a request for armour was cancelled. By evening he had already dismissed some officers; the following day saw the first of his damning reports on 50th Division, and blistering assessments of some of the officers (of whom Auchinleck, during his short spell as Corps Commander, had presumably uttered no criticism). The whole corps was to be reorganised and, in general, shaken up. 'Monty had V Corps at Clive House, Tidworth,' said Auchinleck. 'I used to go and listen in to his lectures – no coughing, no smoking, runs before breakfast – all very inspiring and made me feel a bit inadequate. But I doubt if runs before breakfast really produce battle winners of necessity. However, we got on though we had one row.'* *One row* was a magnanimous view of their relationship. Montgomery's memoirs suggest that the row was continuous: 'In the 5th Corps I first served under Auchinleck, who had Southern Command. I cannot recall that we ever agreed on anything.' Montgomery had no inhibitions about criticising his fellow officers, whether senior or not. Auchinleck had found 50th Division well up to expectations: Montgomery had found it unfit, of poor morale, and lacking in a spirit of urgency; and Auchinleck's gentle suggestion to him that his low opinion of the division was by no means justified was disregarded.

On the defence of Britain, Montgomery's ideas were very different from Auchinleck's, whose policy was to resist on the beaches. In his memoirs Montgomery wrote:

I found myself in disagreement with the general approach to the problem of the defence of Britain and

---

* John Connell, *Auchinleck: A Critical Biography* (London, 1959).

refused to apply it in my corps area, and later in the South-Eastern Army. The accepted doctrine was that every inch of the coastline must be defended strongly, the defence being based on concrete pill-boxes and entrenchments on a linear basis all along the coastline.

My approach was different. I pulled the troops back from the beaches and held them ready in compact bodies in the rear, poised for counter-attack and for offensive action against the invaders. After a sea crossing troops would not feel too well and would be suffering from reaction; that is the time to attack and throw the invader back.

On the beaches themselves all I would allow was a screen of lightly equipped troops, with good communications and sufficient firepower to upset any landing and cause it to pause.

From this it seems that in order to defy the wishes of his commander, Montgomery was prepared to use tactics which he knew could not possibly be right. If the Germans were seasick they would be at their worst on landing – that was the time to 'hit them for six', in his favourite expression. He could not really have believed that once the Germans had put a substantial force ashore, brushing aside the 'lightly equipped troops', anything could check them. He did not expect the Germans to employ such a policy in 1944 on the French coast: he expected stiff resistance on the beaches and was not disappointed. But in 1940 it served as a lever to undermine the authority of Auchinleck.

Auchinleck was none too pleased when Montgomery wrote asking that he should be allowed to have his own way and reverse his superior's policy of beach defence. Auchinleck wrote back immediately, thanking him and expressing agreement with some points, but:

I want to make it quite clear, however, that I wish the instructions as to the urgent need for the completion of the defences so as to admit of the withdrawal of men for training, which I issued to the Corps just before I left . . . carried out.

Montgomery, however, was determined. The War Office apparently turned a blind eye, and he got on quietly with the job of reversing Auchinleck's plans. There was another aspect of Montgomery's reorganisation of V Corps worrying the GOC. Auchinleck had, under protest, been obliged by the War Office to issue orders for the transfer of officers with British Expeditionary Force experience from the V Corps formation to others. In August he learnt that Montgomery – like himself loath to lose good officers – had, instead of referring to him, gone direct to the Adjutant-General on this subject.

Military standard practice – and normal courtesy – decreed that any approach to officers in higher formations should be routed through one's immediate superior. It is not always practised, but in previous wars an officer making a direct request to someone not his immediate senior was likely to receive a very chilly answer, perhaps a formal reprimand. Montgomery undoubtedly knew exactly what he was doing. He could see Auchinleck ahead of him all the way to the highest posts and realised that his superior's character would probably cause him to condone such offences, seeing them perhaps as over-enthusiasm rather than signs of calculating ambition. Auchinleck could on occasions lose his temper, but would quickly recover it; he could not imagine that others could really be less highly motivated than himself, an attitude which went back to his early training. But on 15 August 1940 Auchinleck was sufficiently incensed to write Montgomery the following, fairly mild, letter:

My dear Montgomery,

I want to draw your attention to your 84/A of August 7th. In this it is stated that you interviewed the Adjutant-General on the transfer of personnel with BEF experience.

There are two points with regard to this minute. I am quite aware that it is common practice in the Army for all ranks to visit the War Office, but in this case it appears that you interviewed the Adjutant-General on a matter which directly concerned my Headquarters, in that they had issued orders for certain transfers to take place. I do not consider that this is the proper manner in which this, or any other matter of this nature, should be handled. When orders are issued from these Headquarters, whether they come from the War Office or direct from these Headquarters, and you wish to make a protest, from whatever point of view against these orders I wish such protests to be made to these Headquarters and not to War Office officials over my head.

The second point is that I think it is unfortunate that, having interviewed the Adjutant-General, special reference should be made in the memo to which I have referred above to this fact, thereby indicating to your subordinates that you had gone over the head of my Headquarters to deal with the problem direct with the War Office.

I would like to add that the subject of transfer of personnel with BEF experience from your formation to others in England had actually been made the subject of protest both by my predecessor and myself to the War Office, in order to save formations under your command from being depleted of their trained personnel, and moreover these protests were made as the result of representations made by the 5th Corps. These protests having been turned down by the War Office there was no alternative but to issue orders for the transfers to take place, and these should have been obeyed without any further reference to anybody.

I am afraid I must ask you to cancel the memorandum in question. You will, I am sure, understand that my sympathies are entirely with you in this matter and that my object in writing to you as I have is to ensure that our common object shall not be defeated by the 'short cut' method of conducting business, which in my experience nearly always ends in confusion, however efficient it may appear at the time.

Yours sincerely . . .

Montgomery's reply to this is not on record. In any case he had now proceeded well beyond the original cause of the letter – an attempt to prevent the loss of experienced officers by postings to other units – and he was now (perhaps taking his cue from the War Office's action) busily engaged in poaching from other units. Nowadays such actions might not seem at all immoral: the practice of 'head-hunting' is accepted commercial behaviour. It was not accepted behaviour in the Army, but once again Auchinleck's response to this latest manoeuvre was unexpectedly mild:

> It has come to my notice that in your understandable desire to get the best officers available in your corps you have been dealing direct with the branches of the AG's department at the War Office, and asking them to post officers to specific appointments in your corps from units and headquarters of other formations in this Command. You will no doubt recall one or two incidents.
>
> I want you to realise that this procedure, however justifiable it may seem to you, is likely to cause extreme annoyance to the Commanders of the formations and units concerned, more particularly where, in their opinion, your selections do not tally with their ideas as to who is the best man in the unit concerned for the job for which you want him. I am sure that you do not mean to cause friction or to give offence, but I am afraid that unless you first consult the commander you will do so and I do not want friction.
>
> I shall be grateful therefore if in future when you want a particular officer for a particular appointment from another formation in this command you will either approach me or the formation commander first. I am sure that generally your wishes can be met.

Auchinleck decided that the Adjutant-General should be left in no doubt of what was going on, since the latter probably assumed that Montgomery had received Auchinleck's sanction for the direct approach. Such an approach was very unusual, and the Adjutant-General was almost certainly unaware of the direct requests which were being made to his staff, who complied under the impression that all was agreed at top level. Auchinleck now clarified matters with the following letter:

You probably know that Monty, commanding the 5th Corps, is in the habit of going direct to branches of your department in order to work transfers of officers from other formations to his own corps. He has done this recently more than once I think.

I sympathise with his desire to get the best and his energy (binge he would call it) in making personally sure that he gets what he wants. Heaven helps those who help themselves. However, this practice tends to cause friction and I have had complaints from the commanders of formations from which Monty had kidnapped officers, to the extent that his selections do not always coincide with their own ideas as to the relative efficiency of officers in the units concerned, and that consequently the officers passed over by these personnel selections become disgruntled. I know the whole subject is a very difficult one but I daresay you will agree that it is undesirable that this practice should become prevalent.

Auchinleck must have disliked writing these letters intensely; it was humiliating to be defied by Montgomery in the first place and even worse to have to let the Adjutant-General know that his subordinate had not only ignored his original mild reprimand but also gone on to deserve a stiffer one. Auchinleck had lost a trick here. He was a soldier, not a politician; Montgomery was both.

Had the officer-poaching been an isolated occurrence Montgomery's activities might have been overlooked, and certainly not regarded as disloyal; but, when added to his defiance of Auchinleck in tactical matters – the reversal of the beach-defence policy – it must have made his attitude very difficult for Auchinleck to tolerate with equanimity. And there were plenty of problems for Auchinleck to consider in August and September 1940 without having to worry about insubordinate practice by divisional commanders. The German air force began steadily hammering at what were considered to be vital areas. Dover and the Channel ports received the first onslaught, which then moved inland to airfields and communications centres. An imminent invasion was clearly on the cards, but the War Cabinet learnt from Ultra – although it was at that stage still not very far developed – that the Germans were having trouble with their plans for Operation 'Sealion' (the invasion of Britain) and that the Luftwaffe was not claiming air superiority, and regained their confidence to the extent that, on 10 August, it was decided that Britain could spare a considerable quantity of men, guns and tanks for the Middle East. Britain duly sent 154 tanks (in three regiments), forty-eight anti-tank guns and 250 anti-tank rifles, twenty Bofors (anti-aircraft guns), forty-eight 25-pounders and 500 Bren guns. What was left of Auchinleck's beach-defence plans was thus destroyed. Yet an invasion was a dangerous possibility – even after 17 September when Hitler postponed it, for it could have taken place as late as November – and those men, tanks and guns could have made the vital difference to the defence of Britain had the Germans invaded. Although ultimately correct, the War Cabinet's decision to deplete Britain's meagre resources for a distant campaign seems a remarkable one: either long-sighted wisdom or the utmost folly – even today it seems hard to decide.

Auchinleck issued a number of forthright instructions for the defence of the area at this period, not omitting the Home Guard, for which he had a special affection. In his view the Home Guard possessed certain invaluable assets. They were fighting for their lives on their own home territory and no one could ask for greater motivation than that. They had expert local knowledge of tracks, roads and features, and that knowledge would make them quickly aware of any unwelcome intruder bent on sabotage or other mischief. (Auchinleck may perhaps have overrated their local knowledge. Any motorist becomes quickly aware that few people have accurate knowledge of a place outside their immediate area, and not always of that.) Country people are used to moving around in the dark – or were then – without the aid of torches or lanterns. They were also better than townspeople at crossing obstacles whether hedges, woods or ditches. Many of them could ride horses, thus increasing the range of a patrol. He pointed out that even if the immediate danger of invasion passed the Home Guard training would not be wasted, for they could then take over the general duty of Home Defence. One point in particular strikes one as showing his complete imaginative grasp of the situation in which the Home Guard found itself:

> To make up for their relative weakness in arms and equipment it is essential that all defence works to be manned by the Home Guard should be sited with the greatest care and cunning. An enemy is most unlikely to hit works which he cannot see, however powerfully armed he may be, and it is vitally important that every possible artifice and trick should be used to hide any defences wherever they may be made. In the circumstances in which the Home Guard will have to fight, concealment is 90% of the battle. No defence work should be recognisable for what it is at over fifty yards range. Much well-intentioned work which was done in the earlier stages of the battle for this country, suffers from being too obvious and it is necessary to put this right without delay. The mere sight of a sandbag is enough to put an enemy on his guard. A good deal of the earlier work is not proof against rifle fire and is therefore an actual danger rather than a safeguard.

This instruction led to some ingenious efforts in camouflage. Guns were concealed in haystacks, roundabouts, wood piles and other apparently innocuous settings. The fact that some of the pill-boxes are easily visible today should not be taken as an indication that they were always so. Skilful camouflage with shrubs and branches meant that sometimes it was possible to walk right up to the muzzle of a gun without realising it was there. Pevensey Castle, for instance, had an ingenious piece of medieval-looking masonry added to it, thus enabling machine-guns with an excellent field of fire to be concealed.

It was at this time that Auchinleck first met Edward Seago, the painter: 'I met Ted Seago for the first time as a camouflage officer and liked him from the start. We had some fun together camouflaging Chesil Beach. He invented a wonderful camouflage material made out of horsehair which was the best I have ever seen, but the

War Office said there were not enough horses to provide the necessary hair.' Years later, Seago's friendship and his encouragement of Auchinleck's painting were to have a great effect on the Field-Marshal's life in retirement.

Although large numbers of soldiers were apparently doing very little, Auchinleck was quick to repudiate the idea that they could be more usefully employed. To many people, including the writer of an article in the *Spectator*, dated 27 September 1940, there were plenty of soldiers who could have been relieving some of the civil defence services, either by fire-fighting, clearing up the debris left by air raids, or digging out air raid victims. With over 5000 people being killed each month by air raids the strain on civilian services was immense. There were many occasions when troops were called in to help, but that was a very different matter from taking over duties completely. If the invasion came there would not be much gain in having large numbers of soldiers deployed on ARP and similar activities. Auchinleck wrote to Brooke about the article which he considered 'a most dangerous statement'. However, at the beginning of November, although the threat of invasion was by no means past, and would not be until the Germans committed themselves in Russia the following summer, he was taken out of this vital command.

The custom of moving army officers from one post to another often seems inexplicable to many civilians. For the first part of his posting the new commander is learning his job, then he makes a few changes and sees how they work; then suddenly he is off again. The theory is that a new look and new ideas keep everything up to date and set the blood of the unit coursing, but in practice the benefits are often hard to discern.

On 21 November he was officially appointed Commander-in-Chief, India, succeeding General Sir Robert Cassels who was due to retire. The hand of Leopold Amery, who was Secretary of State for India and Burma from 1940 to 1945, may be detected here; he had always had a high opinion of Auchinleck and believed that if anyone could mobilise the resources of the sub-continent, then he was the man to do it. India was not threatened with invasion at this time, but if Britain became too pre-occupied with Europe there was every chance that the Japanese, the third factor in the Berlin–Rome–Tokyo axis, would seize any opportunities there if they occurred. Furthermore, the demands made on the Indian Army for troops for the Middle East might well, in the future, provide Indian political agitators with inflammatory material. If, however, the Army was at one with the Commander-in-Chief – as it would be with Auchinleck – the danger could be discounted.

Auchinleck's post in Southern Command went to Lt-Gen. Alexander, his old friend from Indian campaigning days. Many thought his former command might have gone to Montgomery, who already knew the area and the units involved well. Had it done so Auchinleck's subsequent career might have been very different.

Among his first farewell messages was one to the Home Guard:

It is with the greatest regret I now say Goodbye to you.

The Germans are still in a position to launch a large-scale attack on this country and this state of affairs may last for many months to come. I am firmly convinced that in meeting this threat the Home Guard will have a great and increasingly important part to play.

The more I see and hear of your work the more sure I am that to make yourselves fit to shoulder this great responsibility you have only to go on as you are doing. I have no doubt whatever that you will.

Everywhere I go I am amazed by the originality, ingenuity and efficiency shown by all ranks. Your keenness and self-sacrifice are beyond praise and an example to all soldiers. You are now firmly established as an indispensable part of the single Army we have formed and I hope that the bond between you and the Regular troops serving side by side with you in the Command may not only be maintained but strengthened.

I thank you all most sincerely for what you have done to help me to make this part of the country secure against the enemy and I wish you the best of luck in the future.

On taking over as Commander-in-Chief, India, Lt-Gen. Auchinleck would be promoted General and addressed as 'Your Excellency', and he was also awarded the GCIE (Knight Grand Commander of the Indian Empire). His appointment was greeted with enthusiasm by the units of the Indian Army who were already performing distinguished service in the offensive against the Italians in the Western Desert – the offensive made possible by the dispatch of tanks and weapons from hard-pressed Britain.

The next stage was anything but prestigious. On 27 December the Auchinlecks embarked on a Sunderland flying-boat in Southampton Water. As they could not fly over Europe they had to proceed via a wide sweep into the Atlantic, out of the likely range of German aircraft, then land at Estoril in Portugal. Since Portugal was neutral all visitors had to be civilians, which, for Auchinleck, meant wearing a suit and using an assumed name and a different occupation. He became Mr Smith, businessman, but his wife, 'Mrs Smith', owing to a clerical oversight was described in her passport as 'Army Officer's Wife'. Such details were not of vast importance in Portugal, which then abounded with spies with assumed identities; the Auchinlecks subsequently described the occupants of their hotel as 'the biggest collection of riff-raff imaginable'. The journey onwards was most unpleasant, taking them to Las Palmas, Sierra Leone and Port Harcourt, thence by small aircraft to Kano, Khartoum and Cairo before going on to New Delhi, which they reached by the second week in January 1941. Auchinleck's stay at Cairo gave him the opportunity to discuss the Middle Eastern situation with Wavell, the C-in-C there, little realising that the latter's headaches would soon be his own.

8

'GENERALLY ACCLAIMED'
C-IN-C, INDIA

Before leaving Khartoum Auchinleck had taken the opportunity to visit 4th and 5th Indian Divisions, which were at Kassala in Abyssinia (now Ethiopia) waiting to invade Eritrea. It was probably the happiest moment in an uncomfortable journey. Lady Auchinleck remembered the journey as farcical rather than arduous; she was not one to complain of the occasional rigours and discomforts of being married to an army officer (as some do!). She was looking forward to returning to India, which she loved. The winter of 1939–40 had been worse for the Auchinlecks than for many for they had come from a warm climate to near-Arctic conditions and found coal for domestic heating was severely restricted.

India seemed calm, but many Indian politicians were quietly resentful of the fact that they were now in the background rather than the makers of news. They had a further cause for resentment: the Indian Army – several divisions of it – was bringing credit to the country by its performance in the Middle East, but there were those who felt it should not have been sent there at all. There was a general awareness that the British Empire was locked in a desperate struggle and that India was one of the keys to success, but the complex bureaucratic machine of peacetime military and civilian affairs was not going to be altered quickly, if at all.

In 1940 Herbert Morrison, Minister of Supply, had appointed a committee under Sir Alexander Roger, a businessman of distinction, to examine and report on the potential of India as a source of war supplies. The brief was vast but the recommendations were gratifying in that their implementation enabled India to provide vital supplies both for the Middle East and, later, the Burma campaign. Auchinleck was well aware, however, that the East was full of the graves of men who had tried to hurry it, and was not surprised to find that a spirit of urgency was almost totally lacking in India.

India was not as remote from the war as many supposed. Japan, though not yet in the war, was increasing in her belligerence, and posed a threat which, while it was not considered to be immediate, could not be discounted. To threaten India the Japanese would have to come through neutral Siam (Thailand) and British Burma, or past the supposedly impregnable naval fortress of Singapore. Even the most fanatical Japanese would be unlikely to venture on such a risky policy unless those areas were so denuded of defensive forces by European demands that they were exceptionally vulnerable. But the Japanese had a nuisance value in that it was necessary to maintain at least some forces in those areas as a deterrent.

It was heartening that Lt-Gen. Richard O'Connor had, by February 1941, crushingly defeated a vast Italian army in the desert campaign, but in the same month there were reports – well founded, as it turned out – that German troops had now entered the theatre, under Lt-Gen. Erwin Rommel, who had commanded a Panzer division with distinction during the conquest of France. So far the German force was small, but its effect on Italian morale was likely to be considerable.

The general situation was made much worse by the fact that the Greeks, who, since 28 October 1940, had held off Italian attacks without much difficulty, were in considerably worse case when the Germans went to the assistance of their allies in April 1941. The details of the campaign do not concern us, but the effects do. In order to assist her ally's courageous stand Britain sent, or rather General Wavell sent, 50,000 men and 8000 vehicles from Middle East Command to Greece, which had already received a smaller British force and some RAF squadrons. Retained in the desert, these troops could well have enabled Wavell to clear the remaining Axis forces, including the newly arrived Germans, out of North Africa. But it was not to be. Instead the Germans conquered Greece and the island of Crete, though whether the retention of Crete would have been worth the effort – it was a battle Britain nearly won and which cost the

Germans dear – is debatable. But the need to make an effort to protect a gallant ally could not be denied.

In the meantime another set of troubles had come to light, this time in Iraq. Even before Auchinleck left England (on 27 February) to take up his post as C-in-C India, Iraq had been worrying him, for he firmly believed that Allied control of that country was essential for the safety of India. In early February he was involved in plans for British intervention in the Middle East. Operation 'Sabine' – aimed at a British occupation of Basra – was of particular importance to him; on 8 February he wrote to Wavell, the C-in-C Middle East, emphasising the need to make early preparations for this plan: 'time is getting short and the situation in Iraq looks none too pleasant.'

Remembering from the Mesopotamian campaign of the First World War the hazards and confusion arising from the division of command between Basra, India and London, Auchinleck wrote to Wavell and General Sir John Dill, by now CIGS, on 21 February, stating his opinion that the task of occupying Basra should come under his command. Wavell – at the time much involved in Greece – did not share Auchinleck's sense of urgency; indeed, he considered, along with a substantial body of 'experts', that intervention in Iraq would arouse the hostility of the entire Arab world. On 8 March, however, he agreed to Auchinleck's proposition.

Auchinleck started preparations immediately – and none too soon, for on 3 April a revolt in Iraq established a pro-German government there under Rashid Ali. On the 8th Auchinleck sent a message to Wavell offering to dispatch an infantry brigade to Basra immediately, with two more to follow within three weeks. Such positive action won Auchinleck Churchill's approval and, on 10 April, the War Cabinet accepted his offer, although Wavell – under whose command Iraq fell – was still reluctant, suggesting instead the use of diplomatic means to overcome the situation. The Marquess of Linlithgow, Viceroy of India, wholly supported the Auchinleck viewpoint, however, endeavouring at the same time to reconcile the views of Auchinleck and Wavell, whom he knew to be friends. He wrote to Amery saying that, delicate though the situation might be with regard to Arab feeling, it was as nothing to the perils which would confront the Allies if Iraq and the Gulf came under German control.

On 18 April Auchinleck's Indian Army force arrived at Basra, taking the Iraqis by surprise and reaffirming British treaty rights. Rashid Ali thereupon signed a secret treaty with Axis representatives and regained enough confidence to prepare for an offensive against the Allies. But Auchinleck had already dispatched more troops, who arrived in Iraq on the 29th. On 2 May the British cantonment and RAF base at Habbaniya were besieged by a force of 9000 Iraqis. After some fighting, however, Rashid Ali's troops were defeated and he himself forced to flee, being replaced on 31 May by the government he had ousted.

The most unfortunate aspect caused by the Iraqi crisis, as we have seen, is that it brought Wavell and Auchinleck into conflict, and caused Churchill to take a critical view of Wavell – unjustly, for Wavell was bearing other burdens in the Middle East. On 11 May Admiral Darlan, the effective leader of the Vichy French government, had allowed the Germans and Italians to establish air bases at Damascus, Palmyra and Syris in Syria. Britain feared that, under its Vichy Governor, General Dentz, Syria would soon become another German satellite, threatening oil supplies from the Gulf and Wavell's eastern flank.

The Allied forces available for dealing with the new threat in Syria were limited, consisting of 7th Australian Division, a part of 1st Cavalry Division, and a Free French force of six battalions with a squadron of tanks and a battery of artillery, plus seventy aircraft and some naval support. The force was outnumbered at all points by the Vichy forces, which fought much harder than had been expected, but by 11 July – by which time Auchinleck had taken over from Wavell – victory in Syria had been gained. In a campaign in which all fought well it is invidious to mention names, but the presence of two brigades from 10th Indian Division played a valuable part. British, Free French, Australians, Arab Legion, and Commandos all added to their laurels.

In August, following the German invasion of Russia on

22 June, a joint Anglo-Russian force occupied Persia: until then and the victory in Syria there had been a reasonable chance that a sudden thrust by the Germans might disrupt the West's oil supplies. The success in Iraq, Syria and Persia all stood to Wavell's credit, though he may be justly criticised for giving support to the unsuccessful attempt to save Greece. But he was much less happy with the campaign in the Western Desert.

The arrival of Rommel and his German forces had led to a complete reversal of British fortunes. O'Connor had been forced to return troops to be sent to Greece, and by 11 April the British had been pushed right back into Egypt. O'Connor himself was captured, and only Tobruk, which could be supplied from the sea, remained in British hands, though virtually besieged. Operation 'Battleaxe', which began on 15 June, was designed to relieve Tobruk, but after an encouraging start had the worst of an encounter with Rommel (who had anticipated British moves) at Sidi Omar, and 'Battleaxe' was broken off after three days. The new Crusader tanks, from which much had been expected, broke down at the most inconvenient moments and the slow and undergunned Matildas were no match for the Germans. But the decisive factor of the battle was the ability of the Germans to feint an attack and then turn to retreat, by which tactic British tanks would be lured into the sights of well-concealed German 88-mm guns, the first time British armour had come across this highly effective weapon. (The gun had been designed as an anti-aircraft weapon, but Rommel discovered its potential as an anti-tank gun.)

All this gave Churchill the impression that, while Auchinleck might be a lucky general, Wavell was not. Actually, Wavell had achieved miracles in the past, but the past was the past, the present was the present, and what was needed was luck and bright ideas for the future. Churchill wrote:

General Auchinleck's forthcoming attitude in sending at our desire and with the Viceroy's cordial assent, the Indian Division to Basra so promptly, and the readiness with which Indian reinforcements were supplied, gave

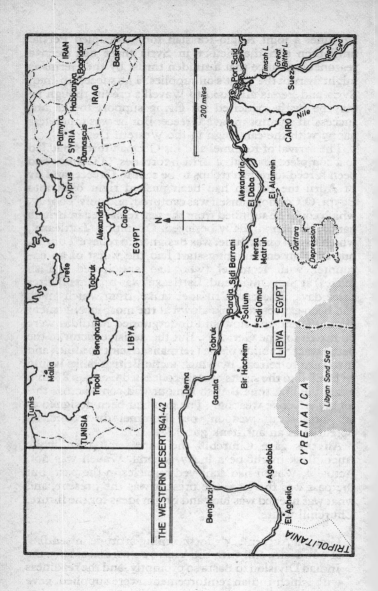

THE WESTERN DESERT 1941-42

200 miles

N

us the feeling of a fresh mind and hitherto untaxed personal energy.

In the third volume of *The Second World War* Churchill gives a clear indication of how his mind was running: 'At home we had the feeling that Wavell was a tired man. It might well be said that we had ridden the willing horse to a standstill.' He goes on to criticise Wavell's handling of the Cretan situation and of 'Battleaxe'. But:

> I admired the spirit with which he had fought this small battle, which might have been so important, and his extreme disregard of all personal risks in flying to and fro on the wide confused field of fighting ... I came to the conclusion that there should be a change ...
> General Auchinleck was now Commander-in-Chief in India. I had not altogether liked his attitude in the Norwegian campaign at Narvik. He had seemed too much inclined to play for safety and certainty, neither of which exists in war, and to be content to subordinate everything to what he estimated as minimum requirements. However, I had been much impressed with his personal qualities, his presence and high character. When after Narvik he had taken over Southern Command I received from many quarters, official and private, testimony to the vigour and structure he had given to that important region. His appointment as Commander-in-Chief in India had been generally acclaimed. We have seen how forthcoming he had been about sending troops to Basra and the ardour with which he had addressed himself to the suppression of the revolt in Iraq. I had the conviction that in Auchinleck I should bring a new fresh figure to bear the multiple strains of the Middle East, and that Wavell, on the other hand, would find in the great Indian command time to regain his strength before the new but impending challenges and opportunities arrived. I found that these views of mine encountered no resistance in our Ministerial and military circles in London. The reader must not forget that I never wielded auto-

cratic powers and always had to move with and focus political and professional opinion.

While all this was happening Auchinleck was travelling around India surveying his command, and receiving news of the Iraqi crisis and the progress of 'Battleaxe'. Communication was by no means as rapid or complete as might be imagined; enormous strides have been made since 1941 and it is sometimes difficult to realise how large a part letters once played. Telegrams were, of course, used, but tended to be over cryptic, and as likely to alarm and confuse as to inform.

In February Auchinleck had received a long letter from Amery which had warned that the Japanese were potentially very dangerous indeed, and that German pressure on Turkey might necessitate sending Indian troops there. There had been a mention of the strategy by which the conquest of Japan would be quickly completed: all Japanese shipping would be immediately captured or sunk, and an advance made from Malaya to the Kra Isthmus, in Siam, as a precaution against land attack.* The Indian Army had already supplied the elements of two divisions to Malaya, although their combined strength only totalled less than 20,000. They were meant to complete their training out there but the shortage of suitable weapons would make this difficult. As no emergency was contemplated the problem of reinforcement did not seem important.

Auchinleck felt, however, that the general outlook in India was encouraging. Munitions production was increasing rapidly, and the expansion of the army was also proceeding well, although equipment was still a problem; there was no point in raising troops not urgently needed if there were no weapons for them. He had, in addition, received a curious request from Singapore for regular officers to command irregular units which it was proposed to raise out there. He refused it, saying:

* British reluctance to infringe Siamese neutrality delayed the operation of this plan: by the time it was put into effect the Japanese had already begun to land on the Kra Isthmus.

I have always been rather sceptical (hidebound – I suppose!) of the value of these specialised small units. I feel that the officers and NCOs they absorb would be of much greater value training and leading regular units on which we must rely to win the battle finally.

The last statement is of no small interest, for Auchinleck has often been criticised for being too prone to allow his armies to be weakened by small splinter groups. It is true that his period of command in the Middle East saw the formation of the highly successful 'Jock Columns' under Brigadier Jock Campbell, and that he gave David Stirling permission to recruit the first sixty-six members of the even more renowned Special Air Service, but since these units were to prove of considerably greater value than mere 'splinter groups' the criticisms of Auchinleck do not seem well founded. Regular officers tend to be suspicious of unconventional units, regarding them as being nearly as disruptive to their own side – in view of the strong feelings they arouse – as to the enemy. But Auchinleck must have wondered later how on earth it was proposed to use such units against the Japanese who did not provide many suitable targets for sabotage tactics.

Despite the encouraging outlook in India the new C-in-C did not think that the Army was getting enough of the right types of Indians for commissions, and he thought that pay differentiation between English and Indian soldiers when both were doing the same job should be abolished forthwith. He saw no difficulty in getting plenty of the right sort of Indian recruits and suggested reviving some of the old regiments with regional associations, as well as creating new ones in previously unrepresented districts. The navy was expanding satisfactorily but the air force gave cause for worry as most of its aircraft were obsolescent and it was difficult to obtain replacements, let alone newer models. One day he hoped to see Indian pilots used in other theatres.

And now, after Auchinleck had been C-in-C India for only a few months, Churchill was proposing that Auchinleck and Wavell should exchange posts. Churchill's claim, with reference to this decision, that he 'never wielded autocratic powers and always had to move with and focus political and professional opinion' might perhaps surprise those who saw generals and admirals shuffled around briskly by the Prime Minister, but the second part of it has more significance than the first. No one would doubt that Churchill at times behaved like an autocrat, and often it was as well for the country that he did, but there was also in him a sense of public opinion. 1941 saw heavy losses in the Atlantic, and in March the Luftwaffe had been on a tour of the British ports, including Portsmouth, Liverpool and the Clyde, killing an average of 1000 people a night. London had a turn in mid-April, when over 2000 people were killed in two nights, then Plymouth, the Clyde and the Mersey had another hammering. Apart from those killed there were the wounded, the homeless, and those under the almost intolerable strain of trying to keep going. Anything that could help morale was vital; equally, any feeling that the war overseas was not being prosecuted with the utmost vigour and skill would cause the Prime Minister's encouraging oratory to fall on deaf ears, or rouse resentment rather than passion.

In Churchill's eyes it was no time for quiet patient progress, however efficient such a procedure might be. That Wavell, who bore a colossal burden of command, had been asked to achieve the impossible and had made a brave effort was not enough. Someone else must take his place and look like a better prospect. It was not that Churchill was playing politics; he was interpreting a national feeling. Those who suffered from his apparently arbitrary moves – Wavell, Admiral Godfrey, Auchinleck himself – knew the pressures which caused such personal injustice.

9

'A NEW, FRESH FIGURE'
MIDDLE EASTERN COMMAND

The decision to change over Wavell and Auchinleck was not made quickly; indeed, it had been mooted as early as April 1941. Amery was not enthusiastic for a direct exchange, and said so. He felt that Wavell should come home and someone else take over in Cairo. He told Churchill that he feared that India would feel she was being given a failed general in Wavell, just at a moment when it was necessary, given the substantial Japanese threat in the East, that Auchinleck's drive should be continued. But Churchill did not want Wavell in London: he knew he would be a disappointed man and he felt he deserved better than to be left unused in England. Dill too, by now CIGS, was lukewarm about the exchange. He had long been an admirer of Auchinleck but felt he was best employed in India.

These objections made no difference to the result. On 21 June telegrams were sent to Wavell and Linlithgow informing them of the decision. Linlithgow, as Viceroy, had by protocol to be informed before the C-in-C, India; the telegram passed on instructions to Auchinleck that he should have an exchange of views with Wavell. Both Auchinleck and Wavell were surprised. Auchinleck, who had a quick though controllable temper, was annoyed at this unexpected turn of events. Wavell, who was equally surprised, showed no emotion.

On 23 June Auchinleck replied:

> Thank you for your confidence in me which I shall do my best to justify. Hope to leave Simla by the first available plane Friday 27th and arrive Cairo by air 30th. As directed by you will confer fully with General Wavell. Am maintaining the strictest secrecy.

Dill's telegram, which went off to Auchinleck on the 22nd, was encouraging but grim:

I welcome you as C-in-C Middle East. No British Commander has been asked to assume greater responsibilities. You can, as you know, count on my whole-hearted support and you have my full confidence.

Amery sent a longer telegram to Linlithgow in which he commended the Viceroy for raising no objection to the transfers, but added that he had urged Churchill to make the change a temporary one, partly because that would be in Auchinleck's own interest but more particularly because of the possible danger of a German breakthrough in the Caucasus region. His telegram was sent on 25 June, three days after the Germans had launched their attack on Russia. Stalin had been warned many times of this impending attack, but did not believe the warnings. They had, of course, come from Ultra, and it had not been considered wise to disclose details of their source on security grounds: the Russians had still been linked to Germany by the Molotov–Ribbentrop Pact. To Amery and others it looked as if the Germans might well have success with their south-eastern thrust and from there turn south, break into Iraq and Persia and soon be at the North-West Frontier of India. If that should happen, Auchinleck's military experience of those areas would be indispensable.

Auchinleck set off from Simla on the 27th. On the way to Cairo his plane touched down in Syria for refuelling. He had landed at a small airfield at Ras Me Quoa, and while he was waiting for the aeroplane to be refuelled and checked he chatted to a group of young RAF officers who had been sent out for the Syrian campaign. One of them was Flying Officer A. R. Hall, who, like the others, was tremendously impressed with this striking but totally unassuming general, who was so natural and friendly, and he never forgot the encounter. He was many years after to go to Morocco as Organising Secretary of the Society for Protection of Animals in North Africa; on learning that Auchinleck had finally retired to Marrakech he looked him up, kept in touch and did much to make life easier for the Field-Marshal.

Auchinleck arrived in Cairo on 30 June, finding no one

there to meet him since the move had been so secret. His meetings with Wavell, which could have been strained in view of the circumstances which had caused them, were warm and helpful. Auchinleck was keen to learn anything which Wavell might be able to tell him, for he was under no illusion about the difficulties of his new high-level appointment. The two generals conferred for several days before Wavell left on 7 July, and from the outgoing C-in-C Auchinleck learnt much about his new responsibilities.

His new Chief of Staff in Cairo was Maj.-Gen. Arthur Smith, who had already been serving Wavell in that capacity; the C-in-C and his Chief of Staff soon became firm friends, and they worked together again later, in India.

He had not brought Lady Auchinleck with him; he intended to live with the army and would have no time for social activities. He missed her companionship but knew that she would understand the reasons for his decision.

Dill had written a letter to Auchinleck before the latter took up his new appointment, but it was much delayed and though dated 26 June did not reach its destination till 21 July. It was a long letter and went beyond the briefing a CIGS might be expected to give a new theatre commander; Dill had doubts about Auchinleck's suitability for a post for which political as well as military qualifications were required. It began with a summary of Wavell's experience in the Middle East. Dill emphasised that Wavell had performed excellently with the resources available, but he pointed out that Wavell had been pushed into Syria too quickly for his resources and that his ill-fated 'Battleaxe' venture was also the result of a premature move. This, said Dill, was not a new situation for a general. Wellington and Haig had both been under pressure from the home government. Such pressure could create very difficult, even dangerous, situations for the commander concerned. He might find himself being asked to take courses of action which seemed quite wrong. The letter continued with a word of advice about the situations in which Auchinleck might find himself. If government pressure, which often derived from 'very broad political considerations', was 'so powerful as to make it necessary to take risks which from the military point of view may seem inadvisable' then Auchinleck should clarify one point at least:

> The main point is that you should be clear what risks are involved if a course of action is forced upon you which, from the military point of view, is undesirable. You may even find it necessary, in the extreme case, to disassociate yourself from the consequences.

The CIGS went on to say that a commander should not sit back and wait for pressure to build up, but should anticipate it and explain his position.

> He should point clearly to the risks he is prepared to accept and those which he considers too great. He should demand the resources he considers strictly necessary to carry out any project and he should make it clear what he can do in their absence....

Dill continued with two other points. One was that in view of Britain's current commitments the Middle East would never be able to have all the resources it needed, and the second was that air co-operation was nowhere as good as it should be. 'You will find the "Air" out to help but they have no complete understanding of what is required of them from the purely Army point of view and how necessary training is.' He welcomed any ideas Auchinleck might have to facilitate better co-operation between military and air forces in ground fighting; this, of course, was before tactical air co-operation had been developed, and long before the era of helicopter gunships.

But the main warning of the letter was obviously: Watch out for Churchill. He will want results and want them quickly. Anticipate his requests, and where they are impossible defuse the situation.

Unfortunately for Auchinleck he was a soldier, not a politician, as Dill well knew. He saw the military scene from a military point of view, and not that of a hard-pressed politician. Generalship had taken on a new character in the Second World War – generals now needed to be spectacular figures inspiring confidence among soldiers and civilians alike; equally they should dismay the enemy. Rommel is an example of this new breed. He was not a politician by inclination, but he performed very well in the role thrust upon him. It is worth bearing in mind, however, that the Germans had no special regard for Rommel – he was not popular with his subordinates in Africa and was criticised in Germany – until the British gave him the sort of treatment a public relations consultant might admire. Indeed, many experts believe that Rommel's particular skills were best displayed at divisional rather than at army level, since with very large formations he was often unable to keep adequate control, a problem which was not alleviated by his habit of being in the forefront of the battle. Commendable though it is for a general to keep himself well forward in the danger area, it is nevertheless not the best place from which to direct a battle or a campaign. In addition, a major contribution to Rommel's success was made by the weapons he had at his disposal, notably PzKW* IV tanks and 88-mm guns.

Auchinleck realised from the outset that his problems would be enormous. Even without Dill's warning he knew that Churchill would be breathing down his neck, wanting immediate action. He had already experienced Churchill's impatience during the Norway campaign, and recalled meeting him in the corridor of the War Office just before he set out for Norway – 'I thought you were on your way, General?' Churchill, he knew, was not interested in explanations, still less apologies; he wanted results because the country needed them. Everyone knew that Churchill had already stopped Britain from losing the war, and that he was the one man who could inspire the country to win it, but most people near him realised that he was so ruthless as to appear at times almost venomous. Even as a schoolboy Churchill had been able to frighten with a look.

* The abbreviation for *Panzerkampfwagen*, 'armoured fighting vehicle', generally just called Panzer.

Auchinleck was not a man to be frightened by anyone or anything, although, as we saw earlier, he knew very well what danger was. Had he stayed in command after First Alamein in 1942, and gone on to win Alam Halfa (Second Alamein) and the October battle (Third Alamein), his great talents would then have been used in another command, perhaps Italy, perhaps France and Germany. In the event, he contributed largely to the victories in Burma and Italy by his drive and inspiration in the Indian base. But there are some who feel that he might have handled the 1944 battle in Europe more skilfully than Montgomery and that, if he had been there, the war would have been over sooner. As it was, his potential was never fully tested, not least because he fell foul of politics in general and Churchill in particular.

But in July 1941 he was totally inexperienced in the conditions in which he was taking command. Most of his life had been spent with the Indian Army, even in the First World War, and the interludes in Norway and Southern Command had been so bizarre, and of such short duration, as to be of little practical value. He did not know the British Army well, as yet, though later all ranks would appreciate his courage, his skill, his integrity and his kindness; the news of 'Sunray'* soon gets round. In general, however, he had not been impressed by the British Regular Army, which he did not find as professionally capable as it should be. If anything, he preferred the intelligence and enthusiasm (where it existed) of the new armies of volunteers, Territorials and conscripts, and he had liked the Home Guard because above all they were keen to learn. In his new command he quickly noticed some scepticism about the traditions of the army. The Western Desert was a battleground in which intelligence, self-reliance and resourcefulness were essential and there was a feeling abroad that these were qualities which the Regulars did not encourage.

Many time-honoured beliefs had been shown to be wrong, not least in the matter of dress. The British Army had acquired an excellent reputation over many years for

* The code-word for a commanding officer.

being able to fight everywhere from the Arctic to the tropics in utterly unsuitable uniform. Battledress had marked a step forward, but was still cumbersome, and groundsheets which doubled as macintoshes did not perform efficiently in either use. KD (khaki drill) was too thin for cold nights in the desert, but battledress rather too warm. Corduroys proved more efficient than KD slacks and were thus more popular, scarves were more comfortable round the neck than sweaty collars, and berets replaced topees. For years it had been believed – especially in Auchinleck's India – that bare heads and exposed spines were a direct invitation to sunstroke. It was now propounded that there was no such illness as sunstroke, but that unsuitable clothing could give a man heat exhaustion, or heatstroke. Spine pads, cholera belts, pith helmets – all became a joke. The Australians had at first evoked horror by their habit of going around stripped to the waist, and sometimes hatless. Before long everyone else was doing the same without harm, provided they did not over-expose too much at first: one of the enduring images of what became the Eighth Army is the variety and informality of its dress.

It was all very novel, a new type of war with new ideas against a highly respected and chivalrous opponent – Rommel, 'the Desert Fox'. From the viewpoint of the General Staff it was an army with plenty of spirit, unorthodox, lively, insufficiently trained but potentially very good indeed. It was not very well equipped in relation to its opponents. It might not be quite as good as it thought it was, if the crunch came. And it was a long way from the relentless machine it would have to become (and did) if it was to clear the Germans out of North Africa.

The Western Desert, as Auchinleck knew, though he had yet to see for himself, is not, as the popular conception has it, a series of sand dunes. It is vast – approximately the same size as India – and extends from the Nile in the east to Libya in the west, from the Mediterranean in the north to the Tibesti Mountains in the south. The northern half is mainly limestone, the southern half sandstone, and within the area are vast sand seas, one of them roughly the size of Ireland. There are oases here and there, while along the northern coastline is a fertile strip about ten miles wide. The temperature ranges from 120° Fahrenheit in June to 0° Fahrenheit in the winter, and the nights at many times in the year can be bitterly cold. The south, though clear of flies, clearly has its problems, mainly with sand; the north is full of flies and dust. Flies would appear from nowhere in the remotest parts and crawl over faces, lips, food, wounds, around the edge of the mug you were drinking from. Dust was in food, hair, ears, engines, guns. It was astonishingly easy to get lost, and many did; on a dark night a man could walk a few yards from his tent to get a breath of fresh air – he could spend the rest of the night trying unsuccessfully to find the tent again.

Had Auchinleck been there in a less responsible capacity, he would have loved the desert. As it was he saw as much of it as he could. He understood it, and the discomforts did not greatly trouble him. Unfortunately he had difficulty in finding subordinates of like temperament.

In old age, looking back over his army career, he told David Dimbleby that 'The best of all commands was commanding a battalion. As a colonel, with 600, 700 good men under you, entirely responsible for them and for the officers, that was the best time of all. As you went on in command you still had the same responsibilities, and bigger ones, but then you hadn't got the same intimate contact with the men under you. The responsibilities got greater and greater, and one became lonelier and lonelier.'

Asked whether he felt that, as he moved to higher rank, he got further and further from people he could trust, he replied, 'I wouldn't say trust, but you get further and further away from people you really knew. In the regiment you could say that if so-and-so is sent on such-and-such a job he will do it. You couldn't say that when you got further up. Certainly not beyond a brigadier: when you were up beyond a brigadier anyway.'

Almost as soon as Auchinleck had taken over from Wavell, Churchill began to bombard him with telegrams. The first suggested he should give urgent consideration to the question of finishing off the Syrian campaign as quickly as possible, or at least not letting operations there flag, and also of taking advantage of the fact that the Germans were now preoccupied in Russia; the second suggested that he should consider General Sir Henry Maitland Wilson for command in the Western Desert. Wilson, later Field-Marshal Lord Wilson of Libya, was at that time completing the Syrian campaign, where he was C-in-C, Allied Forces; he had previously been GOC-in-C, British troops in Greece. Auchinleck agreed about the need to complete operations in Syria, but rejected the suggestion of appointing Wilson, who was already sixty; he replied courteously and fully in a signal dated 1 July. He began with a statement likely to infuriate Churchill: 'No further offensive Western Desert should be contemplated until base is secure.'

He went on to explain that security meant ensuring that Syria, Iraq and Cyprus were all firmly under British control, and continued:

> Once Syria is secure, and this implies consolidation of our position in Iraq, offensive in Western Desert can be considered, but for this adequate and properly trained armoured forces, say at least two and possibly three armoured divisions with a motor division, will be required to ensure success. This is a first essential.

He added several explanatory points. One was that infantry divisions were no good in desert terrain against armoured forces, but that they would, however, be needed to hold captured ground, or perhaps to capture it *after* enemy armour had been destroyed. Another point he made was the need for 'an adequate and suitably trained air component at disposal of the Army for all its needs including fighters, medium bombers, tactical reconnaissance and close support on the battlefield. This is non-existent at present.'

Similarly, 'essential in any offensive operation in this theatre is close support and constant co-operation of Fleet both in close support of the army and harrying enemy sea communications.' Furthermore, he reiterated that Syria must be finished off before there could be any question of a desert offensive.

Churchill came back quickly on 6 July, five days before the French surrender in Syria, emphasising the importance of a victory in the desert. He calculated that by now Auchinleck should have all the armour he needed, in view of reinforcements, including six armoured regiments, already on the way. Air reinforcement was being attended to; he did not think that air strength should be frittered away too much in close air support, as it had been at Sollum in Wavell's 'Battleaxe' offensive, three weeks earlier.

From his signals, it seems that Churchill was already beginning to wonder whether he had appointed the right man. In 1974 Auchinleck said to David Dimbleby, 'I think he was too prone to interfere with the commander in the field. Prodding, you might call it. Prodding people who didn't think they needed prodding. If they wanted prodding he should have removed them. He did make things difficult occasionally because nobody who was not in command of a big operation like that could really understand the difficulties of supply and maintenance and training and that sort of thing. It's all very well to say you've got a whole tank division or a tank brigade or an infantry division arriving, fresh troops. You couldn't throw them into battle in the desert straight away; you had to train them. Fighting in the desert is quite different from anything they have been trained for. I think that was the non-professional mind, the civilian, although he had been a soldier. He failed to understand, really. Of course his whole object was to get things going.'

Churchill, of course, had been a soldier, and a very successful one. After the Dardanelles fiasco, during which he had been First Lord of the Admiralty, he had gone into the infantry (he had originally been commissioned into the cavalry from Sandhurst and had ridden in the charge at Omdurman) and had commanded the 6th Royal Scots Fusiliers in France in 1916. It was no sinecure. But there is no doubt that he was influenced by the charisma of Rommel, whom in his history he described as a splendid military gambler, dominating the problems of supply and scornful of opposition. His ardour and daring inflicted grievous disasters upon us but he deserves the salute which I made him – not without some reproaches from the public – in the House of Commons in January 1942 when I said 'We have a very daring and skilful opponent, and may I say across the havoc of war, a great general.'

A statement such as this was not much help to commanders in the field trying to convey to their troops the idea that Rommel was fallible, not invincible (Hitler himself was of the opinion that much of Rommel's reputation was due to Churchill's speeches), but it showed very well the sort of British general Churchill hoped to discover. Fortunately for Britain, he failed to do so.

Forty years later, it is easier to understand Churchill's actions than it was at the time. The need for a victory to boost morale, the need to instil a spirit of urgency have long been understandable. Latterly, it has been possible to see that the information Churchill was receiving from the Ultra intercepts and from his scientific advisers was enough to drive anyone to distraction. Additionally he was aware that there were many in the House of Commons who were quicker with criticism than support. He was too experienced a politician not to realise that many of those who were now supporting him were only waiting till he had pulled the chestnuts out of the fire to stab him in the back and take the benefits. Even his own personal friends could not be trusted not to let him down. For example, after Dunkirk Beaverbrook had been involved in a plan to make peace with Germany. The Foreign Office had damped this down at the time, but on 25 June 1941 it was brought up in the House of Commons; Churchill had to explain why Beaverbrook was now in the Cabinet, for since that infamous move he had been made Minister of Aircraft Production and then Minister of Supply.

And the problems did not end there. Churchill knew that cities which had been heavily bombed were asking how much longer they were expected to stand it. In the factories workers produced tanks faster in a 'Tanks for

Russia' week than they did for their own countrymen. The Prime Minister realised only too clearly that everything with which he was concerned had a desperate urgency. But even at this hazardous moment he must take measures that would ensure that when Britain had won the war she should not lose the peace. Ultimately he would fail, outwitted by Stalin, misunderstood and eventually betrayed by Roosevelt, even pushed out of power by the very people whose lives he had saved. Had he lost the war the concentration camps and gas ovens would have come to England, and all males between the ages of sixteen and forty-five been deported for forced labour to the Continent; Churchill alone knew the risks Britain ran. He was in no mood to be told that a campaign was impossible, that a risk was unacceptable. He was doing the impossible every day, and the war was being lost because the Germans were taking unacceptable risks and getting away with it. He liked and admired Auchinleck; in some ways they had similar tastes, but he believed firmly that all his generals were too leisurely, too careful. He liked risk-takers – commandos, SAS, Chindits – and he admired, too, flamboyance and luck. Auchinleck knew how to take risks when the position justified them, but as the man on the spot he felt he knew what was acceptable and what was simple suicide.

'Was the prodding an inconvenience or was it actually harmful?' Dimbleby asked Auchinleck in 1974. 'Not to me, or to Wavell. Prodding to attack before you are ready, before the troops were trained, risking everything – that is dangerous. But I don't think it came off. The impression was haste, haste, haste. Mind you, it's no harm – it's no bad thing, really. If a commander was apt to be a bit slow and careful, more careful than he ought to be, it might have hastened him up.'

On 15 July Auchinleck replied to Churchill's telegram with a reasoned statement which, unfortunately, only roused the Prime Minister's fury. He pointed out that the six armoured regiments to which Churchill had referred in his telegram of the 6th had no training on the types of tank, many of them American, which they were now receiving. He agreed that by the end of July he would have about five hundred cruisers, infantry and American tanks, but past experience has clearly demonstrated that for any given operation we need fifty per cent reserve of tanks. This permits twenty-five per cent in workshops and twenty-five per cent available for immediate replacement of battle tanks. Allowing for fifty tanks in Tobruk and requisite reserves I shall not have more than 350 available for active operations ...

Owing to casualties to tanks and numbers in workshop units have had little opportunity for training. Would stress importance of time being allowed for both individual and collective training. 'Battleaxe' showed that present standard of training is not enough, and we must secure that team spirit which is essential for efficiency ...

While I do not intend to alter our present policy of holding Tobruk I cannot be confident that Tobruk can be maintained after September.

This signal made Churchill regret that he had ever appointed Auchinleck. He needed a morale-boosting offensive in the desert, and as for Tobruk – the policy should be to relieve it, not lose it. (The besieged port was, in fact, far more a symbol of Allied defiance than a strategic necessity, but its defence was politically expedient, as we shall see later.)

Quite apart from political questions, Churchill did not seem to realise that much of the equipment sent to the desert had been tested in considerably more favourable conditions, such as on Salisbury Plain, and was often incapable of continuing to function in dust, heat and soft sand. Colonel Norman Berry, who was Chief Mechanical Engineer for XIII Corps and Eighth Army in 1941, took a photograph of a Matilda tank that had encountered an 88-mm gun at Sidi Omar. The shell had gone straight through the front of the tank.

Of the 2-pounder gun, he said:

This was the standard weapon in all British tanks and the standard anti-tank gun in use in the Eighth Army until May 1942. It seems that the War Office considered it was a very good gun. I never came across a single officer or man in the desert who agreed with that view. Unlike our tanks it was beautifully designed, was 100 per cent reliable and had a very long life, but in the view of every tank gunner or anti-tank gunner I knew or spoke to it was simply too small to prove effective against German armour at over 600 yards. As an anti-tank gun it was virtually useless in the desert.

On one occasion I listened in to an OC of an anti-tank battery reporting that his shots were bouncing off thirty German tanks that were attacking him and that this was probably the last that would be heard of him. It was.

I got the impression that the War Office simply did not want to listen to any criticisms of any kind that were made about any equipment that had been sent to the Middle East. It was much easier to criticise the generals.

Churchill's reply to Auchinleck was swift. He wrote on 19 July, and this time he hinted that a consignment of tanks might soon be on their way to boost his strength. The Chiefs of Staff sent a signal on the same day offering 150 cruiser tanks if they would help the relief of Tobruk. At the same time the Prime Minister felt that Auchinleck had made a mistake in sending 50th Division (at that time his only complete British division) to Cyprus, when, according to the Defence Committee,

other troops [presumably inferior] might have been found. The Defence Committee did not foresee any further trouble developing in the Iraq/Syria/Palestine region in the near future but thought that the Germans might make some sort of move against Persia. Germany's entanglement with Russia offered a good opportunity to take the offensive in the Western Desert and Wilson, they felt, was the right man for it unless Auchinleck thought of commanding it directly himself.

Auchinleck felt slightly nettled by this last communication, for the criticism of his disposition of 50th Division and the suggestion for employing Wilson were a direct encroachment on his authority as Commander-in-Chief. He was already running into problems which arose from the mixture of troops in his command. 9th Australian Division and 25 Australian Infantry Brigade were penned up in Tobruk. Although they were theoretically on the defensive, they were in fact very much on the offensive against the Germans encircling them, and were undoubtedly causing a lot of trouble to the enemy. However, they had been there for a considerable time and now, for health reasons, needed to be moved out. This could be done by exchanging them with a British division, for Tobruk was a port, even if a somewhat harassed one, and reinforcements could be brought in by sea, guarded by the Royal Navy. In a letter to Dill on 21 July, replying to the latter's long-delayed letter warning of Churchill's prodding, Auchinleck explained that he had no intention of giving up Tobruk prematurely, that he would probably relieve the Australians with the British 6th Division, and that he had felt that nothing less than a properly equipped division would do to safeguard Cyprus (he probably had an acute realisation of what had happened to an under-garrisoned Crete). He mentioned that he was about to reorganise his command structure, and he thought that a lot of administrative matters could be delegated to Army commanders leaving GHQ to deal with the bigger issues.

One thing I am very anxious to do and that is to get GHQ out of Cairo if I can. There are far too many distractions here, social and otherwise, and the climate is enervating.

What I would like to repeat is that it is not sound to take an unreasonable risk. I am quite ready to take a reasonable risk as I think you know but to attack with patently inadequate means is to take an unreasonable risk in the present circumstances and it is almost certain to result in greater delay eventually than if we wait until the odds are reasonable. I am afraid I shall be quite firm on this point.

On 23 July, having received Auchinleck's replies to his signal and that of the COS, Churchill decided that he had better have a talk with his Middle East Commander. Accordingly, on the 24th he suggested that the C-in-C should come to London, leaving General Sir Thomas Blamey, GOC Australian Forces in the Middle East and Auchinleck's Deputy C-in-C, in command while he was absent.

Auchinleck left on 26 July, taking with him his Private Secretary and Deputy Director of Plans. They travelled in a Sunderland flying-boat, crammed with all ranks. (To travel in such discomfort seems almost ludicrous for a man of his rank but it happened to be the first aircraft available.) On 31 July he presented himself to the War Cabinet in London, and thus began two days of intensive discussion with the Prime Minister and his advisers, political and military. He spent the weekend of the 2nd and 3rd at Chequers with Churchill, who was greatly impressed by him. However,

> we could not induce him to depart from his resolve to have a prolonged delay in order to prepare a set-piece offensive on November 1st. He certainly shook my military advisers with all the detailed argument he produced. I was myself unconvinced. But General Auchinleck's unquestioned abilities, his powers of exposition, his high, dignified and commanding personality gave me the feeling that he might after all be right and even if wrong he was still the best man. I therefore yielded to the November date for the offensive.

Whatever the arguments put to him, Auchinleck remained adamant that he could not attack until he had a greater number of tanks than Rommel, and supplies and reinforcements to back up such an offensive. His forces around Tobruk and Sollum continued to harass the enemy, but any major attack would require a considerable weight of armour, supported by artillery and aircraft. He agreed that an offensive should be launched as soon as practicable, but he would not be hurried into an 'unreasonable risk'; in addition, he privately considered Tobruk and its defence to be less than vital to victory in the Western Desert. His judgement was subsequently

114

proved to be sound, but his stubbornness left its mark in the Prime Minister's mind. Delay, for however good a reason, was something that irked Churchill greatly.

Some of the time was spent discussing matters with the War Cabinet and the Chiefs of Staff, but there was an interlude when Auchinleck was able to spend a few hours alone with Churchill. He was enormously impressed with the Prime Minister's far-ranging mind, and even more by his stamina. He himself found the endless round of talks exhausting, but felt that the visit had been well worth while. (For Auchinleck the most pleasant feature of it had been an informal lunch at the Palace with King George VI on 1 August. It was a frugal meal at which they drank cider cup.)

Auchinleck spent the next week in London with Air Chief Marshal Arthur Tedder, AOC-in-C of the RAF in the Middle East, discussing questions raised by their visit and talks. In the coming months, Tedder was to prove a staunch ally, both as the RAF commander and as a friend. Auchinleck left for Cairo on 10 August, feeling happier about plans for the coming offensive, and with a conviction that important matters had been settled and that relations with the Prime Minister would now be easier. Churchill, unfortunately, had not seen the meeting in the same light. He liked Auchinleck but saw no reason to cease prodding him.

There was, of course, no way by which Auchinleck could really convince Churchill of the essential nature of the problems confronting him. 'The difficulties of the desert were the difficulties of movement,' he said later. 'Desert warfare is quite different from warfare in an ordinary civilised country. Churchill thought that troops could come straight out of a ship and be put into battle in a week, but it would take at least two months before those troops were fit to go into battle. It was like taking troops out of England and putting them into Switzerland. People coming from England and Africa, South Africa, even from India – not from India so much – were completely lost in this country with no features at all.'

On his return, Auchinleck appointed Lt-Gen. Sir Alan Cunningham, the GOC East African Forces, to command the Western Desert Force, though Churchill disapproved of the choice, still preferring Maitland Wilson. It was this choice that provided Auchinleck's detractors with much of their ammunition. Cunningham replaced Lt-Gen. Sir Noel Beresford-Peirse, who had commanded during 'Battleaxe'.

Not least of Auchinleck's difficulties was the variety of the forces under his command, which included British, Australian, New Zealand, South African, Indian, even Polish, Greek and Free French troops. He had already mentioned in a letter to Dill:

> We are going to have trouble I fear and plenty of it from de Gaulle over the Free French position in Syria. If they refuse to see reason and persist in their present illogical and unrealistic attitude I am afraid they will have to be dealt with firmly and drastically.

British and Indian forces were under his direct command, but Auchinleck was well aware that back in India there were politicians who would not be slow to make trouble if there was any hint that the Indian divisions were being unfairly or over used. The Australian, New Zealand and South African theatre commanders always conveyed the impression that their first responsibility was to their own governments, to which they reported direct. Australia and New Zealand had lingering memories of the sacrifice of many of their best troops by what appeared to have been mistaken policies and generalship in the First World War. The Anzacs (Australian and New Zealand forces) were not likely to forget Gallipoli, Messines or Passchendaele, nor the South Africans likely to let the memory of Delville Wood in 1916 fade, whatever their political outlook. (The South Africans would be allowed to fight only on African soil during this war, it had been decided.)

A crisis soon blew up over the then Maj.-Gen. Bernard Freyberg, commanding the New Zealand Division and GOC-in-C, New Zealand Forces. Freyberg had an astonishing record from the First World War, during which he had won the VC, the DSO with two Bars (he was to win a fourth DSO in Italy in 1945), and had been mentioned in Despatches six times. But, although a New Zealander, the greater part of his service had been with the British Army and his qualities were insufficiently appreciated in his own country. He had commanded the New Zealand Division in Greece and Crete with daring and imperturbability, although at one stage he had made the remark, over-optimistic in the circumstances, which he was not allowed to forget: 'I think we can hold Crete.' The Crete disaster led to criticism of Freyberg in New Zealand, and Peter Fraser, the New Zealand Prime Minister, suggested to Dill that perhaps a different commander should be found, one who was more obviously a New Zealander. Freyberg had held a regular commission in the Grenadier Guards and was a perfectionist, but his own exacting standards caused him to take too much on himself and to be somewhat high-handed with his staff. Dill wondered whether it might not be an appropriate moment to promote him Lieutenant-General and post him to an Indian Command – Wavell would be delighted to have him there. Auchinleck promptly vetoed the proposal. He needed Freyberg, whom he sensed would justify himself again as soon as the bullets started flying.

The next pressure came from the Australians, who wished to see their forces united in one theatre under one command. By September one Australian brigade had been taken out of Tobruk, which was chiefly garrisoned by 9th Australian Division under Maj.-Gen. Leslie Morshead, but the rest were still there. Evacuating one brigade had been a major task, and Auchinleck considered that to exchange the remainder would place an enormous, perhaps intolerable, strain on the ships and aircraft likely to be involved. Churchill conveyed this message to Arthur Fadden (the Australian Prime Minister after the resignation of Robert Menzies), hoping that the latter would not insist upon evacuation. In Australia the opposition was hard at the throat of the government over this issue which, properly exploited, might well help to overthrow Fadden's administration and bring the opposition back into power. In those circumstances Fadden had no time for sweet reason. He rejected Auchinleck's arguments that the relief of the Australian division in Tobruk was not 'a justifiable military operation', and said, 'It is vital to Australian people to have concentrated control and direction of the Expeditionary Forces.' There was no more to be done. On 15 September 1941 Churchill replied to the Australian Premier: 'Orders will at once be given in accordance with your decision. The maintenance of secrecy for the present is of the highest consequence of all.'

For Auchinleck it was a distinct slap in the face. He attributed the Australian attitude in some measure to Blamey, the overall commander of the Australian forces and Auchinleck's Deputy. His resentment of Blamey's obstructive attitude was tempered by his admiration for Morshead, who was known to his troops as 'Ming the Merciless'. The Mercilessness of Morshead, however, was directly only towards inefficiency and slackness; in every way he deserved and received respect. Fadden's move, however, failed to save his government and it was replaced by a Labour administration under John Curtin. Churchill made an attempt to persuade Curtin to alter his predecessor's decision, but it was no good. Even a plea that the evacuation should be postponed till after the proposed November offensive (now code-named Operation 'Crusader') met an uncompromising refusal. Here again it looks as if the Australian government was being uncooperative; before passing judgement, however, it should be borne in mind that Australia had sent her best troops (for whom Auchinleck had a very high regard) to the Middle East, where a large number were now pinned down in a besieged garrison of doubtful strategic value, and that all this was happening while the news from Japan was becoming steadily more ominous. It was difficult to persuade the average Australian that it was in their interest to have their soldiers thousands of miles away, when at any moment Australia might need every available man for the defence of her homelands. Between 19–27 September and 12–25 October the greater part of Morshead's division was evacuated from Tobruk, being replaced by the British 70th Division. It was a costly operation – the Germans accounted for seven ships sunk or damaged – and, moreover, one which Auchinleck considered unnecessary, besides his resentment of such interference in his decisions.

Churchill's urgent requests for action in the desert were partly the result of knowing that the Germans were enjoying great success in Russia and might soon be able to spare more men and materials for Rommel, and partly because Beaverbrook, who combined military ignorance with optimistic belligerence, took it upon himself to encourage Churchill to keep up the prodding. Certainly, at this time Rommel's forces were outnumbered, and consisted of two German armoured divisions and one Italian, and one German and one Italian motorised division. There were four non-motorised Italian infantry divisions and one non-motorised German rifle brigade. Some of these formations were under strength. The two German armoured divisions (21st and 15th) made up what was called the Afrika Korps, although that title was mistakenly applied to all Rommel's forces by many journalists at the time. A Panzer division had two battalions made up of four companies and possessed a total of 194 tanks. A motorised infantry regiment had three battalions and sufficient vehicles to carry all its personnel when it wished to move; normal infantry might occasionally be 'lifted' from place to place but, as they did not possess sufficient trucks of their own, they were not as fully mobile as their counterparts.

However, the first essential for victory in the desert was adequate tanks; the next was adequately trained personnel to man them. Obviously there were other requirements, such as supply and reinforcement, anti-tank weapons and artillery, and air support, but both Auchinleck and Rommel agreed that the primary weapon was the tank. Rommel was well aware that his own forces were much better trained than their potential opponents. He himself had had years of experience; some of his opposing commanders had very little and the general appointed to command the army in the Western Desert had virtually none. Cunningham was a Gunner whose experience as a general had been in the command of infantry divisions, with which he had done well in Ethiopia. He was now to command two corps, one of infantry and one of armour, against an avowed master of armoured warfare in the desert. (His brother, Admiral Sir Andrew Cunningham, was the Naval Commander-in-Chief in the Middle East; somewhat confusingly the commander of the Western Desert Air Force was Air Vice-Marshal Arthur Coningham.)

Subsequently Rommel set out his theories of armoured warfare:

1. The main endeavour should be to concentrate one's own forces in space and time, while at the same time seeking to split the enemy forces spatially and destroy them at different times.

2. Speed of movement and the organisational cohesion of one's own forces are decisive factors and require particular attention. Any sign of dislocation must be dealt with as quickly as possible by reorganisation.

These points, and many more like them, were set out in the Rommel papers (subsequently edited by Captain B. H. Liddell Hart). In his letters home to his wife, Rommel gives the impression that the delay in a British attack, which he knew was bound to come sooner or later, was by no means to the German advantage. He, and others, were extremely uncomfortable. 'A quite atrocious heat, even during the night. One lies in bed tossing and turning and dripping with sweat.' – 'Yesterday I was away eight hours; you can hardly imagine what a thirst one gets up after such a journey.' – 'Bagged two more bugs this morning. There are endless swarms of flies ...' – 'Some of the others are having a bad time with fleas.' On 6 October 1941 he wrote, 'Unable to write yesterday, my stomach struck works again. We had a fowl the evening before last which must have come from Rameses II's chicken run. For all the six hours' cooking it had it was like leather and my stomach just couldn't take it.' Rommel, of course, was perpetually plagued by stomach troubles, but the discomfort he mentioned shows that his forces were no less plagued than the Allied troops by the creatures of the desert.

Rommel's messages, both to his wife and the German High Command (the OKW), were almost all intercepted and read by British Intelligence working through the Ultra intercept system. They were passed to Churchill and his Chiefs of Staff, who formed the opinion that Rommel was near the end of his tether, and that the sooner Auchinleck attacked and finished him off the better for the British war effort (it will be remembered that this was the autumn of 1941, several months before America was directly involved in the war – that fateful day would arrive in the following December). Rommel's endless complaints about his health, his lack of supplies and the incompetence of his Italian allies built up a false picture in everyone's mind – except Auchinleck's.

It is interesting to learn that after defeating Wavell in the 'Battleaxe' operation Rommel wrote:

Wavell's strategic planning of this offensive had been excellent. What distinguished him from the other British Army commanders was his great and well-balanced strategic courage, which permitted him to concentrate his forces regardless of his opponent's possible moves. But he was put at a great disadvantage by the slow speed of his heavy infantry tanks, which prevented him from reacting quickly enough to the moves of our faster vehicles. Hence the slow speed of the bulk of his armour was his soft spot which we could seek to exploit tactically.

Of those tanks (the Matildas) he said:

The gun they carried was far too small and its range too short. They were also supplied with solid, armour-piercing shell. It would be interesting to know why the Mark II Matilda was called an infantry tank when it had no high-explosive ammunition with which to engage the opposing infantry. It was, as I have already said, far too slow. In fact, its only real use was in a straight punch to smash a hole in a concentration of material.

In the winter battle of 1941–2 the enemy Mark VI

Cruiser tank made its first appearance. [This was the Crusader which gives its name to the November offensive, to which Rommel is referring.] With its tremendous speed, more than 40 mph, this was an extremely useful tank. But its gun was far too small and it could not make up for its lack of calibre, and thus of range, by the heavy armour it carried. Had this tank been equipped with a heavier gun it could have made things extremely unpleasant for us.

Rommel did not in fact know that fifty Crusaders had been used in the 'Battleaxe' operation; he might otherwise have been privately more optimistic about the future than he was. In theory the 2-pounder was a better gun than the German 50-mm anti-tank gun (a $4\frac{1}{2}$-pounder), or even than the short 75-mm gun, as mounted on the Panzer IV tanks. But theory and practice are often very different in battle, as we have seen from Colonel Berry's note on the 2-pounder.

But Churchill's attitude, his continual demand for action, become more understandable when one realises that he believed that every one of Rommel's successes was not only due to daring, but also was achieved in spite of shortages and deficiencies of every possible kind. Yet here were British generals, with supplies of new tanks and with nearly 600,000 men at their disposal, complaining that they could not take the offensive because they were not yet ready for it, nor would they be for some time.

Auchinleck, with greater experience of the way field commanders tend to minimise their advantages and maximise their deficiencies, was wary of putting his army into any traps laid by Rommel. To launch an inexperienced tank squadron into battle against one possessing veteran skills is like putting a brave but inexperienced boxer against a master of ringcraft – the inexperienced man will wonder why his blows never seem to land, why his opponent is never where he should be but seems able to hit him from unexpected angles. It is the same with armoured warfare, barring accidents.

On 2 September Auchinleck gave General Cunningham his brief for the next offensive, agreed with Churchill in London early in August. He had already discussed it with Admiral Cunningham and Tedder. The objective would be 'to drive the enemy out of North Africa, first by capturing Cyrenaica and secondly by capturing Tripolitania'. It would be a combined operation, but it was left to General Cunningham to decide the tactical approach. At the end of September he submitted his plan. Maj.-Gen. Willoughby Norrie's XXX Corps, comprising the bulk of the British armour, would advance across the line from Sidi Omar and Fort Maddalena, heading north-west towards Tobruk. Meanwhile, Maj.-Gen. Godwin-Austen's XIII Corps, chiefly infantry, would push forward along the coast to the area between Bardia and Tobruk, driving the enemy from his positions on the border between Libya and Egypt. The attack, to be called Operation 'Crusader', would begin on 11 November.

The 'prolonged delay' which Churchill had criticised had been used in strenuous preparations. Rommel did not suspect that the British would attack at this time, but himself had every intention of capturing Tobruk. Auchinleck now had the advantage of a Special Liaison Unit for keeping him in touch with the Ultra interceptor. The SLUs were small parties of specialist signallers who received the messages from the decoding centre at Bletchley Park in Buckinghamshire and passed them on to the commander concerned. It was difficult for them to conceal the nature of their highly secret activities, but throughout the war the SLUs managed to do this successfully; they acquired an expertise for blandly explaining their presence without disclosing their real work or purpose. Unfortunately there was not much information of future plans from Ultra during the autumn of 1941 – Auchinleck probably guessed that Rommel would make an attack on Tobruk before long. What was useful, however, was to have Rommel's own figures of his strength, which he sent periodically to the OKW in Berlin. Rather less useful was the fact that Churchill had received them too, and noted that Rommel's petrol supply position in September was distinctly better than it had been in the previous two months; this confirmed Churchill in his view that Auchinleck should have begun

'Crusader' earlier, whether the troops were trained or not.

To make sure that Rommel had no suspicion of the coming offensive, British Intelligence, organised by the Director of Military Intelligence in that area, Brigadier John Shearer, and Lt-Col. Raymund Maunsell, spread the news that Britain was planning a drive up from Palestine to help Russia protect vital oilfields. The deception was made possible by using a captured German agent and, to give greater credibility to this piece of fiction, on 3 October Auchinleck left for a brief visit to Palestine and Syria – where spies would report his presence – as if making plans for that event.

On 26 September Auchinleck's army received the title it was to carry so long and so honourably – Eighth Army. Previously it had been referred to either as the Western Desert Force or (chiefly by Churchill) as the Army of the Nile. Consulted whether the soldiers of the Western Desert Force would like or dislike being called the Eighth Army, Auchinleck replied: 'I don't think they would care what they were called!' Rightly, he knew that it is only when a name has won distinction in battle that men care about it. In the remarkable way the bureaucratic mind works it was later decided in the War Office that the figure 8 could not appear on a campaign ribbon unless the wearer had fought at Third Alamein – Montgomery's battle – and after. The rule, so unjust and unnecessary, was described by many soldiers as '—typical of the deskborne brigade'. Auchinleck protested vigorously at this injustice but failed in his attempts to have it rectified. It is interesting to speculate whether Montgomery played a hand in this petty decision; as one historian remarks, Montgomery did Auchinleck 'and his troops and their predecessors a grave wrong by denying them the Africa Star.'*

As the day for the start of 'Crusader' approached, hopes, particularly Churchill's, rose high. If this offensive succeeded Britain would be well on the way to clearing North Africa and opening a second front in Italy. The

---

* Ronald Lewin, *Montgomery as Military Commander* (London 1971).

Prime Minister was slightly disappointed when, early in November, he learnt that the offensive had had to be postponed for a week to the 18th, but accepted the explanation without demur. The reason was that on 2 November Maj.-Gen. George Brink, the 1st South African Division commander, had said that his troops, which would be in the forefront of the battle, needed the extra time to be ready for their task. They had arrived after an excellent campaign in Ethiopia but had spent much time since on extending the Mersa Matruh defence, and too little on learning desert warfare, of which they had no previous experience. In the event the delay made no difference.

The night before the offensive, 17/18 November, is notable for being the date which gave the Special Air Service its birthday (17 November). Since the previous July there had been a somewhat unorthodox unit called 'L' Detachment, SAS Brigade. There was at that time no SAS Brigade (it was merely a deception title), just a small number of highly enterprising men drawn from the disbanded 8th Commando. 8th Commando, which had been largely recruited from the Brigade of Guards and was based in Egypt, had been part of a force to be used in an optimistic plan to capture Rhodes, led by Brigadier Robert Laycock. His force – 'Layforce' – was then to be used for commando raiding along the coast; shortage of naval resources, however, soon ended that aspiration (although, also on the night of 17 November, Laycock led a force of commandos in the daring, though tragically abortive raid on what had been Rommel's HQ behind the Axis Lines). At this point David Stirling, a young lieutenant in the Scots Guards, decided that if the commando could not travel by sea it could do equally well, if not better, by air. With others of similar temperament he acquired fifty parachutes which, intended for India, had been unloaded by mistake in Alexandria. Neither he nor his friends had any experience of parachuting but they managed to borrow an old Valentia bomber for learning. The Valentia was totally unsuitable for parachuting; was, in fact, highly dangerous, but this did not deter them. Stirling managed to crash his way into GHQ and eventually to bring his proposal to the attention of Auchinleck. He was given permission to recruit sixty men and to train at Kabrit in the Canal Zone. Training was arduous in the extreme; with it went research into time-pencils and the art of placing bombs on airfields. The plan was to drop near a German airfield, approach unnoticed, place bombs on all the parked aircraft, and disappear as the results accumulated. The operation, which, together with the raid on Rommel's HQ, formed part of the build-up to 'Crusader', obviously required courage, stamina, field-craft, intelligence and perfect discipline. All were there in ample measure. The Germans in North Africa had far superior aircraft to the British at this stage, notably Messerschmitt 109s, and had recently been reinforced with the latest type, the Me 109F, equipped with a cannon. There was scant chance of destroying such planes in the air with the Desert Air Force's few overworked fighters, chiefly Hurricanes and obsolete Gloster Gauntlet biplanes, but there looked to be a fair chance of doing so on the ground. In the event the first operation, on 17 November, the day before Auchinleck launched his offensive, was a disaster which would have destroyed the faith of anyone except Stirling. Soon after take-off the weather deteriorated rapidly. In the ensuing sandstorm, with gusts of up to 90 mph, the planes were blown miles off course, and many of the parachutists were lost. The twenty-two survivors were eventually picked up by the Long Range Desert Group, another formation of enterprising desert venturers but who made a speciality of reconnaissance rather than destruction. Stirling's reaction to this appalling setback was that if the LRDG could cover vast distances in the desert by vehicle, then the SAS could do likewise, completing the trip if needs be by a walk of fifteen miles or so. His optimism appeared absurd, even fantastic to many at the time, but was soon shown to be justified when the SAS destroyed over 350 German aircraft on the ground in a series of daring raids.[*] Unfortunately, on the morning of 18 November the Me 109Fs remained intact.

* See Philip Warner, *The Special Air Service* (London 1971).

On the evening of 17 November, as British forces moved up to their starting points, the weather broke. A violent rainstorm, accompanied by the same very high winds that had thwarted the SAS, fell upon the waiting troops, Allied and Axis. Auchinleck retained his customary calm; he was not even slightly nervous about 'Crusader'. He had delayed the offensive until he was ready, and had resisted the prodding of others who lacked his head for strategic realities. In doing so he had sown doubt about his aggressiveness in the minds of some at home – he would see whether the coming days would bring his vindication. He himself was sure, and more than that, he was ready.

10

'IMMENSELY HEARTENED'
THE 'CRUSADER' BATTLES

In terms of relative strength the outlook for 'Crusader' seemed good. Auchinleck had 600 tanks, 100,000 men and some 5000 soft-skinned (unarmoured) vehicles. They moved forward on 17 November, ready at last, but not without difficulties. That night came the storm, and the rain which followed the wind was so merciless that it appeared to penetrate everything. It put an end to any chance of air or naval support, and drowned the battle area in icy water. It was, however, the same for both sides.

What was not the same for both sides, as the armies soon discovered in the very confused battle which now began, just after dawn on 18 November, was the relative value of the tanks. Even now, official figures vary according to their sources, but it seems that the Panzer IIIs and IVs were a match for the Stuarts, better than the Crusaders, and considerably ahead of Matildas and Valentines. Rommel had some indifferent tanks on his strength too, but not enough to make a difference to the essential balance of forces.

In Cunningham's army, XIII Corps, under Godwin-Austen, contained the 4th Indian Division, the New Zealand Division and 1st Army Tank Brigade; XXX Corps, under Norrie, contained the 7th Armoured Division, 4 Armoured Brigade, the 1st South African Division and the 201st Guards Brigade Group. In reserve were the 2nd South African Division and the 29th Infantry Brigade Group. In the Tobruk garrison was 70th Division, 32 Army Tank Brigade and the Polish 1st Carpathian Infantry.

There were also the 'Jock Columns' – named after their initiator, Brigadier Jock Campbell. These were small, self-supporting and highly mobile strike forces drawn from many Eighth Army units and devised at this time specifically to deal with Rommel's army in the desert.

They proved their worth on a number of occasions, for they were an easy method of paying Rommel back in his own coin. The 'Jock Columns' had their limitations, however, as they were too large to be very nimble but too small to handle anything but raiding.

'Crusader' then took the following course. XXX Corps met stiff opposition from the Italian Ariete Division at El Gubi, but a part of the Corps swung to the north and captured the high ground to the south of Sidi Rezegh on the 19th. This split in the main armoured force was to prove nearly fatal to the offensive in the ensuing days. Owing to their lack of enthusiasm for fighting in the earlier stages of the war the Italians had gained a reputation as poor fighters – they were fast losing it. Some units were now fully as good as the Germans, and in certain activities, such as night fighting, even better. Rommel sent some German armour as reinforcements into this sector to see if he could recover the position, but XXX Corps held him, and by the 21st Sidi Rezegh and the surrounding area was in XXX Corps' hands, though not in any great strength, since other armoured units of the Corps were well to the south.

XIII Corps, meanwhile, were working along the frontier at Sidi Omar, which was captured by 4th Indian Division. The Corps turned north and began to move towards Tobruk, and Rommel now looked to be in danger from 70th Division, who were breaking out from Tobruk to link up with the advance. The German commander was not to be caught so easily, however. He held 70th Division and, knowing Sidi Rezegh to be the key to the battle, launched his counter-attack there. On 22 and 23 November the 21st Panzer Division stormed Sidi Rezegh and drove the British armour from the area, virtually destroying one infantry brigade. Some forty miles east of the main battle were German garrisons at Halfaya and Bardia, which had been by-passed by the British advance. In order to prevent them being overrun, and to build on his success at Sidi Rezegh, Rommel made a fast swoop with two Panzer divisions right through the rear of the XXX Corps position on 24 November, driving the British east and south-east. This unexpected counterstroke, combined with the loss of Sidi Rezegh, caused unbelievable chaos – the Eighth Army wondered what had happened, what to do next, where to go. Elements of XXX Corps HQ took refuge in Tobruk, XIII Corps HQ was in complete disorder. To Cunningham it looked like a sudden overwhelming victory for Rommel, and it seemed to him that the British force could do no better than withdraw as best they could to the prepared defences at Mersa Matruh, some 150 miles to the east, and regroup there. On the evening of 23 November, however, having been apprised of the defeatist attitude in Eighth Army HQ, Auchinleck had appeared on the scene. He grasped the situation at once, ordered Cunningham to stand fast at all costs and to attack wherever possible, and refused to be shaken out of his coolness even when, on the morning of the 24th, Rommel's Panzers swept eastwards towards the Egyptian border. On 25 November he replaced Cunningham with Maj.-Gen. Neil Ritchie, the Deputy Chief of the General Staff at GHQ in Cairo, who arrived on the afternoon of the 26th. Auchinleck himself had returned to Cairo the day before.

In the confusion the two corps managed to stay firm, aided not a little by Ritchie's view that Rommel was becoming desperate, and his belief, which he shared with his C-in-C, that the Panzers' 'dash to the Wire' could not possibly be backed up by adequate supplies, and that numbers of serviceable German tanks must be running low. The RAF were paying constant attention to Rommel's supply lines, while to the west elements of XIII Corps had pushed to within striking distance of Tobruk, and XXX Corps had regrouped south of Sidi Rezegh. Faced with being caught between two forces and cut off from the rest of his army, Rommel decided that enough had been gained for the time being and began to withdraw on 27 November. On the 29th elements of XIII Corps managed to link up with the Tobruk garrison, while troops from both corps succeeded in re-taking Sidi Rezegh as the Germans fell back. They received as good as they gave, however; by 30 November the area was again in German hands and an advance to Tobruk baulked a day later. The British continued to attack, however, and badly mauled German counter-attacks near the border on 2 December. By 4 December Auchinleck's firmness, and his speed of reinforcement, began to tell; on the 7th Rommel withdrew westwards, with the Eighth Army in pursuit. 'For the first time in his life, Rommel was in retreat—a mortifying experience', as one of the German's biographers wrote. The offensive had cost him dearly: he left 400 damaged tanks behind him, having suffered some 24,000 casualties and lost a further 36,000 men who had been taken prisoner. By 15 December, the Eighth Army occupied Gazala, followed by Benghazi on the 24th; on 6 January 1942 they pushed the Germans back to El Agheila, and here the pursuit was called off. For the loss of 18,000 men, 'Crusader had cleared Cyrenaica and relieved Tobruk, which was finally cleared of the ring of besiegers on 8 December, some 240 days after it had first been cut off.

Auchinleck had vindicated the faith placed in him, and in doing so had proved himself more resourceful than his enemy. For a time, Rommel *had* succeeded in mesmerising Cunningham and others: his 'dash to the Wire' (the British defences on the border between Egypt and Libya) had bred near-panic in HQs and in units confronted by the racing Panzer columns. But Auchinleck and Ritchie had known the move to be strategically unsound, and had kept the Eighth Army on the offensive, restoring morale and forcing a swift and elusive enemy to stand and fight. 'Crusader' was a complicated series of battles ranging for considerable distances over the desert; Auchinleck's cool certainty that, however bad it was for the Eighth Army, it must be as bad or worse for Rommel, allowed him to ignore the confusion and concentrate upon destroying the German armour while keeping it from its supplies and reinforcements. He had waited until he was ready to fight and, despite setbacks (the split in Norrie's XXX Corps early in the battle, and the problems caused by Rommel's dramatic counter-attack), he had known what to do to be assured of victory. Auchinleck had become the first British general in the Second World War to defeat a German general – the man he defeated was the almost legendary Desert Fox, and he was to do it again.

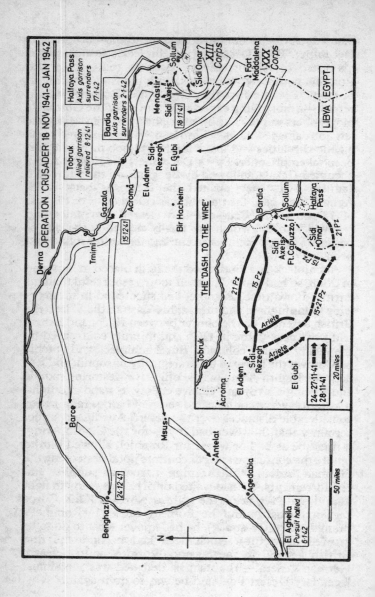

OPERATION 'CRUSADER' 18 NOV 1941-6 JAN 1942

Halfaya Pass
Axis garrison
surrenders
17.1.42

Tobruk
Allied garrison
relieved 8.12.41

Bardia
Axis garrison
surrenders 2.1.42

Sollum
Sidi Omar?
Menastir
Sidi Azeiz
18.11.41
XIII Corps

Fort
Maddalena
XXX Corps

LIBYA
EGYPT

El Adem Sidi
Rezegh
El Gubi

Gazala
Acroma
15.12.41

Derna
Tmimi

Bir Hacheim

Barce

Msus

Antelat

Agedabia

Benghazi
24.12.41

El Aghelia
Pursuit halted
6.1.42

N

50 miles

THE 'DASH TO THE WIRE'

Tobruk

Acroma
El Adem
Sidi
Rezegh

El Gubi

Ariete

Ariete

21 Pz

15 Pz

Bardia
Sollum
Halfaya
Pass

Sidi
Axeis
Ft.Capuzzo
Sidi
Omar

21 Pz

15+21 Pz

24-27.11.41
28-11.41

20 miles

After a series of successes and reverses Auchinleck's men were now poised to drive home their success. For this, however, they needed reinforcements. The only reinforcements earmarked for the Eighth Army at the time were the well-equipped 18th Division, already on their way to the Middle East. On 8 December, however, the Japanese had landed in Malaya, a day after the infamous attack on Pearl Harbor. III Indian Corps, in Malaya at the time, under the command of Auchinleck's old schoolfriend Lt-Gen. Sir Lewis Heath, had been forced to withdraw down the peninsula, and reinforcements were urgently needed. So on 12 December it was decided that 18th Division and all its equipment should be diverted to Singapore. Accordingly, some 20,000 men arrived at their destination – after a short period of acclimatisation in India – too late to save the situation, and having lost most of their equipment with the sinking of the *Empress of Asia*, just in time to be surrendered along with the rest of Singapore garrison on 15 February 1942: Auchinleck's much-needed reinforcements had been denied him, only to become Japanese prisoners of war virtually straightaway.

In consequence, Rommel, so far from being crushed, was able to recover and attack again in January, driving the Eighth Army back from El Agheila to the Gazala-Bir Hacheim line. But, as we shall see, Auchinleck saw that he did not escape unscathed from this further venture.

Auchinleck's preparations for 'Crusader' had not been assisted by the fact that he had constantly to mollify Churchill even as the launching date for the offensive grew nearer. General Sir Hastings Ismay, Chief of Staff to the Minister of Defence,* had already explained in August that Auchinleck needed to use what would now be called the 'public relations approach' with Churchill. In September he had advised:

> If you had said the demands of modern armies in desert warfare are so insatiable that we are still 'short' you would have made your point and he would have been

---

* As well as being Prime Minister, Churchill was also Minister of Defence.

perfectly happy. As it is he regards the epithet 'appreciable' as a reflection on or at least a grudging acknowledgement of the efforts and sacrifices made at Home to keep you well supplied. [Auchinleck had described the level of reinforcements he was receiving as 'appreciable', in a restricted military sense.] But the main point is – do write him long personal chatty letters occasionally. I know normally you would recoil in your modesty from doing so. But he isn't a normal person (Thank God), and these aren't normal times.

Auchinleck took Ismay's advice and his next letter to Churchill, on 16 September, had been much fuller and less formal. He had not, however, answered one of Churchill's ventures into military tactics when the latter had written:

I still feel there is a place where the 'I' tank with its short range might play an important part. It is not a question of moving far out into the desert or capturing El Adem [Rommel's HQ at the start of 'Crusader'] at this stage but simply of forcing the enemy to fire off his scanty ammunition and use up the life strength of his troops, cumbering himself also with wounded.

To have committed the slow and undergunned Matildas and other 'infantry' tanks to such a policy would have been madness. In the superb tank country provided by the desert the superior German armour, far from wasting ammunition, would merely manoeuvre out of range, and use its more powerful armament to destroy the 'I' tanks at will. If ever Auchinleck had wished to draw attention to Churchill's total inability to understand the desert position he would only have needed to quote the last sentence of the signal. But he never did; he did not even resent it. Ismay's advice, seemingly so reasonable, was totally misplaced. The more Auchinleck told Churchill, the more the latter tried to direct the desert campaign from Whitehall. An example of this came on 21 October, when Churchill sent a crisp message:

The War Office Movement Branch state that the three MT ships and two out of the three personnel ships arrived on October 2nd and remaining personnel ship two days later. We do not understand why when every day was of measureless consequence it took nearly a fortnight to unload these 150 vehicles from three separate ships.

Auchinleck neither explained nor excused the time taken; he realised that to try to do so would merely provoke Churchill into a comparison using statistics made elsewhere and applying to different cargoes and a different time. On receiving no answer to his point Churchill assumed that the reprimand had been accepted as just, and that there would be no similar delays in the future!

'Crusader', like all battles, produced much that was unexpected by both sides – the phenomenon known as 'the fog of war'. Whatever the plan, whatever the ability of those concerned, from the moment the opposing forces approach each other confusion begins. Messages go astray, vehicles break down or are delayed, orders and counter-orders are misunderstood. 18 November and succeeding days had had an added bonus of torrential rain, though this would not stop later stages of the battle being fought in clouds of dust and smoke. One of Auchinleck's staff officers, Lt-Col. F. W. de Guingand, who succeeded Shearer as Auchinleck's Director of Military Intelligence in February 1942, said:

Our armoured brigades were commanded with great dash but not perhaps with comparable skill. When once they came into contact with Rommel's forces very heavy casualties occurred. The tank returns that came into Army Headquarters were positively frightening. At this stage Rommel undertook a very bold and well-timed armoured raid deep into our area. During this fighting a New Zealand casualty clearing station was overrun by the enemy. Rommel found time to walk round and talk to some of the patients. He certainly had something about him this German General.

It was an interesting moment, and one that contributed greatly to the Rommel charisma. There are those, however, who are certain that it only happened because Rommel himself was lost and did not for the moment know what to do next.

Auchinleck's Dispatch (his official report to London of Middle East operations during his term as C-in-C) gives a vivid description of the events of 22 November:

Desultory fighting broke out again on the aerodrome [Sidi Rezegh] on the morning of November 22nd, and in the afternoon developed into a pitched battle in which the enemy employed at least a hundred tanks, besides large numbers of anti-tank guns and infantry. On our side, in addition to the wearied Support Group and 7th Armoured Brigade, all three regiments of the 22nd Armoured Brigade were involved. The fog of war literally descended on the battlefield, for the clouds of dust and smoke raised by tanks and bursting shells made accurate shooting impossible and at times it was difficult to tell friend from foe. At the conclusion of the battle, which raged until after dark, our armoured brigades were finally driven off the aerodrome.

De Guingand goes on to say that after six days British losses had been so heavy – the armour being no match for the enemy anti-tank guns and tanks – that doubt arose in the Army Commander's (Cunningham's) mind about continuing with the original plan if the cost was as high as appeared; indeed, he considered withdrawal to Mersa Matruh. It was at this moment, the evening of the 23rd, that Auchinleck arrived on the scene and took stock. De Guingand said:

I understand that he arrived at a moment when orders had actually been issued for the move of the Army's Headquarters back into Egypt. [Apparently the Brigadier, General Staff, Brigadier A. Galloway, had realised that the situation might not be as bad as it seemed, and was therefore delaying any moves for retreat; he also informed GHQ in Cairo of the position.] It was then that the Commander-in-Chief showed great courage and leadership. He decided to make a change in command to drive the Army forward in spite of what they had suffered.

The change, of course, was to replace Cunningham with Ritchie. There is little doubt that the appointment of Cunningham in the first place was a mistake, but whether the appointment of Ritchie in his place was equally misguided seems debatable. Cunningham had not had the right sort of experience for this sort of fighting, but then there were few who had. It is said that at fifty-five he was probably too old for this type of warfare, and the action he had seen had been of a very different kind. He had been a heavy smoker but as it was said to be affecting his eyesight he had recently given up the habit: when Auchinleck saw him on 23 November he had begun smoking heavily again. It seemed to Auchinleck that at this moment Cunningham was exhausted, but might perhaps rally. He therefore gave orders that the attack should be renewed. In his appreciation he said, 'It is clear to me that after the fighting of the last few days it is most improbable that the enemy will be able to stage a major advance for some time to come.' Auchinleck's rapid assessment of the situation was generalship of the highest order. He had arrived in haste in an aircraft which had frequently been forced close to the ground by low cloud and rain, and reasoned that if the British Army was close to the end of its tether the Germans were even more so. As he said of Rommel in the presence of Randolph Churchill, then a war correspondent, 'He is making a desperate effort, but he won't get very far. That column of tanks simply cannot get supplies. I am sure of this.'

On the 25th he returned to Cairo, where he received an encouraging message from Churchill:

I cordially endorse your views and intentions and HM Government wish to share your responsibility for fighting it out to the last inch whatever may be the result. It is all or nothing but I am sure you are the stronger and will win.

Am immensely heartened by your magnificent spirit and will-power.

For Auchinleck to have to dismiss a man he liked in the middle of battle was a most unpleasant task. The key paragraphs in his official message on 25 November to Cunningham were:

I have formed the opinion that you are now thinking in terms of defence rather than offence, and I have lost confidence in your ability to press to the bitter end the offensive which I have ordered to continue.

You will realise, I hope, that this is an extremely painful decision for me to make. It is all the more painful because I realise that I owe you a deep debt of gratitude for your conduct of the battle up to this moment.

At the same time he sent a less formal letter in which he said:

It is no use, I am afraid, my telling you how I hate to have had to do this thing, but I must act according to my belief and I have done so. It is most painful to me because I like you and respect you a very great deal, and I never thought I should have to act in this way towards you.

(Cunningham's career was not finished, despite the dismissal. Subsequently he became Commandant at the Staff College, Camberley, and also High Commissioner and Commander-in-Chief, Palestine.)

When, in 1976, David Dimbleby asked him about this situation years later Auchinleck answered, 'Cunningham came to me at about the same time as I came to Egypt. He had been in Central Africa I think where he had considerable success on a very small scale against the Italians, and I put him in command because I thought he had the idea of mobile warfare. I think he did very well but his health cracked up eventually and I had to remove him.'

It was pointed out that Cunningham had only fought

for eight days, and with his C-in-C present for the last forty-eight hours, and that he appeared to have split up his forces too much. Auchinleck's answer was this:

> It is very difficult to concentrate in the desert. In the desert movement is possible anywhere provided you can get water. In this case perhaps it was wrong to choose Cunningham but on the face of it he had a very good record but he lost his nerve. I went up to visit him and found him in a very shaky condition. You see in the normal way the Chief Staff Officer should tell you if the Commander isn't fit to carry on but loyalty is so great that very few people think of doing that. They should have told me. But the man is dead and he has no defence, it is not fair to say these things now.

When pressed Auchinleck said he did not feel there were any special military lessons to be drawn from this event. He had misjudged Cunningham's potential, and overrated his health. Cunningham had, of course, been working continuously and without adequate leave, and had moved from one important job to another. But this did not, of course, alter the fact that eventually the strain overcame him, as it might anyone.

It should not perhaps be overlooked that Cunningham, as a field commander, did not receive Ultra decrypts, though naturally he was given intelligence summaries. Without knowing the exact source and full range of Ultra information it was impossible for a commander to believe that information about his opponent's deficiencies in equipment were as accurate as was asserted. Like many generals, Cunningham probably mistrusted intelligence reports, preferring the evidence of his own eyes and ears. These did not suggest that Rommel was at the end of his resources; they suggested he had a limitless reserve enabling him to take extravagant risks.

The events of the early stages of 'Crusader' give the first indication that Auchinleck might be the outstanding general of the war. He had known when to arrive and what to do when he reached the heart of the battle; he had taken all the right decisions and, above all, he had reassured by his presence. Before his arrival panic was abroad in the Eighth Army: there are stories of officers shaving then, realising that German tanks were upon them, leaping still naked into trucks and driving top-speed for 'the Wire'. Everyone was tired and bewildered, information was either scanty and incomplete or too detailed and confusing. It was a battle lost. Defeat could have been explained perfectly adequately as being due to the enemy having better tanks and better guns, handled by more experienced troops, commanded by a general of dash and imagination. But Auchinleck was not going to accept defeat. He might have had Churchill's words on his lips: 'We are not interested in the possibilities of defeat. They do not exist.'

They did in fact exist, but he realised that they existed for his opponent too. Rommel had done well in spite of differences of opinion with General Ludwig Crüwell, the Afrika Korps commander, and a belief that the Italians had done less for him than he might have expected. Rommel was in many ways a military genius, and opposed by an inferior general he would have been unbeatable. But he was not. He was opposed by a superior general all the way from 'Crusader' to First Alamein, then by another very high-quality general who had the advantage of enormous material superiority. Had Rommel survived the war his testimony would have confirmed what was already deducible from results. This is not to say that Auchinleck was invincible. He had been unable to achieve a great deal in Norway and would not have been able to do much in France before Dunkirk. It is doubtful also whether he could have salvaged the disasters in Malaya and Burma once the Japanese had achieved air and naval superiority. But in a battle which appeared to be lost but might still be won he was unequalled.

Having pulled the battle round and appointed Ritchie to command Eighth Army, Auchinleck left him to get on with it. On 1 December he himself returned to Eighth Army HQ to see how matters were progressing, and stayed till the 10th. In the meantime the battle had changed from armoured warfare to one of infantry. The tanks were temporarily out of it; there is a limit to the performance of tanks under desert conditions and they had reached it. Reserves were moving up, but the stage was not yet ready for another clash of armour. There was much for Ritchie to do to consolidate the victories which had been won. Tobruk had to be safeguarded against any sudden drive by the Germans to reinvest it or capture it.

The next stage was to move right on to the offensive and make a drive for Benghazi, using a mobile force under Brigadier W. H. E. 'Strafer' Gott, commander of the Support Group in 7th Armoured Division. Meanwhile the New Zealander Division, part of XIII Corps, mounted a sweeping-up operation south-east of Tobruk, taking many prisoners and capturing stores the Germans could ill afford to lose. Rommel was now on the defensive. Experience had already shown, however, that the moment when the German commander appeared to be at the end of his tether was the moment when he could usually manage a disconcerting strike back.

This was such a moment. Between 29 November and 3 December he rallied every usable tank, gun and vehicle and hit hard at XIII Corps south of Tobruk and around Sidi Rezegh, and at other points nearer the border. Success here would have enabled him to reinvest Tobruk. Despite closing the corridor to the port and retaking Sidi Rezegh, the effort seemed likely to fail. Ritchie was unperturbed and Auchinleck signalled to Churchill: 'I am absolutely confident.'

Not the least source of Auchinleck's satisfaction at this moment was Freyberg, who was doing all that could ever be expected. The New Zealanders of his division, refusing to be shot to pieces from a distance, had gone in with the bayonet. Casualties were high, but less than expected. On 3 December Rommel aimed a new blow at Menastir and Sidi Axeiz but this was broken up by Brigadier Jock Campbell's 'Jock Columns'.

Sir David Hunt, at that time an Intelligence Officer with XIII Corps (and later Ambassador to Brazil), makes the point that:

since our standard anti-tank weapon, the 2-pounder, had neither the range nor the killing power, the 25-

pounder was the only weapon on which we could entirely rely to kill a tank. Each column ... was a method of carrying the 25-pounder to the enemy tank with sufficient infantry to protect it, and armoured cars or other reconnaissance vehicles to act as feelers. At a later period, when the commander of the Eighth Army had under his orders far more troops than General Auchinleck ever had, and both the 6-pounder and the 17-pounder anti-tank guns were in standard supply, it was fashionable to decry the use of columns. The answer I suppose is that if the circumstances had been different the employment of columns would have been wrong. ... It was Rommel who began the practice and he carried on with it after we had given it up. He clearly thought the method had its advantages for a General operating in the desert with comparatively small forces.

By 5 December Auchinleck felt that Rommel was probably beaten for the moment, and would have to withdraw and regroup; he planned to help him make up his mind by constantly prodding him with the 'Jock Columns.' Auchinleck, of course, knew from Ultra that the German supply position was not good, but he did not discount the fact that further supplies could arrive unheralded and upset the balance again. While at Eighth Army HQ for the second time (1–10 December) he wrote to Lt-Gen. Sir Arthur Smith, his COS in Cairo:

I am not hoping for too much and it may take a little time yet. However the Prime Minister seems happy. Isn't he grand? A wonderful chap. All well here and everyone fighting like hell. The Air Force is magnificent and our 'Jock' columns have been doing awfully well.

In a further message to Smith of the same day (6 December) he went on to describe the virtues of the 'Jock Columns'. Referring to the fact that these had been mentioned in communiqués as mobile 'patrols' he said:

Our 'Jock' columns are balanced forces of all arms, as

we used to say, and are most offensive and distinctive. They work with definite objects and are co-ordinated by higher commanders. They are the answer to this kind of fighting to the centre of no-man's land besides being most valuable gainers of information. They have been in close and continuous touch with the enemy on a wide front, and shell his troops and transport continually, besides taking prisoners.

This clear description of the character and tasks of the 'Jock Columns' did not prevent later critics from suggesting that Auchinleck's tactics against Rommel were wrong in that they were too similar to the North-West Frontier punitive expeditions, and more suitable for India than for the desert. The criticism is quite unwarranted, though: a North-West Frontier expedition resembled a minor army of occupation; a 'Jock Column' was a fast-striking force – and the armoured column was certainly not a feature of Indian warfare. And, in spite of their limitations, 'Jock Columns' were effective enough in countering Rommel's thrusts at this stage of the war in the desert to become a legendary aspect of the Western Desert.

In his reply to Auchinleck's encouraging message, Smith said: 'I note you write "I can't come back yet" – I can't help wondering if the word "can't" should not have read "won't"!' The COS went on to express his fears about the losses to Allied shipping likely to result from the relief of Tobruk, since the port could now be used more fully.

Enemy air is likely to be reinforced for this purpose. Anti-aircraft defences on merchant ships is inadequate. I have ordered therefore that the first priority of captured Bredas* shall be to the Navy for this purpose. I have just seen Lumsden [Maj.-Gen. H. Lumsden, commander of 1st Armoured Division] who tells me that not a single tank arrived from England complete with equipment and one was quite empty except for a tow rope.

* Italian machine-guns.

The date this message was sent, 7 December 1941, saw a rapid widening of the war. The Japanese attacked Pearl Harbor, crippling the American Pacific Fleet, thus bringing America into the war; on the 8th they landed in Malaya, and on the 10th in the Philippines. It was now undoubtedly a world war. The fact that the full weight of American power would now be wholeheartedly committed to the Allied cause was a great comfort to Churchill, but strategically the immediate outlook seemed bleak. It seemed bleak too to Rommel, who wrote to his wife on 9 December:

> You will no doubt have seen how we are doing from the Wehrmacht communiqué. I've had to break off the action outside Tobruk on account of the Italian formations, and also the badly exhausted German troops. I'm hoping we'll succeed in escaping enemy encirclement and holding on to Cyrenaica. You can imagine what I'm going through and what anxieties I have. It doesn't look as though we'll get any Christmas this year.

On the 12th he wrote, 'Don't worry about me. It will all come out all right. We're still not through the crisis.' On the 20th, 'We're pulling out. There was simply nothing else for it. I'm very well. I've now managed to get a bath and a change having slept in my coat for most of the time for the last few weeks. Some supplies have arrived – the first since October. My commanding officers are ill – all those who aren't dead or wounded.' But on 30 December he was cheering up again: 'Heavy fighting yesterday, which went well for us. Their new attempt to encircle us and force us back against the sea has failed.' This was a counter-attack near Agedabia, sixty-odd miles east of El Agheila, in which the Panzers destroyed two-thirds of 22 Armoured Brigade's tanks.

In fact, as his Intelligence Officer, Major Friedrich von Mellenthin, pointed out, events were now turning to German advantage. As they retreated, in good order, harassed but not put into disarray, their supply lines shortened and the British lines of communication lengthened. There was developing precisely the sort of situation which Rommel had a genius for exploiting. He still had better tanks and guns than the Eighth Army could muster, as Ritchie pointed out to Auchinleck. Benghazi had been taken without fighting on 24 December, but its loss probably meant little to Rommel at the time. On 6 January the Germans withdrew from Agedabia and made El Agheila their strongpoint. Owing to the difficulties of approaching El Agheila nothing more could be done for the moment, but the Eighth Army was heartened by the capture of Bardia, over 200 miles to the east and isolated since Rommel's withdrawal early in December 1941, which had capitulated on 2 January. 8000 prisoners were taken. The Axis garrison in Halfaya, south of Bardia and also cut off, put up rather more resistance, but also surrendered with the loss of over 5000 prisoners. All looked well for the British.

Unfortunately, Rommel received another consignment of supplies at the beginning of January. In December a convoy of German shipping was on the way across the Mediterranean when, by virtue of Ultra intercepts, its presence became known. It was intercepted and two of its ships were sunk, taking forty-five tanks to the bottom. One of the survivors, however, the *Mongevino*, landed twenty-three tanks at Tripoli on 19 January and another, the *Ankara*, reached Benghazi, also on the 19th, just before the town was captured; the twenty-two heavy tanks she carried were hastily unloaded and rumbled off to join 15th Panzer Division. This incident provided an example of the problem that, although it was a magnificent advantage to be able to break the German codes and read their signals, it did not mean that British knowledge of what was happening was complete. The assumption in British Intelligence in December 1941 was that even if the *Ankara* did reach Benghazi, there were no facilities for berthing a ship of that size, and that even if there had been it would have been impossible to get the tanks off and away in the limited time available to the Germans. That the assumption was wrong became clear when, a month later, Rommel came on to the attack again; he was using those forty-five tanks. Had the British known that the ship had been designed to carry railway locomotives they would have realised how suitable she was for transporting and unloading tanks. Brigadier Shearer, Auchinleck's DMI, was blamed for the wrong intelligence assessment, although Shearer was relying on information he had received from the Navy that even if the *Ankara* arrived she would be unable to unload. Since he had been proved wrong, however, he was dismissed in February on the advice of Brooke, the CIGS, although Auchinleck at first wished to retain him. The *Ankara* feat undoubtedly enabled Rommel to mount his unexpected offensive on 21 January 1942. His timing was further influenced by another intelligence lapse when a British armoured regiment, the Queen's Bays, sent a wireless report on the number and serviceability of its tanks *in clear* by mistake. The information was joyfully received by the enemy, particularly when they realised that the only serviceable tanks were the Crusaders. Of the Crusaders, Colonel Berry said:

> Shortly before Operation 'Crusader' was about to begin it was found that the suspension arms of the Crusader tanks were breaking off like carrots, in large numbers. This proved to be due to faulty casting in the manufacture in England, but a cure was effected by welding reinforcing plates to each arm. As there were ten arms to each tank and each arm weighed about two cwt this put an enormous strain on the already overstrained field workshops. This suspension trouble was not a design fault, it was a fault in the manufacture of a certain batch of tanks, it was cured and had no effect on operations. The lack of mechanical reliability was a very different matter and had a profound effect on the whole of the desert fighting in 1941 and 1942.
>
> Like the Matilda* the engine of the Crusader tank was not designed as such. It was a 12-cylinder 400 hp aero engine left over from the 1914–18 war. The engine was produced in America when she came into the First World War and was supposed to contain the best

---

* Of which the power unit was two London bus engines.

features of the British Rolls-Royce and Sunbeam aero engines in use by the RAF. As an aero engine it proved to be very reliable and had a good performance.

Unfortunately the cooling problems in a tank are very different from those in an aeroplane, and here the troubles began. In an aeroplane there is, or was, no need for cooling fans as the air rushing through the radiator at over 100 mph is sufficient to cool the water in the radiator. In a tank big fans have to be provided to do this. In the Crusader the engine was modified by the fitting of two fans and two water-pumps driven from the engine crankshaft by a long chain. This was a disaster. As soon as the tank was used in the desert sand got in the chain, the chain stretched and started to jump the crankshaft driving sprocket. It was a three-day job to change the sprocket.

Worse still, the water-pump would not stand up to the sand and heat of the desert and soon leaked very badly. A re-design was necessary but unfortunately the manufacturing facilities did not exist in Egypt.

In January 1942 we had pushed Rommel right back to El Agheila and he seemed to be nearly finished. I think he would have been finished if we had not had two hundred Crusader tanks under repair in the XIII Corps workshops. The situation was so critical that the Corps commander signalled that four hundred water-pumps should be flown out from England, by flying boat if necessary. The reply came back: 'Regret not available in UK.' If those water-pumps had been available Rommel's counter-attack could never have succeeded and there would not have been a battle of Alamein, first, second or third.

Colonel Berry added another point about the anti-tank guns. In November a captured German anti-tank gun was brought in:

I was asked to inspect it and report on it. I could not believe my eyes. It was a British three-inch AA gun manufactured by Vickers and fitted to a Russian gun carriage. It was a very effective and powerful weapon.

Clearly it had been sent to Russia, captured by the Germans, serviced and sent to the Middle East.

When the three-inch guns in London were replaced by the 3.7-inch guns, several hundred three-inch guns became redundant. If these had been fitted to twenty-five-pounder gun carriages and rushed out to the Middle East, the whole course of the war would have been changed.

Perhaps it was fortunate for Auchinleck that he did not know about the 3-inch guns back in Britain; he certainly had enough to ponder upon from what he knew of the lack of reliability of the Crusader tanks. It was a story all too familiar to those on the spot. 'The equipment is excellent, it has been tested in Britain and we have made a great effort to supply it.' A few days in battle and it would be found to be virtually useless. There were many examples of unsatisfactory equipment which varied from anti-tank rifles which were probably only effective if one poked them into the turret and shot the driver, to aircraft which were found to have severe blind spots and became veritable flying coffins.

But one advantage of the *Ankara* incident was that it caused provision to be made against such an oversight occurring in the future. On Shearer's staff in Cairo was a Major Enoch Powell, formerly a Fellow of Trinity College, Cambridge and a Professor of Greek in Sydney, Australia, who had enlisted originally in the infantry but had been transferred to Intelligence. It was clear to Enoch Powell that all available information was not being adequately co-ordinated and assessed, and he therefore applied his energies to seeing what could be done to make sure that it was. The result was a committee, which met daily, under Group Captain Long, consisting of another RAF representative, two naval officers, and Powell. As it received the latest information from Ultra and other sources the committee was able to apply the laws of logic and probability to enemy moves. Thus, the information that a convoy had left Naples, presumably bound for Tripoli, did not mean that two days later it would be at Point X. It could very well have taken a somewhat different route and instead be at Point Y. The need for preserving the Ultra secret meant that the convoy would have to be 'accidentally' discovered, and then an aircraft would have to be directed to fly over its probable route; the aircraft would be delighted to report its 'spotting'. The result of this type of approach was a spectacular rise in the number of Axis ships sunk in the Mediterranean, and even elsewhere. As has been said, however, one of the great difficulties with Ultra information was acting on it without arousing suspicion as to the source.

Once more, Rommel's new offensive, on 21 January, was unexpected both in timing and direction. Although the British did not anticipate a counter-attack, the assumption was that if one occurred it must be in the north; thus the Eighth Army was astonished to find that it came from the west. There were two main thrusts. The principal reason why the attack caught the Eighth Army totally by surprise was that Rommel had informed neither his superiors nor his Italian allies of what he was proposing to do, and there was, therefore, no information from Ultra. Then the northern thrust by 21st Panzer came quickly by Mersa el Brega, while 15th Panzer took a more southerly route by Wadi Faregh. They converged at Agedabia on the 22nd, raced on to Antelat, swerved towards Saunnu, then split again before coming together on Msus. Another quick thrust gave them Benghazi (again) on the 29th and thus through Barce to Derna. From Derna they pushed on to Gazala, forty miles west of Tobruk, where a defensive line was established by the British on 4 February. Meanwhile the southern prong, which had taken the Charruba-Mechili route, also managed to reach the British positions on the Gazala line. Once more Rommel had slashed the Eighth Army to ribbons. The British troops so unceremoniously swept out of his way, with severe losses of tanks and other equipment, were not, however, cowed or disheartened, though they were very considerably disorganised. They referred to the withdrawal as the 'Second Benghazi Handicap', the first having been O'Connor's retreat in April of the previous year.

Initially Rommel's drive had not gone all that well, as

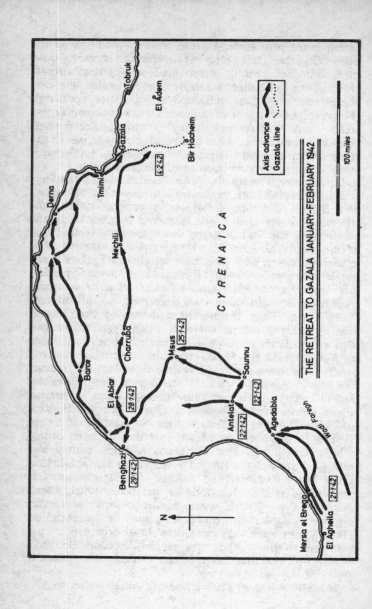

THE RETREAT TO GAZALA JANUARY–FEBRUARY 1942

Tobruk

El Adem

Gazala

Bir Hacheim

Tmimi

4.2.42

Derna

Mechili

CYRENAICA

Charruba

Barce

Msus
25.1.42

El Abiar
28.1.42

Saunnu
22.1.42

Benghazi
29.1.42

Antelat
22.1.42

Agedabia
22.1.42

Wadi Faregh

21.1.42

Mersa el Brega

El Agheila

N

Axis advance
Gazala line

100 miles

15th Panzer had been held up in the sand dunes near Wadi Faregh on 21 January. Soon afterwards, however, success came within his grasp, and the Luftwaffe assisted his troops greatly with accurate dive-bombing. Both the RAF and the British armour were short of fuel, for their original overstretched line had taken them far ahead of their bases, and Benghazi had not come into use as a supply base, being full of magnetic mines thoughtfully dropped by the Luftwaffe as they abandoned it. It was soon clear that the Eighth Army must do its utmost to avoid losing whole regiments as prisoners as a result of the wide-sweeping Panzer movements; it was clearer still from the efforts to check those movements that the British equipment was no match for the German. On 25 January there was a clash of opinion between Godwin-Austen, commanding XIII Corps, and Ritchie over the deployment of the former's forces, though subsequently it seems that Godwin-Austen was right in his reading of the situation. By the beginning of February the battle had stabilised, since Rommel was virtually out of petrol, and at that point (2 February) Godwin-Austen, feeling he had been over-ruled wrongly, tendered his resignation, which Auchinleck reluctantly accepted, replacing him with the redoubtable 'Strafer' Gott, now a major-general.

The German estimate of the battle was that the Eighth Army had shown plenty of courage but insufficient awareness of possibilities; this had been true in the battle as much as before it. But the Germans then proceeded to underestimate the ability of the Eighth Army to prepare another offensive in the near future. Only some 1400 British casualties were recorded during the retreat to the Gazala line. Forty-two tanks were destroyed and thirty more abandoned, and a similar number of guns was lost. The most serious aspect of the reverse, however, was that it showed that Ritchie, whose grasp of the 'Crusader' battles had been effective and courageous, had not perhaps been as good a judge of matters as he should have been; his tendency to over-optimism would have disastrous consequences later. And it demonstrated once again that British tanks and guns were no match for those of the Germans, nor were they handled to the best advantage; this last was again a matter of training. It should be remembered that the Germans had been concentrating on armoured warfare in the years between the wars, and had also learnt many useful lessons in France and the Low Countries.

On 25 January Auchinleck, fully aware that the situation was becoming ugly, flew up to Tmimi. The previous day had seen a heartening attempt by 1st Armoured Division, part of XIII Corps, to check 15th Panzer near Msus. The Division had already been badly mauled during the retreat eastwards and was down to almost half its original strength; its attempted stand failed sadly, and it fell back on Charruba. The reason for this failure lay not only in 1st Armoured's equipment but also in its lack of training in the execution of tactics. The RAF flew continuous sorties to harass the German armoured columns but in spite of inflicting considerable damage could not stop them. On the 27th Auchinleck wrote to Churchill:

There is no doubt, I fear, that our armoured forces failed to compete with the enemy satisfactorily and that they have had heavy losses without the prospect of being able to inflict comparable damage on the enemy. Cause of this is not clear but probably that our troops, being dispersed widely, were unable to concentrate for concerted action against enemy compact mass ... Meanwhile object is to regain initiative, close in on enemy, destroy him if we can, otherwise push him back. Am confident General Ritchie is fully determined to effect this object. Tedder and I will be staying here for the present.

Disturbed though he was by this, Churchill replied:

Many thanks. I have complete confidence in you and am glad you are staying up ...

I am most anxious to hear further from you about the defeat of our armour by inferior enemy numbers. This cuts very deep. [He was referring to the report that eighty tanks of 1st Armoured Division had been outfought at Msus by fifty of the enemy.]

Auchinleck sent an account of the battle to General Smith on 28 January.

> The enemy started moving again before lunch yesterday as you know and, true to form, has taken the bold stroke of dividing his forces in diametrically opposite directions from a base which cannot hold any real reserve of supplies. At least that is how it looks. Without being too optimistic, it seems as if he may have once again under-estimated our capacity to recover and hit back after a reverse – for we have had a reverse – there is no getting away from it. However, I feel that Neil [Ritchie] has the situation very well in hand. In fact it looks as if the enemy is doing the very thing that Neil was hoping he would do, except that he did not anticipate him splitting his force as he has done. This again may give us an even better opportunity of hitting him.

This optimistic view was qualified in the second portion of the message which ran:

> Neil has just heard from Godwin-Austen that [Maj.-Gen. Frank] Messervy says that 1st Armoured Division is reorganised and ready for offensive action. It has been ordered by Godwin in anticipation of orders from Neil to strike south-eastwards against the enemy moving on Mechili. [Maj.-Gen. Francis] Tuker and the 4th Indian Division are to hold El Abiar and strike east and south against the flank and the rear of the enemy moving on El Abiar, which would seem to offer a good chance of success, though a report just in, indicating movement of small columns of enemy tanks and MT northwards from Agedabia, may hamper this move. There is no doubt that today may be critical and much will depend on the skill and boldness with which 1st Armoured Div is handled, and the ability of 4th Indian Div to hold off the threat from the south while striking east. Both sides are taking big risks and I hope we can play that game as well as Rommel. He is running absolutely true to form and putting everything in the shop window. So are we, I hope. The difference is, I think, that our

situation ought to be better than his and that our air is, for the moment, having everything its own way.

I should not be at all surprised to learn that the apparent failure of 1st Armoured Div to deal with the enemy in the present operations was due largely to the divorcement of the armour from the infantry.

I shall stay on here for a bit, I think, and I fancy AOC-in-C [Tedder] will stay too. The RAF have been grand – morale sky high and full of hate.

Auchinleck returned to Cairo on 1 February, by which time it was all too clear that any previous optimism had been unjustified. While the letter to Smith was being written, Rommel was leaping forward to other disconcerting successes. Ritchie, clearly realising that this was a moment for desperate measures, issued direct orders to Tuker about the way 4th Indian Division should be used. Godwin-Austen, under whose command Tuker's division came, not unnaturally felt that this was a direct reflection on his own ability and on the 2nd asked to resign, as has been mentioned. (Apparently Auchinleck bore Godwin-Austen no resentment for resigning at a critical point in the battle for he accepted him as his Quartermaster-General in India in 1945; perhaps by that time Auchinleck felt some sympathy with him over his conflict with Ritchie.) Auchinleck had more than enough to occupy him at this time without worrying about a clash of personalities in one of the corps. He knew that the loss of Benghazi would distress Churchill deeply, since it had been held for only a month. In fact, Churchill had taken the bull of potential criticism by the horns on 29 January and asked for a vote of confidence in the House of Commons:

I feel I am entitled to come to the House of Commons, whose servant I am, and ask them not to press me to act against my conscience and better judgement and make scapegoats in order to improve my own position, not to press me to do the things which may be clamoured for at the moment, but which will not help the war effort, but on the contrary to give me their encouragement and give me their aid.

This disarming appeal, following as it did a long and detailed account of 'Crusader', had the desired effect. Only one man refused to vote for him.

The news that the pressure of home criticism was temporarily off Churchill was encouraging to Auchinleck, but did not solve his own problems. He wrote to Smith on the 30th, saying he had not yet received the full figures of the tank losses, but:

> We have got to face the fact that, unless we can achieve superiority on the battlefield by better co-operation between the army and more original leadership of our armoured forces than is apparently being exercised at present, we may have to forgo any idea of mounting a strategical offensive, because our armoured forces are tactically incapable of meeting the enemy in the open, even when superior to him in numbers.

This was the crux of the matter, and it led to:

> Another very serious aspect which is obtruding itself more and more is the growth of an inferiority complex amongst our armoured forces, owing to their failure to compete with enemy tanks which they consider (and rightly so) superior to their own in certain aspects. This is very dangerous and will be most difficult to eradicate once it takes root, as I am afraid it is doing now. It becomes therefore all the more important to weld the three arms together as closely as possible.
>
> I have put this matter very plainly to the Prime Minister, as the military authorities at home, including Martel*, must realise what they are up against, and it is no good just counting tanks or regiments and pretending that ours are individually as good as the German because they are not. Before we can really do anything against the Germans on land, they have got to be made as good and better both in equipment, organisation and training.

* Lt-Gen. G. Le Q. (later Sir Giffard) Martel, the eminent tank pioneer and at that time Commander of the Royal Armoured Corps.

As you know I am not inclined to pessimism but I view our present situation with misgiving, so far as our power to take the offensive on a large scale is concerned.

On the same day Auchinleck sent a telegram to Churchill. In it he regretted the loss of Benghazi 'but hope loss is temporary only'. He questioned whether the German tanks were inferior in numbers to British on the day reported (1st Armoured Division's defeat near Msus on 25 January) but thought it possible, But, he continued,

other and at times irremediable causes which I have already mentioned to you in a letter are short range and inferior performance of our two-pounder guns compared with the German guns and mechanical unreliability of our cruiser tanks compared with German tanks. In addition I am not sure that the tactical leadership of our armoured units is of sufficiently high standard to offset German material advantage. This is in hand but cannot be improved in a day unfortunately.

I am reluctantly compelled to the conclusion that to meet German armoured forces with any hope of decisive success, our armoured forces as at present equipped, organised and led, must have at least two to one superiority. Even then they must rely for success on working in the very closest co-operation with infantry and artillery, which except for their weakness in anti-tank guns are fully competent to take on their German opposite numbers.

General Ritchie and I are fully alive to Rommel's probable intentions but whatever these may be he will certainly try to exploit success by use of even smaller columns until he meets resistance. Plans are in train to counter such action.

Like many explanations this dealt with the matter for the time being, but did not provide much hope for the future. It may seem almost incredible now that Churchill should have been criticised at this time, particularly in the House of Commons, when it must have been clear to everyone that if he were not there to win the war no one else could. But Churchill above everyone appreciated the right of others to criticise him, a right that was part of what he was fighting for. Undoubtedly at the beginning of February 1942, when the Eighth Army had dug in on the Gazala line and when it looked as though the unpredictable Rommel had been stopped for the moment, Churchill himself needed a victory, however small, to revitalise his own confidence. The reverse in the desert, after the tangible success of 'Crusader', was not the only setback of that grim winter. German armies were pushing the Russians back at all points; Japan had met with considerable success in Burma, Malaya, the Philippines and elsewhere; in the Mediterranean naval shipping losses had been severe and, to cap it, the *Prince of Wales* and the *Repulse* had been sunk off Malaya. It was a hard winter in every sense of the word.

11

'YOU MUST COME HOME' STORM IN THE DESERT

General Sir Alan Brooke, who had taken over from Dill as Chief of the Imperial General Staff in December 1941, lost no time in communicating his confidence in Auchinleck, blaming Shearer's intelligence estimates for the setbacks. Privately, however, Brooke had doubts about Auchinleck, particularly after Benghazi fell. Shearer was an obvious scapegoat for the underestimate of Rommel's strength although, as we have seen, he had no means of making a different one. Brooke was not the only person to criticise the unfortunate DMI, and although Auchinleck felt the general opinion was unfair he had to face the fact that confidence in the accuracy of intelligence could not return until Shearer had been replaced, blameless or not. In consequence, on 23 February he agreed to the appointment of F. W. de Guingand. De Guingand was a lieutenant-colonel working in the planning department of GHQ Cairo when he was told to report to Auchinleck. In his own words:

Auchinleck looked up from his desk. 'Freddie, I want you to take over DMI.' This was a shattering thing for a lieutenant-colonel with no previous intelligence experience to be told. When I recovered my breath I replied 'But I have never done anything of that sort before, sir.' 'Excellent,' said the Auk. 'That's why I've chosen you, you'll do it all right. I want you to take over at once.'

Stunned though he was at this sudden promotion to Brigadier and the leadership of a department with which he had previously been unfamiliar, de Guingand was soon aware, as were others, that this was a job for which he was exceptionally well fitted. One of his early moves was to pick out two young officers to join his staff. Both were university dons: one was Major E. T. Williams, later to become Sir Edgar Williams, Warden of Rhodes House, Oxford; the other Captain J. Ewart, who sadly was killed in a car crash soon after the war. Another significant appointment at this time was that of Maj.-Gen. Richard McCreery to take charge of policy for training and leading the armoured formations. Lt-Gen. Arthur Smith, Chief of the General Staff in Cairo, was replaced by Lt-Gen. T. W. Corbett, at that time a corps commander in Iraq. This last appointment raised some eyebrows, for Corbett had had little experience of desert warfare.

In view of dire reports from the Far East Churchill took this moment to send Auchinleck a personal message. It was dated 12 February 1942 and read:

Have been thinking much about you and your affairs with complete confidence you will come out on top.

Evidently the Prime Minister felt that morale in the Middle East should be maintained. The news all round was gloomy enough, and the message was a timely one. Singapore seemed certain to fall, and did on 15 February; in Burma the Japanese had entered Moulmein and further disasters for the British Army were obviously in store. In view of these setbacks the Chiefs of Staff decided that Australia, India, Ceylon and Burma must now have top priority. On 17 February Brooke warned Auchinleck that the 70th Division would have to go to bolster the remaining defences in Burma, 9th Australian Division, which had been replaced in Tobruk by the 70th, would have to return to the Pacific area, and there might be others to follow; 18th Division had already been lost for no purpose in Singapore. He agreed, however, that these withdrawals might endanger the chances of a Western Desert offensive. Yet Auchinleck was now pressed to begin a new offensive in Cyrenaica, partly to frustrate any plans which Rommel might have, and partly to take pressure off Malta. On 20 February the Governor of Malta, Lt-Gen. Sir William Dobbie, had stated very clearly to the Chiefs of Staff that the recent advance by Rommel had taken over the airfields from which the RAF would normally operate to protect the Malta convoys. The view was not shared by Auchinleck and many others, who felt that the main threat to Malta came not from the Germans in Cyrenaica but from the Axis airfields in Italy and Sicily. Unfortunately it was held by Brooke.

On 26 February Auchinleck received a telegram from Churchill which suggested that further offensive action in the Middle East must begin shortly:

I have not troubled you much in these difficult days, but I must now ask what are your intentions. According to our figures you have substantial superiority in the air, in armour, and in other forces over the enemy. There seems to be a danger that he may gain reinforcements as fast or even faster than you. The supply of Malta is causing us increased anxiety and anyone can see the magnitude of our disasters in the Far East. Pray let me hear from you. All good wishes.

Auchinleck replied promptly and fully on the next day, with seven pages of military appreciation. In essence, he said that he did not feel that the Eighth Army would possess adequate armour to launch an offensive before 1 June; any offensive launched before that date might well end in disaster. He pointed out that he would be building up this force as rapidly as possible, that he was strengthening the present frontier positions, that he would be extending the railway from Sollum to El Adem and that he was establishing dumps in forward areas with a view to supplying the coming attacks. He also said that a minor offensive to capture airfields in the Derna–Mechili area was contemplated, provided it did not in any way prejudice later plans.

Unhappily, this letter crossed with one from the Chiefs of Staff, telling Auchinleck that he must recapture the Cyrenaica air bases immediately in order to enable a vital convoy to get through to Malta. The timing was particularly unfortunate because, if Auchinleck had realised that the Chiefs of Staff took this view, he might have struck a slightly more optimistic note in his appreciation to Churchill. It is clear, with hindsight, that Churchill needed to feel that every effort was being made to show enterprise; Auchinleck's appreciation had, therefore, angered him greatly. Part of the problem was that it was impossible for anyone not in the desert to realise how dangerous any rash, or incompletely prepared, move against Rommel would be.

Some of the more enterprising ideas thought up by those actually in the desert were tested at a series of 'war-game' discussions which Auchinleck held at this time – one of the reasons why he has been criticised for listening too much to the views of others, almost practising a form of generalship by committee. An example of one such idea, mentioned by de Guingand, was called 'The Cowpat Theory'. The plan was to establish a series of bases ahead of the present front-line position, like a series of isolated cowpats. They would be well stocked, and they would contain armoured units, infantry and artillery. The thinking behind the idea was that they would force Rommel to attack and thus make himself vulnerable to a counter-attack on his lines of communication. The weaknesses of this theory were shown in a game in which McCreery and de Guingand took the role of the Germans. It became clear that the principal advantages would lie with Rommel who would be able to deliver concentrated attacks in areas where the Eighth Army had dispersed its forces.

One advantage in this type of exercise, as de Guingand mentions, was that the Eighth Army was extremely fortunate in having a very accurate account of the numbers and types of German tanks and other vehicles. This was provided by the Long Range Desert Group, whose primary function was to probe deeply into the German lines, lie up unobserved and then, miraculously undetected, report on the German strength. Other information along the same lines was provided by the SAS which combined reconnaissance with destruction. In view of the fact that the SAS raids roused the Germans and Italians to a frenzy of search-and-destroy operations it was surprising that the LRDG, whose whole wish was to be undetected, remained so amiable and co-operative with the SAS. De Guingand, as DMI, was especially appreciative of the fact that the LRGD managed to send in a report every twelve hours.

Another enterprise which Auchinleck favoured, but which the Intelligence Chiefs did not, was the 'German cell'. The proposal, made by Amery to Auchinleck on 25 June 1941, was to segregate a small number of officers whose function would be to keep apart, think German, and therefore try to visualise what the Germans might be likely to do in any given circumstance. It was clear to de Guingand that a small unorthodox body such as the German cell might be the source of fanciful views which would conflict with those of regular Intelligence circles. Rather than say this outright he played for time, stressing the problems of finding the right officers and the right accommodation. Auchinleck, realising the unpopularity of the venture as much as its impracticability, allowed the scheme to drop after a short time.

De Guingand admired Auchinleck, but could see faults in him. As he also had the opportunity to observe Wavell and Montgomery from close quarters, he was able, after the war, to make useful comparisons of the dangerous months of 1941–2:

Auchinleck has never been given sufficient credit for his leadership during those anxious days. It was a situation that required great determination and courage. I admired him very much during this period and really enjoyed – if that's the right word – that exciting home in the desert.

Like many others at GHQ I was immediately impressed by Auchinleck when he arrived in Cairo. He certainly looked the part and had a warm-hearted and attractive personality.

We planners had been struck by his robust attitude towards the Rashid Ali rebellion in Iraq. He was all for 'having a go' while Wavell opposed intervention and even suggested a political solution. In the end Auchinleck's view prevailed and he successfully directed the operation. His achievements during his term of command were considerable and although he was relieved of his appointment after about a year the British people and their allies have much to thank him for. To start with, he was immediately responsible for producing a new spirit in the Middle East, more confidence, a feeling of expectancy, a more robust outlook and altogether a raising of morale.

This then was the feeling throughout Auchinleck's command in the early days of 1942, despite the reverses of January and February. Subsequently, in view of the fact that he was replaced, there was a tendency to imply that Auchinleck had been somewhat lacking in dynamism in these days because of his reluctance to attack; that is not, however, the view of those who were with him at the time.

Although at this time Auchinleck's mind was concentrated on the immediate problem of achieving victory in the desert and keeping the Prime Minister happy during the period of build-up, as had been the case with 'Crusader', there were other events in the background of which he was aware, whether he liked them or not. One was that Iraq and Persia, formerly the responsibility of the C-in-C, India, now came under his command, following a proposal put by Churchill in December 1941. The former title of 'British Troops in Iraq' was changed to Tenth Army. The post of Minister of State in the Middle East, which up to mid-February had been held by Oliver Lyttelton, now became vacant as Lyttelton went home to become Minister of Production. He would be greatly missed, for he had had the experience to shoulder many burdens which would otherwise have fallen on the Commander-in-Chief. His office in Cairo had become a centre for inter-Service co-ordination, and for generally considering and coping with the economic and social problems of the surrounding countries: the Sudan, East Africa, Palestine, Syria, and Iraq. Above all, Lyttelton was in touch with the Home Government; to him came many matters of policy which were scarcely the province of the Commander-in-Chief, but which, without the Minister of State, would have fallen to the already over-burdened holder of that onerous post. Rather surprisingly, Richard Casey, the Australian Minister to the

United States, was appointed to succeed Lyttelton at the end of February, although he would not be able to take up the post till 5 May. Pending his arrival Sir Walter Monckton, Director-General of British Propaganda and Information Services in Cairo, acted as Minister of State, a task he performed with considerable skill.

These changes happened just when Auchinleck needed a very close, established link with the Home Government to bridge the gap in thought which was now beginning to show. In retrospect, it is simple enough to see the problem. On the one hand was the Commander-in-Chief, fully aware of the deficiencies in his own forces, knowing that any offensive with less than a two-to-one superiority could be an invitation to possible disaster, but knowing also that, given time, all would be well. On the other hand was the Home Government, alarmed by the spate of recent disasters and quick to criticise Churchill; there in the background were the Chiefs of Staff whose views at this moment happened to coincide with those of Churchill and, worrying everyone, was the dire plight of Malta which, after a heroic stand, now seemed at the point of collapse. Above all there was the Prime Minister, with his ceaseless prodding in the quest for a decisive victory. Auchinleck felt some frustration at being asked to do the impossible; Churchill and his colleagues felt frustrated beyond belief by this obdurate general who refused to stir himself and move forward in spite of the increasing numbers of men and materials he was receiving. Churchill was hoping that Auchinleck might name a date around 15 March for his next offensive; Auchinleck in the meantime was thinking that 1 June or, more probably, 1 August was the key date, and had said so in his appreciation of 27 February. He wondered how those at home could imagine his forces were being strengthened when the news was of withdrawing divisions, and less air and naval support.

One encouraging appointment at home had been that of Sir James Grigg to be Secretary of State for War. Grigg was an old friend; he had been Finance Minister to the Government of India from 1934–9, and Auchinleck had known him when C-in-C, India. He now wrote to Grigg explaining the difficult situation which had arisen over

Indian Army officers being appointed to posts in British formations. (As Indian Army pay was higher than British, these postings caused individuals to lose financially, resulting in some hardship to their families.) Furthermore these postings away from their own Army would probably be a disadvantage to their careers. Auchinleck commented, 'I know that this should not weigh with individuals whose sole thought should be to win the war, even if their families starve, but human nature being what it is, it does weigh with them and must therefore affect their efficiency.' The tone is ironic; he felt little sympathy with the complaint, but was concerned with the effect on morale.

The size of the grievance was considerable. In Middle Eastern Command were 190,000 Indian and 270,000 British soldiers. He made the point very clear: 'I must dilute all my staff, from GHQ downwards, with Indian Army Staff officers, and this is now going on. This means that these officers have a substantial grievance or think they have, and efficiency without a reasonable degree of contentment is hard to attain.'

Auchinleck also raised the point of ranks being appropriate to the job. He explained that he appreciated that one did not want to create 'inflated staffs and hordes of generals' but for certain important posts it was only sensible to have the appropriate rank. He felt that the army was much too rigid in its organisation and pointed out that they had 'moved far from the days of rigid organisations which are supposed to be suitable for every part of the world. We must get flexibility and the power to improvise quickly and without disorganisation right down to the smallest formation. The German does it every day.'

He was not concerned only with the larger problems of command, however. As C-in-C, he told Grigg, he was annoyed by the policy of the Military Secretary who 'either fails to realise the meaning of psychology or, if he does, lacks the courage of his convictions.' Auchinleck was criticising the policy which allowed awards to be announced to the individuals concerned and published in orders but not to be announced in the local press until the

King had approved them for publication at home. He was quite sure that the King would approve if he knew, and that the present policy was bad psychology.

At the beginning of March the Chiefs of Staff Committee unwittingly did Auchinleck a bad turn, though with the best possible motives. Churchill, infuriated by Auchinleck's appreciation and ruminating upon the C-in-C's apparent inertia in the Middle East, drafted a telegram on 2 March in which his own feelings were very clearly expressed – 'Soldiers were meant to fight' was one of its phrases. The Chiefs of Staff tactfully intervened and reworded the signal, which was sent on the 2nd. Even then it emphasised that action in Cyrenaica was essential, that by action alone could Malta be saved, and that, apart from this consideration, delay might actually worsen the position, since it might result in the Germans receiving even more supplies than the British. It concluded ominously:

> Viewing the war situation as a whole we cannot afford to stand idle at a time when the Russians are straining every nerve to give the enemy no rest, and when it is important to increase by every possible means the drain on the German armed forces.
>
> If our view of the situation is correct you must either grasp the opportunity which is held out in the immediate future or else must face the loss of Malta and a precarious defensive.
>
> Please reconsider the matter urgently and telegraph your views.

Auchinleck was well aware whose views were being expressed, and replied courteously but forcibly to Brooke on 4 March:

> I find it hard to believe in view of your telegram of February 17th [Brooke's message warning of the withdrawal of troops] that COS241* had your approval as it seems to fail so signally either to appreciate facts as pre-

---

* Chiefs of Staff followed by the number of message.

sented from here or to realise that we are fully aware of the situation as regards Malta in particular or the Middle East in general. We are here trying to face realities and to present to you the situation as it appears to us, not as you would like it to be.

He followed this with a statement of the number and types of tanks received in January, which included forty-eight Grants and seventy-six Stuarts. He listed the tanks in workshops or out of commission for various reasons; 528 reparable or under repair, forty-eight serviceable reserve tanks, and 591 tanks with units. Against these figures the untried reinforcements of January made a poor showing, certainly not one to suggest that they tipped the balance between possible defeat and certain victory.

The CIGS replied equally crisply two days later. Among other points he said:

The situation has changed considerably since my tele-gram of February 17th was sent. At that time the full gravity of the situation in Malta was not apparent, also the decision not to withdraw further from the Middle East and to leave the Indian Division, which it was previously intended to withdraw, had not then been taken.

The greatest difficulty I had here was in reconciling your figures of tank strengths. In your statement dated February 23rd you showed 660 serviceable tanks yet in your appreciation of February 27th you have allowed only for 430 tanks on April 1.

At that moment Auchinleck, suppressing any stronger reaction, must have wished that Brooke and his colleagues were out there in the desert seeing just how well a tank tested in Britain could cope with the totally different conditions in Africa. Unfortunately the frustrations of the situation appear to have clouded his judgement at this point, for he missed a golden opportunity to resolve his differences with leaders in England. It was, if he had realised it, vital to his own future.

On 7 March Churchill sent a telegram:

> The situation disclosed by your appreciation is very
> serious and not likely to be adjusted by correspondence.
> I should be glad therefore if you would come home
> for consultation at your earliest convenience, bringing
> with you any officers you may require, especially an
> authority on state of tanks and their servicing.

The implication that Auchinleck might know less about
tanks than one of his subordinates did not pass unnoticed.
He signalled Brooke on the 8th:

> Beg you to use your influence against this idea which
> can in no circumstances do any good. In any case I am
> not prepared in present situation to absent myself from
> my command for even shortest period and still remain
> responsible for it.

On the following day he addressed a telegram to
Churchill:

> Am certain I cannot leave Mideast in present circum-
> stances. Situation is entirely different from that obtain-
> ing last July [the date of his previous visit to London]
> and am not prepared to delegate authority while
> strategical situation is so fluid and so liable to rapid
> change. I can give no more information regarding tank
> situation than I have already given, nor would my com-
> ing home make it more possible to stage an earlier
> offensive.
> I earnestly ask you, therefore, to reconsider your re-
> quest. If you desire it I will gladly send senior staff officer
> who can explain tank situation in more detail.

This was Auchinleck the soldier – courteous, reasonable, but giving the underlying impression that he did not
suffer fools gladly. For a man of his imagination, so
clearly shown in his compassion and his dealings with
inferiors, he seemed at that moment singularly unaware
of the importance of the particular problem he was facing.
Churchill had rallied Britain after Norway and Dunkirk,

he was maintaining contact with difficult allies, he had recently had the shock of unimaginable disasters, particularly the losses of capital ships which symbolised so much to him as 'Former Naval Person'.* He admired Auchinleck as a man and as a soldier, but he was not going to be patronised as a civilian politician by a visit from 'a senior staff officer who can explain the tank situation in more detail', instead of the man to whom he wanted to talk about the entire strategy of the war.

The principle of British politics – as Churchill well knew, for he had been in politics a long time – was that a Minister does not have to be an expert in detail but he has to be a man capable of seeing the broader issues. A regular Service background makes this fact hard to grasp. From the moment he joins the Services the recruit is taught that there is something special about the regular Services, something no civilian can ever understand. Thus, even when he goes to the highest rank, there lingers in the Regular this belief that although the Services are subordinate to Parliament, Ministers will never really be able to see matters as the Services do. The explanation perhaps lies deep in the history of warfare, but the existence of the feeling was realised by Churchill who, like Auchinleck, had been at Sandhurst. His subsequent military experience was not inconsiderable, but he felt in 1942 that if he had allowed the laws of military probability to govern his life in 1940, he would long ago have disappeared into the hands of the Gestapo. Churchill stood for making the impossible possible; Auchinleck believed in the calculated risk. It was now that Churchill, for the first time, actively considered the replacement of the C-in-C, Middle Eastern Command.

On 9 March Brooke sent another telegram to Auchinleck:

> Other COS are in full agreement with me that you should if possible come home for consultation in these matters.

---

* Having been First Lord of the Admiralty, Churchill always signed himself thus in letters to Roosevelt.

We wish, therefore to impress on you the urgency for such a visit, provided you are not expecting to be engaged in active operations within the next week or so.

As Auchinleck was by now on a visit to Iraq, it was three days before Brooke got his reply, which re-emphasised the impossibility of leaving and suggested that a solution to the problem might be found in a visit by Brooke himself to Cairo.

Churchill was furious. He was so angry that he thought that the only solution would be to replace Auchinleck. He refused to allow Brooke to go.

Three days later Churchill sent a fairly mild telegram which listed probable reinforcements for the Middle East but did not comment on Auchinleck's refusal to come to England. But, also on the 15th, Churchill began a letter with the blunt statement:

Your appreciation of February 27th continues causing deepest anxiety here, both to the Chiefs of Staff and Defence Committee. I therefore regret extremely your inability to come home for consultation. The delay you have in mind will endanger safety of Malta. Moreover there is no certainty that the enemy cannot reinforce faster than you, so that after all your waiting you will find yourself in relatively the same or even a worse position. Your losses have been less than the enemy, who, nevertheless, chance fighting.

Then followed more details about tank strengths before continuing:

I have done everything in my power to give you continuous support at heavy cost to the whole war. It would give me the greatest pain to feel that mutual understanding had ceased. In order to avoid this I have asked Sir Stafford Cripps to stop for a day in Cairo about 19th or 20th on his way to India and put before you the view of the War Cabinet . . .

On the 17th was added a sharp sting to the former message:

> I ought to have added the following to my message of March 15th. If, as a result of all discussions, it is decided that you must stand on defensive until July, it will be necessary at once to consider the movement of at least fifteen air squadrons from Libya to sustain Russian left wing in the Caucasus.

The CIGS protested strongly to Churchill about the content and wording of this telegram, but was overruled with the words 'It will be a whip to him'.

It was now clear to all, except perhaps the principals, that the Churchill–Auchinleck clash had reached a point from which there could be no withdrawal. Auchinleck was not by nature obstinate, but he was determined to do what he felt was right for his army, which was not necessarily what others thought was right. He had memories of those suicidal head-on attacks in Iraq in the First World War, when his own regiment had been sacrificed without much result.

Churchill could now see that whatever Auchinleck's merits as a field commander his refusal to take what, to the Prime Minister, seemed to be the only course meant that a successor must be found. But to send Stafford Cripps, at that time Lord Privy Seal, was a sign of Churchillian flippancy rather than statesmanship. In the event it rebounded on him, for Cripps, who was accompanied by the Vice-CIGS, Lt-Gen. Sir Archibald Nye, found everyone in Cairo 'most co-operative'. He wrote on 21 March: 'I have no doubts of Auchinleck's offensive spirit but I think his Scottish caution and desire not to be misled by optimism cause him to overstress in statement the difficulties and uncertainties of the situation.' He went on to suggest it would be a great help if Churchill would reassure the C-in-C 'that all misunderstandings are at an end and there is no more questioning of his desire to take offensive'. He continued: 'It would, I am sure, help if you could send Auchinleck a short friendly telegram expressing your satisfaction that he will have all possible help from you to hit the target at the appointed time.'

Churchill's reaction was, 'I was very ill-content with this and the long telegrams of technical detail which accompanied it.' Cripps and Nye had clearly seen the sense of Auchinleck's view and had completely failed to convey Churchill's own feelings, to which Cripps himself had subscribed before his meetings in Cairo. Not least of Churchill's misgivings was the fact that, in spite of his constant urging, mid-May was still given as the earliest date on which an offensive could be launched. Brooke then intimated to Auchinleck that the situation now demanded that some action be taken: 'I am certain that any further delays will be unacceptable unless you produce overwhelming reasons.' Auchinleck's obstinacy had, however, produced the results desired since Churchill had to bow before united opinions on the danger of attacking too soon. But his refusal to come home and his defiant resistance to the prodding were to damage irreparably his relations with the Prime Minister.

An attempt to pour oil on troubled waters came from Ismay on 2 April in a letter to Auchinleck:

> The outstanding point is that although the PM is *at present* at cross-purposes – and even at loggerheads – with you this is a purely temporary phase of a relationship which is marked by mutual esteem and, I might almost say, affection.
>
> You cannot judge the PM by ordinary standards, he is not in the least like anyone you and I have ever met. He is a mass of contradictions. He is either on the crest of the wave, or in the trough; either highly laudatory or bitterly condemnatory; either in an angelic temper, or a hell of a rage; when he isn't fast asleep he's a volcano. There are no half measures in his make-up – he apparently sees no difference between harsh words spoken to a friend and forgotten within the hour under the influence of friendly argument, and the same harsh words telegraphed to a friend thousands of miles away – with no opportunity for 'making it up'.

At the end of his long explanation of Churchill's character and manner Ismay urged Auchinleck:

You must do what you did with such happy results last time YOU MUST COME HOME. I know how hard it is for you to leave your command at this juncture, but nothing matters so much as the removal of the wall of misunderstanding which has grown up between you two. I know that at heart the PM thinks the world of you, but he will never confess this, even to himself, until you have got together again and had the whole thing out.

Throughout April Malta continued to hang on. (Field-Marshal Lord Gort, VC, had replaced Dobbie as Governor in that month.) That the island was vital to the desert campaign was clear to everyone, but at this moment Malta was so much under pressure herself that she had nothing to spare to attack the convoys of material which were going to reinforce Rommel. Malta needed a desert offensive to take the pressure off herself; equally the desert offensive required that Malta should be in a position to harass enemy supply lines. On 23 April Churchill gave an account of the war situation to a secret session of the House of Commons. It was a grim picture. The Germans were pressing hard on Russia; British shipping was being lost at an alarming rate; and in the Far East the Japanese had made far greater gains than anyone would have imagined and were almost at the gates of India. These views were expressed to Auchinleck in a Chiefs of Staff signal of the same date.

Later that month (the 27th) Auchinleck set out his views on the situation for the Middle East Defence Committee in Cairo; this too presented a grave picture. He noted that the enemy were gaining command of the sea in the Eastern Mediterranean and that the Allies had not the forces to prevent them. Likewise, British forces were too weak to establish any form of air superiority in the coming battle, and would not even be able to beat off an attack on the Egyptian bases. Malta was in a precarious position; if lost it would be of enormous value to the enemy. Auchinleck had sufficient land forces to hold a serious attack against Iraq or Syria. It was most unlikely, he thought, that any reinforcements would now be sent to the Middle East as anything available would probably go to India. Although he was preparing for an early offensive in Libya, too much should not be expected from it; he should probably not have the required tank superiority and at the height of the battle might find that much of the air force would have to be withdrawn to operate on the northern front (Iraq, Syria, Turkey). One of the risks of an offensive at the planned mid-May date was that it would mean leaving the easily defensible Gazala position between Tobruk and El Agheila, to which Ritchie had retired the Eighth Army following Rommel's successes of January and February.

Of the risks involved in taking an offensive at that time he had this to say, on 3 May:

> If the immediate political and strategic results of an even partially successful offensive in Libya were likely to affect decisively the course of the war in this, or in any other theatre I would not hesistate to advocate it. Even if fully successful, however, such an offensive could not materially affect the chances of a successful defence of our Northern Front, nor could it arrest the Japanese progress towards India and the Persian Gulf. It could have little material effect on the coming campaign in Russia.
>
> On the other hand failure on our part in Libya is likely to have an immediate and most far-reaching effect not only on the Middle East but on the whole world situation.

Surprisingly, he concluded by saying they should

> devote every resource that can be spared to the reinforcement of India in order to check the Japanese advance before it is too late.
>
> I am urgently examining the possibility of sending troops from here to India or Ceylon in the immediate future.

Auchinleck stressed these views in a long letter to Brooke, also dated the 3rd. He said:

The matter most in my mind at the moment is the threat to India . . . I am seriously perturbed and cannot help wondering whether the dependence of the Middle East on India, strategically and materially, is fully realised at home.

He pointed out that there were over 200,000 Indians in the Middle East, 'which is very nice for us but hardly in keeping with her own apparently very urgent need for all the trained soldiers she can muster.'

He continued:

We are still dependent on India for great quantities of munitions. For instance we drew from her in March about 90,000 tons. We are particularly dependent on India for steel.

How it is proposed to replace India as a source of men and munitions should she be invaded by the Japanese I do not know. Moreover, what the attitude of the Indian troops will be if this situation arises is doubtful, to say the least of it.

I believe myself that there is no shadow of doubt that we cannot afford to lose India or even to contemplate the loss.

Auchinleck explained why this was so:

I feel very strongly that the time has come when we must decide what is vital to our continued existence and what is not. We lost Singapore and then Burma chiefly because we did not or could not decide to concentrate our resources on holding what really mattered while letting less important places go. If I had to choose now between losing India and giving up the Middle East I would not hesitate. I believe that we can still hold India without the Middle East but that we cannot for long hold the Middle East without India.

Other points were that an advance as far as El Agheila would take three months, and that if that objective were not reached there would need to be a withdrawal, which would be particularly bad for morale. Some details of tank strengths and the use to which the Valentines and Matildas could be put then followed.

This letter, with its suggested postponement of the offensive, merely succeeded in enraging Churchill still further. He was now talking of replacing Auchinleck with Alexander, but Brooke dissuaded him from making this precipitate move. Churchill sent off a cynically worded telegram on 5 May:

> While we are grateful for your offer to denude the Middle East further for the sake of the Indian danger we feel that the greatest help you could give to the whole war at this juncture would be to engage and defeat the enemy on your Western Front.

On the 8th the Prime Minister, still feeling that Malta was in greater danger than India, again re-emphasised the need for attack:

> We are all agreed that in spite of the risks you mention you would be right to attack the enemy and fight a major battle, if possible during May, and the sooner the better. We are prepared to take the full responsibility for these general directions, leaving you the necessary latitude for their execution.

On 10 May Churchill sent a further telegram, beginning:

> The Chiefs of Staff, the Defence Committee and the War Cabinet have again considered the whole position. We are determined that Malta shall not be allowed to fall without a battle being fought by your whole Army for its retention . . .
> We therefore reiterate the views expressed in paragraph 2 of our telegram of May 8th with this qualification – that the very latest date for engaging the enemy which we could approve is one which provides distraction in time to help the passage of the June dark-period convoy.

2nd Lieutenant Claude Auchinleck, Indian Army*

Illustrations marked thus have been kindly lent by the family and
friends of the late Field-Marshal Sir Claude Auchinleck

Gyantse, Tibet, in 1907—Auchinleck watching his
62nd Punjabis march past*

Mesopotamia, 1916. Auchinleck (with pipe) and fellow
officers prior to Maude's offensive on Kut*

As GOC,
IV Corps in 1940*

Cairo, June 1941.
'A new, fresh figure'
—Auchinleck,
the new C-in-C,
Middle Eastern
Command (left)
conferring with
Wavell, the
outgoing C-in-C*

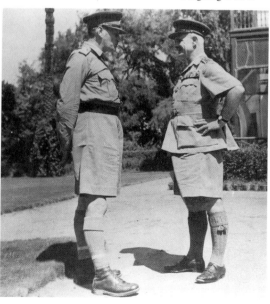

The retreat to El Alamein, 27–30 June 1942.
Auchinleck studies positions from his command car*

El Alamein, July 1942.
Auchinleck talks to an Indian sentry during the battle.

Auchinleck's wife Jessie (far left) with her husband and other relatives in Delhi before the break-up of their marriage*

'The troops loved him because he was such an honest-to-God soldier.' Auchinleck chatting to men of the 2nd West Yorkshire Regiment some ten miles north of Rangoon, August 1945*

A relaxed Auchinleck with his CIGS, Field-Marshal Montgomery,
at a cocktail party during one of the latter's visits to India
before Independence. The photographer has caught to a nicety
the characteristics of the two men

On 4 August 1947, ten days before the last Indian Army Order,
Auchinleck was made an Honorary Doctor of Laws at Aberdeen University,
an honour he received in July 1948 with Lord Wavell (left)*

'It would certainly make a very luxurious dressing gown'—
Auchinleck (left) in the Mantle of the Bath
during a procession of the Knights Grand Cross of that Order,
Westminster Abbey, 29 October 1964

The Supreme Commander's last parade.
The Farewell Guard of Honour provided by the Royal Scots Fusiliers
in front of the C-in-C's House, Delhi, 24 November 1947.
Seven days later Auchinleck left India for retirement*

Auchinleck, 'the lonely soldier' as C-in-C India during the war, looking from the window of his aircraft*

This telegram, like that of May 8th is addressed to you as Military Commander-in-Chief, the Air having been placed under your general direction for the purposes of major operations.

The implications of this were clear enough. Auchinleck had been ordered to attack, and they now awaited the date of the offensive or his resignation. But Auchinleck left the matter open. He merely thanked Churchill for his kind suggestion about putting Air under his command but said that

I do not think its application would do good and I am pretty sure it would do harm. I do not therefore propose to act on it. My relations with Tedder are excellent as they have always been and his support and co-operation could not be bettered ...

But on the 17th Churchill sent a telegram which Auchinleck could not avoid answering:

It is necessary for me to have some account of your general intentions in the light of our recent telegrams.

Two days later came the reply:

My intention is to carry out the instructions in paragraph 2 of your message of May 10th [i.e. attack by the June dark-period at the latest].

He went on to say that this would be a full-scale offensive, not merely a diversionary move to assist the Malta convoy, that the Germans might themselves launch an offensive before that date and that this would affect his own timings, and that:

I feel it is of the greatest importance that in the first instance no publicity at all should be given to our intentions to carry out a major offensive even after it has been launched. Still less should the public be led to hope for a speedy and striking success.

Churchill immediately signalled his pleasure at the news and said,

Of course we realise that success cannot be guaranteed. There are no safe battles . . . but we have full confidence in you and your glorious Army, and whatever happens we will sustain you by every means in our power.

I should personally feel even greater confidence if you took direct command yourself as in fact you had to do at Sidi Rezegh. On this, however, I do not press you either way.

Not surprisingly this brought the reply:

Much though I would like to take command personally in Libya I feel it would not be the right course to pursue. I have considered the possibility most carefully and have concluded it would be most difficult for me to keep a right sense of proportion.

It was as well that Auchinleck was a man who thrived on long hours and hard work, because the drafting of these long, complicated signals to Churchill and Brooke used up time badly needed for consideration of other matters. The fact that he was living close to his army, not insulated in a remote rear-headquarters, probably enabled him to preserve some sense of balance. And, in spite of his various worries, Auchinleck never lost his understanding of the problems of others, nor his patience. Mr Robert Dyer, at the time a corporal serving in the desert, tells of one instance of Auchinleck's humanity:

A private soldier, having received disastrous news concerning his family in England, together with certain information that no help was forthcoming from any Official Body or Private Persons, in his despair gate-crashed General Auchinleck's office at GHQ and blurted out his problem. The Great Man heard him out most courteously – incidentally rebuking and sending out the outraged Sergeant-Major who charged in with the intention of throwing out this unofficial intruder –

and, on receiving documentary proof of the unhappy soldier's problem, wrote out immediate orders for him to be transported back to England on the next available ship. This charitable act concluded, he then gently but firmly pointed out to the man that his highly unorthodox act was contrary to Military Discipline. The man agreed and was duly sentenced to 'Jankers'* the duration of which was arranged to coincide with the ship's voyage and to be served solely on the ship: the moment she docked in Britain he was to be a free man with a month's leave on full pay and a rail warrant to his home railway station.

At this time Auchinleck sent to all staff officers an apt quotation from the Duke of Wellington to the then Secretary of State for War. It ran:

My Lord
    If I attempt to answer the mass of futile correspondence that surrounds me I should be debarred from the serious business of campaigning.
    I must remind your lordship – for the last time – that so long as I retain an independent position I shall see that no officer under my Command is debarred by the futile drivelling of men quill-driving in your Lordship's Office from attending to his first duty which is, and always has been, so to train the private men under his command that they may, without question, beat any force opposed to them in the field.

I am, My Lord
Your Obedient Servant
Wellington

As a footnote, Auchinleck added the words:

I know this does not apply to you, but please see to it that it can never be applied to you or to anyone working under you.

---

* Military punishment, in this case probably involving a few extra drills and confinement to the barracks.

As he directed that the notice should be circulated, Auchinleck must have envied the ability of the Great Duke to be able to make his point so crisply. Paper accumulates in large organisations, as is well known, but bleatings about the need to restrict it usually have no effect at all: sometimes they seem to increase it. Combatant units are often driven to distraction by the futile, meaningless verbiage directed at them from headquarters. Everybody deplores it, yet it goes on. But on 26 May there was little time for churning out more paper. Rommel attacked.

'THESE CRITICAL DAYS'
GAZALA AND MERSA MATRUH

Rommel's attack had come at an inconvenient moment, but the situation could have been worse. Even while bombarded by correspondence from Britain, Auchinleck had found time to write at considerable length to Ritchie on 20 May, not to interfere but in order to make absolutely certain that Ritchie was aware of all possibilities. There were two main threats: an attack enveloping the southern front and then turning north to Tobruk, accompanied meanwhile by feints and diversionary actions which could be mistaken for the real thing; and an attack in the north on the Gazala position with the aim of slicing through the British defences, on a narrow front, and rushing on to Tobruk. This area was full of British minefields, but the attack would be so concentrated and so well supported by the Luftwaffe that it would probably burst through. Auchinleck went into some detail about possible positioning of troops, but particularly stressed that the armoured reserve should be positioned well to the north, so that if Rommel did break through in that area on the way to Tobruk that reserve could then come into the battle and hit him very hard. The aim, as he concluded, was that 'if the enemy attacks, you will deal him a blow from which he may find it difficult, if not impossible, to recover.'

Maintaining a continuous line of defence in the desert was impossible with the number of troops available. In consequence, the only possible method was to establish strongpoints, known as 'boxes', at strategic points, with an extensive network of minefields in between each box. One of the problems of the incessant pressure from Churchill to attack was that the Eighth Army was partially deployed for the offensive. Since, however, it was known from Ultra that Rommel had every intention of attacking in May, although the exact date was not known, Auchinleck had given considerable thought to the tactics his ingenious opponent would be likely to pursue. But on 26 May 1st Armoured Division was just south of the Trigh Capuzzo, immediately to the south of Tobruk, with 7th Armoured Division some ten miles south of that. Neither, therefore, was in the position Auchinleck had suggested.

Ritchie, unfortunately, was full of confidence in his own dispositions. It was hardly surprising. He had been promoted to command an army when – as he probably knew – there were many who said that his ceiling was a division (he commanded a corps on D-Day). He reassured Auchinleck that, whatever happened, 'our main strength is the counter with our armour to destroy him. We are ready for this – and I feel confident that our armed forces are prepared to operate either to the south or to the north-west.'

Auchinleck replied on 22 May: 'I am quite happy about the positioning of the armoured divisions, and I am glad we were thinking on the same lines.' At this time Auchinleck did not know that the armour was so far back from the front line, nor so far to the south. Two days later Ritchie began another confident summary:

I am so pleased you are happy about the positioning of the armour.

Personally I am satisfied that we can fight in this position now. I do not for one moment suggest it could not be improved but I would say that it is fightable as it stands today.

Auchinleck was less happy, and on 26 May, the day Rommel attacked, he wrote to Ritchie:

My opinion for what it is worth is that the great majority of the indications point to a very heavy attack on the northern sector of your front...

Have you considered the desirability of altering the infantry and artillery dispositions in this sector, I wonder ... I would like to stress the absolute necessity for preventing him establishing defensive flanks if he does try to attack in the way I have suggested.

On the afternoon of the 26th Rommel opened the attack: as expected, he forced a way forward in the north between Gazala and Sidi Muftah with XXI Italian Corps and supporting troops under Crüwell. It was, however, a diversion. Panzers were told to show themselves and then return to 90th Light Division to the south. That night, by moonlight, the main German striking force – Afrika Korps, 90th Light, and 15th and 21st Panzer – put in a brilliant right hook around Bir Hacheim, the Eighth Army's southern flank, heading for Acroma and El Adem. As Rommel's battle plans were captured soon after the beginning of the operation, the British commanders were able to admire the precision with which these opening moves had been executed.

Some of the flanking movements were observed on the 26th, earlier than the Germans thought, by the patrols of the 4th South African Armoured Car Regiment, and on the following morning the commander of 3 Indian Motor Brigade, stationed around Bir Hacheim to prevent just such a movement, reported to his Divisional Commander that he was facing 'a whole bloody German armoured division'. It was in fact the Italian Ariete, plus some tanks from 21st Panzer, but the Indian brigade gave their opponents something to think about before they were themselves completely overwhelmed, largely due to lack of anti-tank guns and support from the distant British armour.

With Crüwell continuing to attack in the north, and with the Italian Trieste and Ariete Divisions pushing against the line around Bir Hacheim, the Eighth Army was already heavily engaged by the morning of the 27th. The Germans were not having it all their own way, however. The forces engaged on the Gazala line were unable to penetrate the minefields, while Rommel's armoured sweep behind the line and up into the heart of the British position was in danger of coming to a halt as he encountered more resistance and his fuel began to run low.

In addition, the new American M3 Grant tanks the Eighth Army had recently received were proving very satisfactory. They were fast, reliable and carried both 75-mm and 37-mm guns; the result was that they could now deal with the German tanks and anti-tank gunners at far more favourable ranges. And the new 6-pounder anti-tank gun, also newly introduced in British units, gave the Germans trouble they had not experienced in the past. They, however, were able to bring on to the battlefield nineteen of the new Panzer III specials, with highly effective armour-piercing shells launched from a 50-mm gun. Even so, by 29 May the battlefield situation was not looking at all happy for Rommel; his move to encircle the Gazala line was in danger of encirclement itself as he encountered the British armour, he had lost 200 tanks, and his supply position was precarious. He seemed nowhere near the hoped-for breakthrough. Furthermore, Crüwell had been shot down on the 28th and taken prisoner while flying over the battlefield. Field-Marshal Albert Kesselring, who happened to be visiting the African front at this time to look into the supply position, temporarily took over Crüwell's post.

Rommel now brought back his forces east of the Gazala line into the shelter of the British minefield north of Bir Hacheim, protecting them with defensive screens of anti-tank guns. In spite of constant attention by the RAF, he managed to convert this area – soon nicknamed 'the Cauldron' – into a bridgehead, and all attempts by armour and infantry to dislodge him were both costly and unsuccessful. The British strove to move in south of his position and cut his supply lines, but he intercepted and drove off these attacks with aggressive armoured tactics. The Germans were now able to hammer at the centre of the Gazala line from both sides.

Unfortunately, this was the sort of situation which Rommel was good at exploiting. He reasoned that if he could hold the Cauldron position and then capture Bir Hacheim he would have created a significant gap in Eighth Army defences. From this he could probably mount a quick strike to the north and first isolate, then capture, the troops holding the Gazala line. While it looked to many – including the over-optimistic Ritchie – as if Rommel was besieged in the Cauldron and would have to surrender, it did not look that way to Rommel. The principal obstacle to his plans, however, was provided by 150 Brigade, stubbornly holding a 'box' midway between Gazala and Bir Hacheim. Axis troops hammered at the Brigade from all sides by night and day, with tanks, dive-bombers and infantry: eventually, on 1 June, the gallant Northumbrian brigade* was overwhelmed. It seems that scarcely any attempt was made to assist them except by a South African ammunition convoy, which was wiped out, and by 10 Indian Brigade, which had its attempt cancelled before it could concentrate on its objective. Ritchie was beginning to pay the price of scattering his armoured reserve, and Rommel now had a gap in the British defence line. Continued attacks on the Cauldron throughout the first week in June failed to drive the Axis forces out. Also on the 1st, Rommel had once more launched a full attack on Bir Hacheim. The French garrison, under General Pierre Koenig, resisted gallantly for ten days, but was overrun and forced to retire on the night of the 10th. The supply line to German forces east of the Gazala line was now secure. Next day, Rommel drove north from the Cauldron. During the Cauldron battles 7th Armoured Division's HQ was overrun, and its commander, Lt-Gen. Frank Messervy, captured with three of his staff officers. Messervy, however, having taken the precaution of stripping off his badges of rank, was taken by the Germans for an elderly veteran and not closely guarded – he escaped the same evening. By then the disappearance of an armoured divisional HQ without notice had caused considerable consternation, not least to the remainder of 7th Armoured.

A study of Rommel's tactics might have warned Ritchie to expect the Germans to drive forward at this point; Auchinleck was apprehensive but so far did not interfere. On 12 June, however, he flew up to the front to take stock, increasingly convinced that Ritchie's view of the battle was over-confident. Rommel had moved north-east to near El Adem by the 11th, threatening Tobruk, while other Axis elements continued to pound away at the Gazala line from both sides. Supplies and reinforcements no longer presented the Germans with a problem, since

* 150 Brigade formed part of 50th Northumbrian Division.

they would be brought through the breach caused by the loss of 150 Brigade and from the now occupied Bir Hacheim. The Eighth Army's defence line had been penetrated, and it was difficult to know whether it would be better at this stage to take the offensive or to retreat to a new defence line – if the latter, where should that line be? Losses had been heavy on both sides, but the real problem was that the Eighth Army's tank losses – due to Ritchie's failure to concentrate his armour early enough – had been so severe as to leave the initiative with the Germans. The RAF had also taken severe punishment. Auchinleck still did not interfere, however, but accepted Ritchie's view that Rommel could be contained; he returned to Cairo on the next day, by which time that view had been proved shatteringly wrong.

Rommel's next move, on the 12th, was to close a pincer consisting of 15th Panzer and 21st Panzer on to the Eighth Army's 2 and 4 Armoured Brigades, who were deployed in front of the 'Knightsbridge' box, a defensive position south of Acroma. 22 Guards Armoured Brigade tried to help but merely lost tanks, and German attacks on 1 Brigade in the same area completed this tale of disaster. The armoured reserve had been smashed, and the Eighth Army now had about seventy tanks to compare with one hundred German and some sixty Italian. On the night of the 13th Rommel was able to turn his full force on the Knightsbridge box, which was held with tremendous courage by the Gurkha Brigade. On the 14th, being unable to reinforce the Gurkhas, and not wishing to see them and the remnants of his armour totally destroyed, Ritchie gave the order to withdraw, and troops still on the Gazala line were ordered back to conform. He hoped to make a stand on a line running from Tobruk due south.

When, on 14 June, Auchinleck realised what had happened he sent Ritchie a crisp instruction, based on his view that by now Rommel must be nearly, if not completely, exhausted. It stated that Tobruk must be held and that this would be effected by establishing a line west of Tobruk running through Acroma and El Adem: it did not mean retreating and leaving Tobruk in a state of siege once again.

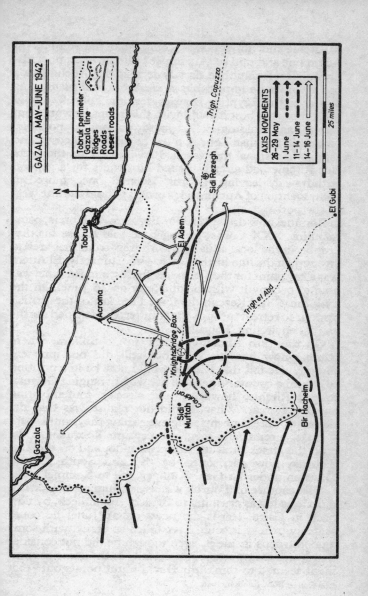

GAZALA MAY–JUNE 1942

Tobruk perimeter ......
Gazala line
Ridges
Roads
Desert roads

N

AXIS MOVEMENTS

26–29 May
1 June
11–14 June
14–16 June

25 miles

Gazala

Tobruk

Acroma

El Adem

'Knightsbridge Box'

Sidi Muftah

Cauldron

Bir Hacheim

Sidi Rezegh

Trigh Capuzzo

Trigh el Abd

El Gubi

Ritchie did not think he could hold the Acroma–El Adem line and said so. Auchinleck said he *must*; no withdrawal. But Ritchie had already decided that Auchinleck's order would be impossible to carry out and planned to retreat to the Egyptian frontier, leaving Tobruk to hold off Rommel as best it could with the troops he would put into it, and holding El Adem for as long as possible. Churchill felt that Tobruk must be held at all costs, and said so in a signal that reached Auchinleck on the 14th. But Ritchie had already issued his orders for a general withdrawal, leaving Tobruk isolated once more, in contravention of Auchinleck's orders to hold the line west of the port.

Rommel now drove hard for El Adem, as Norrie, commanding XXX Corps, having been told to use his discretion in the local situation, withdrew from that area to strengthen the line further back. Unfortunately, El Adem was a key point for the Tobruk defences, and Rommel was able to occupy it without difficulty on 16 June. On the 17th, near Sidi Rezegh, he forced the last of the British armour to retreat towards the frontier, then turned northwards, encircling Tobruk.

On the 18th Auchinleck flew up to Sollum, where Ritchie now had his HQ, but still did not interfere directly. He felt that Ritchie would now be in a position to mount a counter-attack on the widely ranging German forces; Ritchie, however, was already contemplating another retreat. What he did not realise was that the Germans were concentrating everything they could spare – tanks, aircraft and men – to capture Tobruk. On the 20th the attack built up to a crescendo, and on the 21st Tobruk, now garrisoned by the 2nd South African Division under Lt-Gen. Klopper, fell to Rommel.

The capture of Tobruk was as stimulating to German morale as it was crushing to British. Auchinleck, by now back in Cairo, learnt the news on 21 June: he could scarcely believe it could have fallen so easily, with some 33,000 troops inside it, even though he did not consider that it was as important strategically as the home government seemed to think. Sir David Hunt points out* that

* *A Don at War*, London, 1966.

there were many misapprehensions about Tobruk. It was not, in fact, a satisfactory fortress. The perimeter was too big to defend properly, for the need to include the only adequate water supply meant that it had to be longer than was militarily desirable. The strongest point was the south-west corner, where the Italians, during their occupation early in the war, had established an impressive array of defences which included concrete blockhouses, minefields and anti-tank ditches; Rommel had attacked here unsuccessfully on previous occasions. The south-eastern corner was the least defensible, partly because the defences were now weak, much material having gone to strengthen the Gazala line, and partly because that corner was dominated by two hills which an attacking force could use. On 20 June the German attack came in at the south-eastern point, both preceded and accompanied by concentrated bombardment from aircraft and artillery. The defences had been neglected during the previous months under the impression that further attacks on them were most unlikely, and the troops inside were no longer the battle-hardened Australians of the earlier siege. But, worst of all, there had been no serious attempt by Ritchie to counter the German attack on Tobruk, and this further appalled Auchinleck. It was a sad ending to what had been an impressive story. On 22 June Generaloberst Erwin Rommel, commanding the Panzerarmee Afrika, was promoted Field-Marshal – Tobruk had meant a great deal to the Germans, too.

Auchinleck flew up to the front for a few hours on the 22nd, and accepted Ritchie's *fait accompli* reorganisation of his forces around Mersa Matruh. He felt as responsible for the recent disasters as anyone, and on the 23rd sent a message to the CIGS, offering his resignation. If Brooke made a reply, however, it has not survived; undoubtedly, however, Auchinleck's generous offer fuelled existing ideas of dismissing him. On the same day, however, he received a telegram from Churchill, who was in Washington, and had there learnt the news of the loss of Tobruk, which began:

CIGS, Dill and I earnestly hope stern resistance will be

made on the Sollum frontier line. Special Intelligence has shown stresses which enemy has undergone. Very important reinforcements are on the way. A week gained may be decisive.

The 'very important reinforcements' were 300 American Sherman tanks, but unfortunately they did not arrive in time for Auchinleck to use them. Ritchie, of course, had already pre-empted any plans for holding a line on the frontier, considering that he needed to re-organise further to the east.

The telegram concluded with the words:

The main thing now is for you to inspire all your forces with an intense will to resist and strive not to accept the freak decisions produced by Rommel's handful of heavy armour. Make sure that all your manpower plays a full part in these critical days. His Majesty's Government is quite ready to share your responsibility in making the most active and daring defence.

On 24 June Auchinleck replied, pointing out that the Sollum position was not tenable but that the defensive line at Mersa Matruh could be. The chief need was for more armoured units, which would also require time to learn desert fighting, but he did not think that reinforcements could be drawn from the Iraq–Syria area (which did not have armour anyway) as those areas represented a more precarious situation than the one he was at present facing. He himself was heavily engaged at this time in the reinforcement and re-supply of Ritchie's army. In his telegram Auchinleck said that

without exception the troops in the Eighth Army are as determined to beat the enemy as ever they were, which is saying much, and their spirit is unimpaired ... but we are trying to train an army and use it on the battle-field at the same time ... infantry can NOT win battles in the desert so long as the enemy has superiority in armour. Masses of infantry are no use without guns and armour.

This statement about the uselessness of infantry without guns or armour did not prevent Churchill replying on the next day:

I hope this crisis will lead to all uniformed personnel in the Delta and all available loyal manpower being raised to the highest fighting condition. You have over 700,000 men on your ration strength in the Middle East. Every fit male should be made to fight and die for victory. There is no reason why units defending the Mersa Matruh position should not be reinforced by several thousands of officers, and the administrative personnel ordered to swell the battalions or working parties. You are in the same kind of situation as we should be if England were invaded and the same intense drastic spirit should reign.

The signal also contained a message which must have made Auchinleck raise his eyebrows:

The President's [Roosevelt] information from Rome is that Rommel expects to be delayed three or four weeks before he can mount a heavy attack on the Mersa Matruh position. I should think the delay might be greater.

On the same day Auchinleck sent a message to the CIGS:

Am taking over command of Eighth Army from Ritchie this afternoon . . . Shall use Dorman-Smith as my Chief of Staff leaving Corbett to represent me at GHQ.

Auchinleck, like Ritchie, sought to check Rommel at Mersa Matruh, but already he planned to fight his main action further to the east, near a small town close to the coast called El Alamein, only sixty miles or so from Alexandria. By the 25th elements of his forces were consolidating the defences at Alamein – he would draw Rommel on and then break him on the ridges around the little town. The German supply lines by then would be dangerously long, the troops tired and the machinery

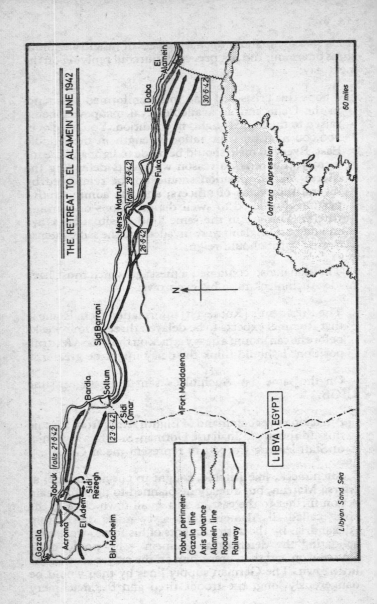

THE RETREAT TO EL ALAMEIN JUNE 1942

60 miles

Qattara Depression

N

El Alamein
El Daba   30.6.42
Fuka
Mersa Matruh   falls 29.6.42
               29.6.42
               26.6.42
Sidi Barrani

Bardia
Sollum
Sidi Omar   23.6.42
Fort Maddalena

LIBYA   EGYPT

Gazala
Acroma
Tobruk falls 21.6.42
El Adem
Sidi Rezegh
Bir Hacheim

Libyan Sand Sea

Tobruk perimeter
Gazala line
Axis advance
Alamein line
Roads
Railway

badly worn, and they would once more be within effective range of the RAF, whose forward airfields had been lost during the retreat from Gazala. But first the Eighth Army must slow down the racing Panzers, and buy for themselves time to consolidate the Alamein position and restore morale after the almost panicky retreat through the frontier, now known scathingly as the 'Gazala Gallop'.

Ritchie had fixed the right of his line, Lt-Gen. William Holmes's X Corps, in Mersa Matruh with Gott's XIII Corps nearly twenty miles to the south. XXX Corps was to the east, falling back on Alamein. Unfortunately, there was a large unmined gap between the two defending corps, since the defences, like those of Tobruk, had been neglected or robbed to provide material for other points. Auchinleck realised the weakness of these dispositions, and on 26 June ordered the Eighth Army to hold the Mersa Matruh line for as long as possible, giving ground to the east in good order. He would husband the shattered remnants of his armour, but above all he would keep the Eighth Army in being as a single force, and not as isolated units to be picked off at the enemy's will.

But by the time the decision to relieve Ritchie was reached, Rommel was already heading for Mersa Matruh, having brushed aside light British resistance at the frontier on 23 and 24 June. Not for the first time had he given a misleading impression to his own High Command – far from consolidating his successes and waiting 'three or four weeks' (as Roosevelt's information from Rome had stated), he would drive his exhausted forces on towards Cairo. Victory in Egypt was within his grasp. On the 26th, as Auchinleck pulled the defences of Mersa Matruh more closely together, 90th Light and 21st Panzer found the gap between 10th Indian Division at Mersa Matruh and the New Zealand Division in the centre of the British line. The confusion in this area was now so great that the Germans were as bemused as the Eighth Army, but on the 27th the New Zealanders were temporarily cut off and took heavy casualties. Auchinleck at once entrusted Gott to organise a fighting withdrawal. His aim was not to make a heroic last-ditch stand in which the remnants of the Eighth Army might well be destroyed, but to keep that army intact, retreating and mauling the German thrusts as it did do. Rommel was determined not to let the retreating British stabilise the position and, by continual pressure, came very near to success. Gott, mistaking the strength of the Panzers in the south, began to fall back, and the rest of the line sought to conform. Rommel raced to cut off Mersa Matruh, which had its harbour facilities and water installations destroyed on 28 June; on the 29th the port fell with the loss of some 2000 prisoners. Gradually the Eighth Army was falling back, more or less in good order, though with considerable confusion. Out of that confusion Auchinleck had to produce a defence that would save Egypt and the Canal, and break Rommel's inspired drive for victory.

13

'THE ADVERSE TIDE'
EL ALAMEIN AND DISMISSAL

By 30 June 1942 the Eighth Army, much reduced after the losses of Gazala, Tobruk and Mersa Matruh, and with its armoured forces severely weakened, occupied a new defensive line between El Alamein and the Qattara Depression. El Alamein is on a ridge close to the coast approximately half way between Mersa Matruh and Alexandria. From Alamein to Quaret-el-Himeimat, twenty-eight miles to the south, is a natural defensive position consisting of a series of parallel ridges extending southwards, and beyond Himeimat is an impassable salt marsh known as the Qattara Depression. Eight miles south of Alamein lies the Ruweisat Ridge, seven miles south of that is Alam Nayal, and a further seven miles to the south of Alam Nayal is the Munassib Depression.

Auchinleck fixed the right of his line at El Alamein itself, held by Norrie's XXX Corps, while from the Ruweisat Ridge southwards to the Qattara Depression was manned by XIII Corps under Gott (X Corps had been sent back to regroup as it had suffered heavily in the previous week). His aim was to force Rommel to waste attacks on three main defensive points – El Alamein, Bab-el-Qattara, and Naqb Abu Dweis – while at the same time striking at the German flanks and rear with mobile forces. The RAF was to play a major role in keeping supplies and reinforcements from the enemy, and continually attacking his forward troops. As a fixed defence, the position left much to be desired, having been hastily thrown up and now mostly manned by troops only recently engaged, to greater or lesser degrees, in rapid flight. But the extraordinary steadfastness of Auchinleck's vision, once Ritchie had lost Gazala and Tobruk, had permitted him to abandon Mersa Matruh in order to draw Rommel on to a position bounded to the north by the sea, and to the south by a desolate area completely impassable to vehicles. With considerable courage, in view of the increasing alarm in London, Alexandria and Cairo – near panic in the two latter cities – he had prolonged the Eighth Army's flight, giving ground in order to keep his force as a cohesive whole, and to bring the bogeyman Rommel to a battle which no amount of brilliant manoeuvring could evade. El Alamein was chosen by Auchinleck even before the actions at Mersa Matruh as the battleground which would save Egypt and, once and for all, ensure that Germany could never win North Africa.

At dawn on 1 July Rommel aimed his main thrust just south of Alamein; 90th Light's attack, however, received a sharp hammering from the South African Brigade to the east and south of the town, and by the afternoon the German advance was halted. Plans to penetrate this area by driving north and south of the Miteirya Ridge and then send one thrust, 90th Light, edging north to isolate Alamein and another, Afrika Korps, south to cut off XIII Corps were blunted by fierce counter-attacks. As 90th Light ground to a halt, Afrika Korps, including 15th and 21st Panzer, fell foul of 18 Indian Brigade on Deir-el-Shein, to the north and west of Ruweisat Ridge. A heroic stand by this largely untried brigade held up Afrika Korps for thirteen hours before the Indians fell back in good order; when 22 Guards Armoured Brigade attacked later in the day, having used to good advantage the delay imposed by 18 Brigade, the German advance was pushed back to the south and west.

A sandstorm at dawn, before the attack began, had contributed to 15th and 21st Panzer tangling together, among other confusions; now, despite their successes of the past weeks the Axis troops, tired and short of vital supplies, were beginning to feel Auchinleck's grip on the battle. By the following day his steady direction and inspiration had held the line together with enough success to make a switch to the offensive feasible. On the 2nd Rommel's attempted advance of his two thrusts ran into Eighth Army counter-attacks. The fighting proved inconclusive, but the British were still very much in possession, and morale was high. Auchinleck – unlike previous Eighth Army commanders – had learnt from his enemy;

first he would let Rommel's armour knock itself to pieces
by running on to British guns, a tactic the Germans had
always used with considerable success. On 3 July spaced
counter-attacks at different points along the line caused
destruction and dismay in the German forces, who were
beginning to reach the limit of their resources. Auchinleck ordered XXX Corps to push hard in the north, while
XIII Corps would drive to the north and west to take
Rommel in the flank. The day went badly for the Axis:
the New Zealand Brigade at Bab-el-Qattara overran and
virtually destroyed the Ariete Division, probably Rommel's best Italian troops, and elsewhere Auchinleck's
armour and artillery, by letting the Panzers come to them,
wrought considerable havoc. By the end of the day Eighth
Army undoubtedly had the upper hand, and the German
commander decided to pull back his forces, replacing
them chiefly with Italian units to hold the line. Auchinleck had once more pushed Rommel on to the defensive;
in doing so he had turned from defence to attack, and had
proved himself, in his switching of counter-attacks from
one sector to another, a master of the mobile warfare
thought to be the chief preserve of the German.

But, although optimistic, Auchinleck was still re-
strained. He anticipated every Axis move by laying minefields, thus strengthening a line originally very weak, and
he sought continually to husband his armour rather than
waste it – as Ritchie had done in the Cauldron battles –
in 'penny packets'. His presence inspired his weary troops
to continue to give of their best, but by 5 July it became
obvious that the Eighth Army was too exhausted to carry
out the encircling move from the south-east. He therefore
changed his plan to one tremendous drive just south of El
Alamein. First, however, he would fool Rommel. Accordingly, on 7 July he pulled back his forces from Bab-el-
Qattara, giving the impression that he was retiring to
consolidate his position. Rommel took the bait and began
to concentrate his forces for a thrust in the now seemingly
undefended southern sector; it was with considerable surprise, therefore, that the German learnt, early on 10 July,
that a massive British attack was in progress away to the
north. Australian and South African units of XXX Corps,

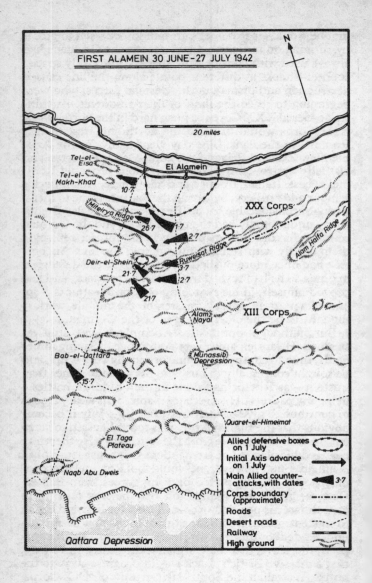

FIRST ALAMEIN 30 JUNE – 27 JULY 1942

N

20 miles

Tel-el-Eisa
Tel-el-Makh-Khad
El Alamein
10·7
XXX Corps
Miteirya Ridge
26·7
1·7
2·7
Alam Halfa Ridge
Deir-el-Shein
Ruweisat Ridge
21·7
3·7
2·7
21·7
Alam Nayal
XIII Corps
Bab-el-Qattara
Munassib Depression
15·7
3·7
Quaret-el-Himeimat
El Taga Plateau
Naqb Abu Dweis
Qattara Depression

Allied defensive boxes on 1 July
Initial Axis advance on 1 July
Main Allied counter-attacks, with dates   3·7
Corps boundary (approximate)
Roads
Desert roads
Railway
High ground

with close support from artillery and aircraft, had fallen upon the Italians west of El Alamein and driven them from their positions on Tel-el-Eisa and Tel-el-Makh-Khad. Rommel raced north and counter-attacked, with some success, but he could not drive the Eighth Army from the area, and by the 11th the positions were firmly in British hands. The danger to the Axis army was considerable, and Rommel rushed forces to the area to prevent a British breakthrough. By 15 July, however, all his counter-attacks had failed to dislodge his opponents from the Alamein area.

Almost at once, Auchinleck switched his attack. Never himself entranced by the Rommel myth, he now began to prove the superiority of his generalship; indeed, for more than a week he had forced his enemy to conform to British moves, a situation which Rommel found both confusing and infuriating. Between 15 and 18 July Auchinleck's troops fell with full force upon the Italian formations around Ruweisat Ridge. Despite some heavy losses to Panzer counter-attacks, he succeeded in picking off the Italian divisions one by one, while Rommel's continual need to drive his Germans back and forth to uphold his scattered allies was exhausting his men and costing heavily in casualties and equipment. Auchinleck had shifted his headquarters well forward on the Ruweisat Ridge; he knew the conditions his troops were encountering because he too was experiencing them. He thrived on it, while Rommel became increasingly exhausted and nervous. Auchinleck had his worries too – about the rest of his command, particularly the German threat from Russia to Persia, Iraq and Syria, and about what might be happening in London – but here he was performing extraordinarily well in a job for which he had an exceptional talent.

On the night of 20 July he attacked again, this time at Deir-el-Shein. It was becoming increasingly apparent, however, that his armoured formations had not yet learnt the art of close infantry support. Panzer counter-attacks on the 21st cost the Eighth Army dear, particularly in tanks – nevertheless, they had not been forced to retreat. On 25 July Auchinleck issued a Special Order of the

Day. Usually such exhortations are received cynically, for the recipients suspect that they are merely the confirmation that a cause is well and truly lost. Not this one, however:

> You have done well. You have turned a retreat into a firm stand and stopped the enemy on the threshold of Egypt. You have done more. You have wrenched the initiative from him by sheer guts and hard fighting and put HIM on the defensive in these last weeks. You have borne much but I ask you for more. We must not slacken. If we can stick it we will break him. STICK TO IT.

On the next day he launched the desperately tired Eighth Army in what proved to be a final assault. The fighting of the last few days had been concentrated in the southern sector of the line; Auchinleck now attacked in the north again, the aim being that XXX Corps should capture the Miteirya Ridge following a diversion in the south by Gott's forces. Lack of armoured support was once more clearly shown; the infantry struggled forward as best they could but took heavy casualties, and by the following day the fighting had come to an inconclusive end. What could he not have done with Churchill's promised 300 Sherman tanks.

By the 27th it was obvious that no further progress could be made for the moment, and the Eighth Army now went on the defensive. Reinforcements of at least two infantry and two armoured divisions would be needed before the offensive could be mounted again. Auchinleck had, however, accomplished a miracle. As Rommel expressed it in his dispatches after the fighting of 26 July:

> The British had again suffered heavy casualties – a thousand prisoners and 32 tanks – and their command now lost all taste for further attacks. The German Italian Front had shown itself to be no longer penetrable by forces of the size they were committing. It was certain that we could continue to hold our front, and that, after the crisis we had been through, was at least

something. Although the British losses in this Alamein fighting had been higher than ours, yet the price to Auchinleck had not been excessive, for the thing that had mattered to him was to halt our advance, and that, unfortunately, he had done.

Auchinleck had halted Rommel and robbed him of his last chance of taking Cairo. As the official history of one British regiment* remarks: 'Sir Claude Auchinleck frustrated the enemy at the eleventh hour, and sowed the seeds of victory.'

Churchill, however, had seen the battle in terms less generous to Auchinleck. On 1 and 2 July, having just returned from America, he had faced a vote of No Confidence in the House of Commons which, though it was defeated by a handsome margin, he clearly considered to be at least in part the result of military failures. He needed a victory, but he no longer believed Auchinleck capable of achieving it for him – the latter's obstinate refusal to accept the prodding had soured the Prime Minister's confidence in him. On the 3rd, the day the Eighth Army began to gain the initiative, Churchill was unable to see that Rommel was not only halted but wrong-footed; on the 4th he chose to dismiss a signal from Auchinleck in somewhat pessimistic terms. On the 12th Auchinleck received a form of ultimatum from Churchill – either defeat and destroy Rommel, or there would be no strengthening of the Middle East's northern front, now seriously endangered by the German advance in Russia. Yet on the following day Rommel suffered heavily in an abortive counter-attack near Alamein, and by the 17th he was telling the Italian High Command: 'Any more blows like today and I do not anticipate being able to hold the situation.' Churchill remained unable to see the fight for Egypt being won almost beneath his nose, and even Brooke held fears for the desert battle and his friend's grip upon it. When, on 27 July, Auchinleck put the Eighth

* *Proud Heritage: The Story of the Highland Light Infantry*, Volume IV.

Army on the defensive once more, Churchill considered his signal announcing the decision to be 'very depressing'.

For some time Churchill had felt that if Auchinleck would not return home, then he and Brooke should go out and see him. Accordingly, on 3 August the Prime Minister and the CIGS both arrived in Cairo. Auchinleck was not there to meet them, being in his desert HQ behind the Ruweisat Ridge, but he returned that afternoon. Field-Marshal Jan Christiaan Smuts was there, however, having just flown from South Africa. Smuts, Prime Minister of South Africa and overall commander of the Union's forces, was one of Churchill's most trusted advisers – Auchinleck had at times been in correspondence with Smuts since many South African troops were involved in the desert fighting. Churchill had asked the South African to Cairo in order to help clear up the problems of command in the Middle East which, he considered, faced Brooke and himself; on the following day Wavell too would join them. Auchinleck had missed his golden opportunity when first asked to go home in March; now he would have to face his inquisitors having come directly from a long-drawn and complicated battle.

Churchill was immensely excited at the feeling that he was now at a battle headquarters. His meeting with Auchinleck was like that of two old friends, and he listened carefully as he was given an account of the military position. Later that night, however, Churchill held discussions with Brooke in which the Prime Minister expressed forthright views. Obviously, he said, Auchinleck must give up command of the Eighth Army as soon as possible – but to whom? It is a measure of how far Auchinleck had fallen in the Prime Minister's eyes that the latter should adopt this view; previously, as we have seen, he had always urged Auchinleck to command the army himself, a course with which Brooke had disagreed. Churchill now suggested Gott (who in many ways was a similar character to Auchinleck), but it was argued that Gott, after the hard battles fought by his XIII Corps, was too exhausted to take on this new post at that moment. Churchill then tried to persuade Brooke himself to take over, but the CIGS realised that this was quite wrong, however attractive. Finally, Montgomery was named, although Churchill still favoured Gott, whom he had never met.

Brooke later claimed that Montgomery was his choice, though he had doubts as to whether this would work, in view of the history of Montgomery's activities in Southern Command, but that Auchinleck raised no objection. This is hardly surprising, since Auchinleck said later that he personally made the suggestion of bringing out Montgomery, and undoubtedly he and Brooke agreed on the 4th on this choice for the Eighth Army. Auchinleck may, of course, have made the suggestion to Churchill on an occasion when Brooke was not present, but there seems to be no doubt at all that he made it, and that he also remembered the trouble he had had earlier with Montgomery. Nevertheless, Auchinleck now thought him to be the best man for the Eighth Army, leaving himself free to direct the campaign from Cairo. He had earlier suggested Corbett to replace Ritchie as a temporary measure, though this had been before Churchill's visit. The Prime Minister, however, took the suggestion as another sign of Auchinleck's failure.

Auchinleck remained ignorant of the portents borne by these arguments over a new commander for the Eighth Army. Brooke considered that Montgomery and the present C-in-C Middle East would never work well together – indeed, he was surprised by Auchinleck's agreement – not, incredibly, because of provocation by the junior man, but because Auchinleck would ride Montgomery on too tight a rein. The CIGS desperately wanted Montgomery for the Eighth Army: if the two men could not get on together then, *faute de mieux*, one must go. And by the 4th Churchill too was considering a greater change than merely appointing a new army commander, for that evening Auchinleck had bluntly pointed out to him that the Eighth Army needed time for reinforcement, training and re-supply before driving Rommel from the Alamein position. However sensible, it was an argument for which Churchill had no time – he had heard it often enough from this stubborn commander. He needed an offensive to back up the coming Anglo-American landing in North Africa proposed for the autumn. And he needed a victory, for political and morale reasons, quite unable to see that there had been a considerable victory achieved since First Alamein began on 1 July. Of Churchill at this time, Lord Moran, the Prime Minister's physician, recorded in his diary for 4 August: 'He is in great heart: he is "the man on the spot". Three times he has said this to me. A great feeling of elation stokes the marvellous machine.' Churchill was then sixty-nine.

On the 5th Churchill and Brooke flew to an airfield in the desert, where they were met by Auchinleck. He drove them first to Alamein, then up to his battle headquarters, a partly fly-proof wire cage. No concessions were made to comfort or ceremonial. Subsequently Churchill wrote:

> There [behind the Ruweisat Ridge] we breakfasted with some men burnt brown by the desert sun. There were flies everywhere. When they were disturbed they rose in a cloud with a buzzing sound ...

Churchill was somewhat disgusted at being received in such spartan and unpleasant conditions, and it helped to make him even more disenchanted with Auchinleck. During this visit the Prime Minister continued to press urgently for an attack, but Auchinleck was adamant that time was needed to regain the Army's strength. Churchill drove back with Gott, still convinced that this was the man to beat Rommel. On the 6th Churchill stayed with Smuts and Brooke all day until evening, discussing proposals that he had been formulating: he would split Middle East Command, giving Palestine, Syria, Iraq and Persia to Auchinleck, while Alexander would replace him in Cairo as C-in-C, Near East Command. Gott would command the Eighth Army. Brooke eventually agreed, and at the end of the day Churchill came out and remarked, 'There is something wrong here. I am convinced there has been no leadership out here. What has happened is a disgrace. Ninety thousand men all over the place. Alex told me there are 2000 officers in Cairo who wear a smart uniform called a gabardine and that they are called the gabardine swine.' His voice rose. 'There must be no cozening. The Army must understand there are very serious penalties for not doing their duty.' Auchinleck, however, was not yet aware of the implications of the day's discussion.

Later, in India, while travelling by plane, Auchinleck told his Press and Public Relations Officer, Major N. Price, that Smuts was the man who had insisted on his removal from the desert command. Smuts, he said, had been deeply concerned at the capture of the 2nd South African Division in Tobruk and felt that his government would cease to co-operate with the Allied war effort if Auchinleck continued as C-in-C, Middle East. Smuts was, of course, a dominant personality, but he had had to use all his powers to bring South Africa into the war in 1939, and only then on the understanding that the Union's troops should fight in Africa alone. Moran said of him, 'He lives to get things done. Anyone who stops in his path is ruthlessly pushed aside. As for his colleagues in the Cabinet, they are kept at arm's length. The whole political apparatus is just a necessary nuisance . . .'

Of Auchinleck at this time, Moran continued:

As for Auchinleck, Brooke tells me he is a man of splendid talent, a very able soldier, and a man, too, of great strength of character. He has come to grief, it would seem, because he could not pick the right subordinates. Those he appointed had so dispersed our forces in the desert that Rommel, with his more effective tanks and guns, had little difficulty in defeating the scattered remnants piecemeal. There is another reason: the Auk does not understand Winston.

Churchill was undoubtedly a difficult man to understand, but it appears, in fact, that Auchinleck did understand him. What Auchinleck did not do, however, was apply the compassion he could feel for his subordinates to his Prime Minister. Clearly he regarded Churchill as a commanding officer who kept on requesting the impossible, but would doubtless be well satisfied with the probable when the time came. As fast as Churchill suggested the impossible, Auchinleck confronted him with the probable or even, at times, the possible. When Churchill came out to Cairo he was only too aware that his next visit would be to Moscow, where he was due on 12 August. He knew that he must have something encouraging to tell Stalin: there were of course to be the Anglo-American landings, code-named 'Torch', in Algiers later in the year, but what he needed now was some British success to recount. Auchinleck's totally realistic appreciation of the desert situation was not what Churchill wanted to hear, and much though he admired Auchinleck as a soldier, knowing him to be a better strategist than Rommel, at the same time, and in the problematic situation he faced, he would have preferred dealing with the latter.

Any open-mindedness the Prime Minister might have had before arrival was rapidly dispelled by the graphic stories about 'The Flap' in Cairo at the end of June, following the retreat from the Gazala line, the 'Gazala Gallop'. Officers based in Cairo had acquired a reputation for luxury, idleness and self-satisfaction, and certainly some were having the time of their lives, enjoying a standard of living they had never experienced before and would never experience again. Nicknames such as 'Groppi's Horse' were applied to the Staff officers whose duties allowed them time to take elegant women to afternoon tea at Groppi's. Officers from units in the desert found Cairo relaxing, if a trifle sickening, while ordinary soldiers on leave found the attractive resorts banned to them and regarded the city with resentment and scorn. After the confusion of the June fighting and hasty retreat a number of officers seemed to have found their way to Cairo without any good reason; separated from their units, with nothing to do and not a little demoralised, they had a bad effect on the morale of soldiers and citizens alike. When it was thought that Cairo might be abandoned to the Germans, officialdom in the city gave an unpleasing display of nerves. Official papers – among them those of the British Embassy – were burnt with such haste that 1 July was nicknamed 'Ash Wednesday'; and towards the end of June the bulk of the British fleet had left Alexandria as a result of the German threat. Corbett, as Chief of the General Staff, Middle East, was subsequently held responsible for the undignified behaviour of those days, and it is said that he approved the order that all officers should carry revolvers at all times, and that the centre of Cairo should be out of bounds from 8 pm to 7 am. These, and other instructions, were probably sound enough if accompanied by reassurances, but the latter were not forthcoming. To most Cairenes, and many British, Rommel's entry into the city was only a matter of time. Corbett was blamed for the panic, and Corbett had, of course, been chosen by Auchinleck: though whether anyone else would have been able to cope with that particular situation better than Corbett apparently did is, of course, hypothetical.

Thus when, on the 4th and 5th, Churchill had broached the matter of when Auchinleck would be able to take the offensive again, what he needed to hear was a resounding message of confidence about a drive forward in the near future. It did not necessarily need to be true; the timing could be changed later, but something was needed to wash away the bad taste of the 'Cairo Flap' and to encourage Stalin to continue the resistance in Russia. Pressed for a date, Auchinleck had mentioned 15 September, to Churchill's fury. Ironically, that date, which the Prime Minister found intolerably delayed, was one month and one week earlier than the start of Montgomery's much-acclaimed battle. Montgomery knew how to handle his Churchill, knew that if he played his cards properly he could be assured of an overwhelming advantage; it was as well for all that he did.

There was another unfortunate thought galling Churchill at this time. That was that if the line had been pierced at Alamein in July Auchinleck would not have ordered the Eighth Army to fight to the last round, but would instead have withdrawn to Alexandria, and if needs be up the Nile Valley. Auchinleck saw his main responsibility as the defence of the oilfields in Persia and of the Suez Canal, and had the worst come to the worst at Alamein, it was essential to keep most of the Eighth Army intact, even if it meant an extensive retreat. Strategically, such a withdrawal would have placed the British forces in a very powerful position and Rommel might have lived to regret the day he reached Cairo, given the existence of a large and experienced army in or near a country he would only recently have conquered.

Not least of Churchill's complaints was the dashing of his hopes. He knew that 44th Division had arrived in mid-July and was at present in the Delta area. Why had it not been sent up to the line? A division was a division, surely – men, soldiers? Patiently Auchinleck went over this well-trodden ground; a newly arrived division needed to be acclimatised and trained. To expect it to be able to go into action straight away, like the unfortunate trench fodder of the First World War, was asking the impossible. (Montgomery, diplomatically, was to send 44th Division to Alam Halfa, in the rear of the Alamein position, where it would have time to accustom itself to the conditions before the next attack was expected.)

After his fly-attended breakfast in Auchinleck's tactical headquarters cage, Churchill had lunched at the Desert Air Force Headquarters, east of El Alamein and near the coast. The RAF had prudently arranged for the meal to be supplemented from Shepheard's Hotel in Cairo. It was a cheerful occasion, but Churchill did not fail to note that the RAF considered the Army to have made a hash of the recent campaign – it had indeed looked that way from the air. The RAF had lost many forward airfields during Ritchie's pell-mell retreat, and the spectacle of a large force withdrawing in haste cannot have been edifying. Subsequently, Tedder's airmen had flown countless sorties in support of Auchinleck's operations during the Alamein battles, often with very marked success, but it is notoriously difficult to comprehend ground actions when viewed from aircraft.

Lt-Gen. Sir Ian Jacob, at that time a colonel serving on Churchill's staff, summarised the situation as he saw it in his diary:

The Prime Minister had found a disturbing state of affairs in the Army in the Middle East. It had received a severe beating in a battle [Gazala] which everybody thought it should have won. The Army was bewildered and was no longer a coherent fighting machine. Some striking change was therefore required to offer a stimulus to the troops. On the other hand the Prime Minister had a great opinion of General Auchinleck and was most averse to the idea that his services should be lost to the state. He felt that if General Auchinleck had been freed from the responsibility of the Levant–Caspian Front and had been able to concentrate on the Western Desert he could have taken command when the battle broke out instead of waiting till the situation was desperate. This might well have turned the scale and given us victory instead of defeat. The Prime Minister was therefore determined that the best possible fighting soldier should be placed in command in the Middle East and that he should have nothing to think of except the battle against Rommel, which he would personally conduct.

Churchill's view of the changes now necessary were furnished to the War Cabinet on 6 August for their approval. Gott would command the Eighth Army, Alexander was to succeed Auchinleck as C-in-C in Cairo, and the latter would be offered the proposed new Middle East Command – Palestine, Syria, Iraq and Persia – since Churchill was loath to lose his services altogether. Alexander had already been appointed to command the British First Army in the Anglo-American 'Torch' landings planned for later in the year, so that post would now be taken over by Montgomery. Auchinleck's two Chiefs of Staff, Corbett and Dorman-Smith, would also be replaced. The War Cabinet expressed doubt about the wisdom of splitting up the Middle East Command, and also of giving one of the resulting new commands to Auchinleck, since they felt it would appear that such a post had been created especially to appease a sacked general. Substantially, though, they agreed to all the Prime Minister's proposals, and their answer reached Cairo on the 7th. Churchill replied almost immediately, insisting on the creation of two new commands and adding a spirited defence of Auchinleck. He expressed the view that had Auchinleck not had the rest of his large command to consider, he might easily have won in the desert, and he pointed out his successes in 'Crusader' and at Alamein, ending 'Nor can I advise that General Auchinleck should be ruined and cast aside as unfit to render any further service.'

Churchill was still in favour of Gott taking over the Eighth Army, in spite of Brooke's opposition and of being told by everyone that the redoubtable 'Strafer' was very tired and much in need of leave. Gott had already been told of his appointment, but the idea was extinguished by his death by enemy action on the 7th. The aircraft in which he was travelling to go on leave had been shot down shortly after take-off, though he had managed to get clear of it. He had realised, however, that others were trapped in the wreckage and had returned to extricate them. The plane blew up, killing them. The news came as a considerable shock both to the Eighth Army and to Churchill and his advisers. On hearing it late that night, Auchinleck, still at his desert HQ, telephoned Brooke and once more agreed that Montgomery should come over and command the Eighth Army. Churchill, whose plans were now 'dislocated', as he put it, toyed with the idea of Maitland Wilson commanding the Eighth Army and clung to it until Smuts and Brooke talked him out of it. He then confirmed his approval of Montgomery's appointment, sending a telegram to the War Cabinet to that effect around midnight.

There now fell to Colonel Jacob the unpleasant duty of handing Auchinleck Churchill's note dismissing him from his post. It was a wretched task for anyone, but particularly for Jacob, who admired Auchinleck greatly. On Saturday 8 August 1942 Jacob flew from Cairo and reached Eighth Army HQ a few hours later, handing over the letter to the C-in-C in person: 'I could not have admired more the way Auchinleck received me and his attitude throughout. A great man and a great fighter.'

The note ran:

Dear General Auchinleck,
    1. On June 23rd you raised in your telegrams to the CIGS the question of your being relieved in this command and you mentioned the name of General

Alexander as a possible successor. At that time of crisis in the Army His Majesty's Government did not wish to avail themselves of your high-minded offer. At the same time you had taken over the effective command of the battle, as I had long ago desired and had suggested to you in my telegram of May 20th. You stemmed the adverse tide and at the present time the front is stabilised.

2. The War Cabinet have now decided, for the reasons which you yourself had used, that the moment has come for a change. It is proposed to detach Iraq and Persia from the present Middle Eastern theatre. Alexander will be appointed to command the Middle East, Montgomery to command the Eighth Army, and I offer you the command of Iraq and Persia including the Tenth Army, with Headquarters at Basra or Baghdad. It is true that this sphere is smaller than the Middle East but it may in the course of a few months become the scene of decisive operations, and reinforcements to the Tenth Army are already on the way. In this theatre of which you have special experience you will preserve your associations with India. I hope therefore that you will comply with my wish and directions with the same disinterested public spirit that you have shown on all occasions. Alexander will arrive almost immediately and I hope that early next week, subject of course to the movements of the enemy, it may be possible to effect the transfer of responsibility on the Western battlefront with the utmost smoothness and efficiency.

I shall be very glad to see you at any convenient time if you should so desire.

Believe me
Yours sincerely
Winston S. Churchill

Auchinleck returned from the desert at midday on 9 August. He saw Brooke, exchanged a few words with Jacob and then went in to Churchill. He was with the Prime Minister for an hour. The meeting was impeccably correct, according to Churchill, but Auchinleck said he was 'disinclined to accept the command of the Iraq–Persia theatre'. Nearly a year would elapse before he received another offer. On the following day he discussed the situation with Alexander, who had arrived on the 9th, and agreed with him the date of 15 August for the transfer of command.

Until he received Churchill's letter, Auchinleck had not known he was to be replaced, though he must have had his suspicions. Churchill had wished to sack him for 'insubordination' when he refused to come home, and as early as January 1942, after the loss of Benghazi, Brooke had committed to his diary his private feeling that Auchinleck was not the man to command in the Middle East. Some of these views must have filtered down to Auchinleck, but believing, as he did, that a general should either be left to get on with it or be sacked, he merely continued with his job as he saw it, regardless of the consequences for his career. He accepted his replacement with dignity and courage, but even in this hour of personal disaster others would try to cut him down yet further. On 12 August the commander-designate of the Eighth Army arrived in Cairo – Lt-Gen. Bernard Montgomery, late GOC-in-C, South-Eastern Command.

Churchill, who had left Cairo for Moscow on 10 August, had suggested the 12th to the War Cabinet as a date for the hand-over, but Auchinleck and Alexander had agreed upon the 15th for the official transfer, since time was needed for the outgoing C-in-C to brief the two newcomers. Montgomery, already enjoying a reputation for taking over commands and making them his own, saw no reason to delay, nor to spare General Auchinleck's feelings. On the morning of his arrival he met Auchinleck at GHQ in Cairo, and there he formed the extraordinary belief, which he was soon disseminating, that the present C-in-C was planning a retreat up the Nile, and possibly into Palestine, by the entire Eighth Army should Rommel attack heavily. The most charitable view of this belief is that Montgomery failed to understand Auchinleck correctly, in which case he was guilty, as Roger Parkinson put it, of 'an acute and unprofessional loss of concentration'. Like any sensible army commander, Auchinleck had made contingency plans for a retreat in good order to keep the army in being should the worst come to the worst; far more important, however, was the existence of his plans, completed by Dorman-Smith on 27 July, for the strengthening and defence of the Alamein line, and for an offensive once the army had had a chance to train and refit. Montgomery, refusing to admit that the withdrawal plan was only a necessary contingency, considered that it had a severe effect on the morale of the army; his attitude gave the impression that Auchinleck had no other plans.

Although, as we have seen, there were contingency plans for a highly improbable retreat to the Delta, Auchinleck's concern was to hold the Alamein line and then attack. Sir David Hunt, who as an Intelligence officer at XIII Corps HQ would certainly know, said:

Plans had been drawn up [around the end of June 1942] by Auchinleck and his staff to meet the eventuality of an enemy penetration of the Alamein front, providing for a defence of the edge of the Delta. This was in the period when the enemy were advancing on Alamein and the plans were in the nature of an insurance policy. For the whole of July it was we who were on the offensive; for the last six weeks of his command Auchinleck had been thinking more of a triumphal drive westwards. Even when it became clear that Rommel would be the one to attack next Auchinleck had no doubt that we should be able to hold our desert position.

During their meeting, Auchinleck informed Montgomery that the official transfer of command would take place on the 15th. On the day after his interview with Auchinleck, however, he drove to Eighth Army HQ and from there sent a signal to GHQ in Cairo: '... Lt-Gen. Montgomery assumed command of Eighth Army at 1400 hrs today.' It was an act of calculated insolence – reminiscent of his take-over of V Corps from Auchinleck in Britain some years previously – though, from his point of view, an effective one, giving the impression of a new broom confronted by a great pile of unnecessary dust. Auchinleck's farewell message to Eighth Army had already been dispatched, and there would be no point in reversing Montgomery's pre-emptive action for what would be a little over twenty-four hours. According to his latest biographer,* Montgomery decided at this point to 'make himself scarce', presumably for fear of Auchinleck's wrath; indeed, the new Eighth Army commander claimed in his diary that the telegram 'had made Auchinleck very angry'. If Auchinleck (who never vouchsafed his views of the incident) was angry, it is only understandable – he had little time for a style of generalship that encompassed ill-manners, bluster, and the denigration of the successes of others.

Auchinleck's last message to his exhausted but once more steadfast troops ended: 'I know you will continue in the same fine spirit and determination to win under your new commander. I wish you luck and speedy and complete victory.'

The Eighth Army would indeed give freely of the first, and achieve, in time, the second; in the process, however, the man who had made it possible would be all but forgotten.

Auchinleck's long battle in the Middle East was now at an end. On 15 August he handed over formally to Alexander and then departed for Rawalpindi and retirement. He would not accept the Iraq–Persia command and told Churchill so; typically, his refusal was not based on pride, but on his belief that the command would feel it had received a failed general, which would be bad for its morale. Churchill by then considered his offer of Iraq–Persia command to be 'high and honourable', adding, somewhat cuttingly, 'it is for him to settle whether he wishes to render further service to the Crown'. This was unworthy – there could be no question of Auchinleck's wish to serve, but he would not do so if, as was the case with this offer, he felt he would hinder rather than help.

In India he at last met up with Lady Auchinleck after their long separation. Outwardly he seemed undistressed at the treatment he had received, but it was impossible for him to hide his deepest feelings from his wife, and she

* Nigel Hamilton, *Monty: The Making of a General, 1887–1942* (London, 1981).

believed he was very badly hurt. (He would deny this, years later, in an interview with David Dimbleby, saying he was 'possibly slightly humiliated, but not hurt'.) Fortunately he did not know that Montgomery's particular style of generalship was capitalising on his own foresight while denying him the credit.

Undoubtedly Montgomery saw his task as one of re-vitalising a beaten army, creating a winning machine, but his method of approaching it seems unnecessarily insensitive. Clearly he thought he had to take *all* the credit and that this could only be done by denigrating the achievements of his predecessor, and he began that process the moment he took over on 13 August. Brooke was impressed when he visited the Eighth Army on 19 August: 'I must confess I was dumbfounded by the rapidity with which he [Montgomery] had grasped the situation.' Brooke might well have been impressed. The plans for the strengthening and defence of the Alamein line, and subsequent offensive, which Montgomery so confidently described to the CIGS had been made by Auchinleck and Dorman-Smith. Montgomery himself denied this, writing in 1962 that he 'took over *no* plans from Auchinleck'. As Roger Parkinson says, however, 'Montgomery must also have seen the appreciation completed by Dorman-Smith on 27 July, approved by Auchinleck, which specified that Rommel would be blocked firmly in August and a full counter-offensive launched in about mid-September.' It was these plans which Auchinleck had outlined to Churchill on 4 August, yet which the latter had considered to represent an intolerable delay. Alexander, Montgomery's C-in-C, wrote, 'I adopted this plan of defence in principle', yet the new Eighth Army commander, to whom Auchinleck must have outlined the plan during their meeting on 12 August, chose only to remember the contingency plans for withdrawal, giving to the world the impression that there was no other plan.

Lt-Col. Brian Montgomery, in his biography of his brother, makes the point that 'we can be certain that Auchinleck felt it his duty to include in his briefing of the new Commander the facts of the official contingency plans as well as his own plans to resume the offensive . . .', adding that 'Bernard's condemnation of Auchinleck on this particular point ... was most unfair and wholly unjustified'. His considered view is that official documents make it entirely clear that Auchinleck was determined to resume the offensive. And Ronald Lewin, while defending Montgomery as honestly believing that he took over no effective plan, says of Auchinleck that 'There can be no doubt that the character of the man, and the conduct of the July battles when he fought Rommel to a standstill, was aggressive.' He adds that 'Montgomery certainly did Auchinleck an injustice by implying that he was craven, as he also did him an injustice by never paying adequate tribute to Auchinleck's fighting defence in July ...'; for Mr Lewin, 'Not even those who think much of Montgomery's military attributes would condone his treatment of Auchinleck on this August day: it besmirches what should have been a day of triumph.'

Montgomery's first success was at Alam Halfa on 30 August, when Rommel tried to break through with his armour. After initial success with a flanking movement in the south, Rommel was 'firmly blocked' on the Alam Halfa Ridge, and called off the attempt on 4 September. Of this battle (Second Alamein), Montgomery said: 'I had to tidy up the mess and to get my plans laid so there was no difficulty in seeing him [Rommel] off.' Montgomery had visited the area the day after he took over. In his *Memoirs* he wrote:

I spent the day examining the ground on the inter-corps boundary and on the southern flank, and at once saw the importance of two dominating areas of ground: the Ruweisat Ridge and the Alam Halfa Ridge. Both were important but the key to the whole Alamein position was the Alam Halfa Ridge. This was several miles in rear of the Alamein line and south-east from the Ruweisat Ridge; it was undefended because there were no troops available.

But what is beyond dispute is that the site of Montgomery's victories was chosen by Auchinleck in June 1942, when the situation was very grim (see Appendix D).

It is highly unlikely that Auchinleck would have failed to draw Montgomery's attention to the Alam Halfa Ridge on 12 August at their meeting; Alexander wrote of Auchinleck's appreciation: 'The plan was ... to threaten any enemy advance south of the [Ruweisat] ridge from a strongly defended and prepared position on Alam Halfa ridge.' Yet of that occasion Montgomery had said:

Plans were being made to move the Eighth Army HQ back up the Nile.

I listened in amazement to this exposition of his plans. I asked one or two questions but I quickly saw that he resented any questions directed to immediate changes of policy about which he had already made up his mind. So I remained silent.

It is difficult to decide which is the most improbable of the statements in Montgomery's remark, but if one thing is absolutely certain it is that any conference which took place in Auchinleck's map room must have devoted some time to the topography of the Alamein position. In any case, Alexander stated in his dispatch: 'A strong position for a brigade had been built on the [Alam Halfa] Ridge in July, defended by wire and minefields.' Montgomery certainly sent forward 44th Division (about whose presence back in the Delta Churchill had complained to Auchinleck) to the position, but it was quite definitely not undefended; even Nigel Hamilton is forced to admit that Montgomery's assertion that 'Alam Halfa was never in the picture at all' is 'an exaggeration'.

It was perhaps understandable that Montgomery, as a new commander, should try to show the stamp of knowledge and authority in his new appointment. He was entirely right to make whatever changes he saw fit and to give the Army an impression that a new revitalised spirit was now abroad. It is perhaps even reasonable that he should have adopted Auchinleck's sound planning as his own brilliant idea. What is not acceptable is that he should vilify his predecessor in the process and fail to correct those statements when he wrote his memoirs fifteen years later, an attitude which even his latest biographer admits 'does him no credit', Of his meeting with de Guingand, for instance:

> I asked him about the morale of the officers and men. He said it wasn't good; the Eighth Army wanted a clear lead and a firm grip from the top; there was too much uncertainty and he thought 'the feel of the thing' was wrong. I did not press him on this point: I knew he was trying to be loyal to his past chief.

Yet in his book *Generals at War*, published in 1964, de Guingand says:

> I found Montgomery more competent and decisive. I would not wish in any way to belittle Auchinleck's achievements, which for the most part were obtained with resources, both human and material, inferior to those after Montgomery's arrival. One can never stress too much the debt we all owed to those who had to fight with inadequate arms and equipment in those early days and by their efforts made possible the victory of Alamein.

Any new commander, particularly one of strong personality, appears on taking over to be like a breath of fresh air; indeed, Tedder had described Auchinleck when he took over as C-in-C in July 1941 as 'first-rate, cool, cheerful and a fighter . . . honest, clear-thinking and full of guts, head and shoulders above any senior soldier in the Middle East.' New appointments are made, new dispositions discussed, the opinions of others sought, new orders given out – the effect superficially is of a radical change of policy. Montgomery, by issuing orders on 13 August cancelling Auchinleck's contingency withdrawal plans while at the same time failing to admit that there was any other plan, sowed in the minds of many the idea that Auchinleck was planning to retreat, and to do nothing but retreat. And as to the poor morale and defeatist attitude which Montgomery claimed had been infused into Eighth Army by Auchinleck and his advisers, there can be no question that this was another of the skilful tricks which made Montgomery such an excellent trainer of troops – if you tell soldiers their morale is low, they will generally strive to improve on it. Eighth Army was very tired, very battered, and in dire need of reinforcement and re-organisation, as Auchinleck admitted, but it had stopped Rommel cold and put him back on the defensive, and that after a confusing and, at times, near panic-stricken retreat lasting some six weeks, with heavy losses. Its commander, in whom there was never the least trace of defeatism, had, if anything, restored the morale of an entire army by his presence and direction, and the testimony of many, from senior commander to private soldier, gives the lie to Montgomery's assertions.

Not least of Auchinleck's efforts was his constant sur-veillance of the potential battlefield. One of his ADCs in 1942 was Captain Angus Mackinnon, MC (who later went on to command the 7th Argyll and Sutherland High-landers), and another was Captain W. M. Cunningham, an 11th Hussar who had taken part in the 'Jock Column' raids. Both ADCs had the intriguing experience of flying over the desert sitting in the bomb bay of a Blenheim, seeking information for their C-in-C. Every time the aircraft made an unusual manoeuvre, possibly in order to obtain a better view of the ground, there was the interest-ing possibility that it was instead taking hopefully evasive action from a Messerschmitt. Both men to this day recall the thoroughness with which Auchinleck surveyed the terrain, outlining areas for minefields and wire.

The explanation of Montgomery's incessant fretting to spoil Auchinleck's reputation probably lies in his private knowledge that Auchinleck was the better general – he must be discredited or men would say, 'Ah, Auchinleck would have done that better.' This applies particularly to Montgomery's failure to follow Rommel and destroy his army after the October–November battle, and it could so easily have applied to Montgomery's handling of his resources after the D-Day landings. It is a sad reflection that Churchill's loss of confidence in Auchinleck was to a great extent based upon the latter's refusal to be rushed into offensives unprepared. Yet Montgomery, whose singular skills lay in the preparation of large set-piece battles and in his ability to force people to believe in him, was the greater delayer – Third Alamein began on 23 October 1942, yet Auchinleck's plan of 27 July had given 15 September as the date for the new offensive. Montgomery's delay in breaking out from the Normandy beachhead in 1944, is, of course, well documented; it was also extremely costly, and the source of soured relations between him and his American allies.

When he took over in the desert in August 1942 Montgomery had to criticise previous arrangements in order to impress upon his superiors the time he needed to prepare a reasonable offensive. In the event, however, he had started receiving reinforcements almost at once, and the vital 300 Sherman tanks, promised to Auchinleck in June, arrived in September. When he went into battle on 23 October he had some 220,000 men and 1000 tanks to Rommel's 108,000 men, of whom half were Italians, and 600 tanks; and British superiority in other weapons and in the air was equally marked. Similarly, Ultra had been of little value to Auchinleck at Alamein in July, since Rommel did not communicate his plans to the OKW as much as he might have done, and also because Ultra could not keep track of a fast-moving battle. But for Third Alamein in October it was a very different story. Montgomery knew what forces Rommel had at his disposal and what he needed: he knew the German plans. The statement that he kept a picture of Rommel in his caravan so that he could study it and deduce the German's thoughts and intentions is somewhat fanciful. He did indeed keep such a portrait, but he had only to lower his eyes to the Ultra decrypts to know what Rommel might or might not do next. Additionally, the quality of the Ultra material he received improved as the months passed.

The fact that in his memoirs Montgomery tried desperately to justify his attitude and behaviour towards Auchinleck seems to show that the recollection was a constant 'Banquo's ghost' to him, one which he tried to exorcise by bluster. At best, it may be said that Montgomery 'exaggerated' Auchinleck's supposed defeatism and the low morale and poor training of the Eighth Army. There is another explanation for Montgomery's criticism of Auchinleck as a military commander. Once Montgomery had command of the Eighth Army he could be sure that Alexander, as C-in-C, would back him and assist him to further promotion, but what he did not want was for Auchinleck ever to be recalled, perhaps to become Supreme Commander for the proposed invasion of Europe. This unfortunately seems to have robbed the Allies of their potentially best general for the remainder of the war. Montgomery, as well as being driven by ruthless ambition, undoubtedly believed firmly that he had a mission to be the Supreme Commander – to him the end justified the means. Auchinleck almost certainly made him feel uneasy and inferior. The senior man, regardless of anyone's views of his ability as a general, was manifestly both courageous and honourable, and many have testified to their feeling that his spirit and bearing were marks of true greatness. His moral qualities were enhanced by his looks and striking physical presence; indeed, years later, Montgomery was to remark to de Guingand, echoing the nursery rhyme, 'Ah, Auchinleck – his face was his fortune.' Sir David Hunt wrote:

General Auchinleck had certainly endeared himself to most people by his fighting command of the Eighth Army in the Alamein line. His intellectual powers were always as evident as his robustness and moral courage. Indeed he seemed to have every characteristic required of a general with the possible exception of the ability to choose wisely in his subordinates and staff. I remember many years afterwards hearing Sir Winston Churchill in private speak with admiration of Auchinleck and saying how remorseful and hesitant he had felt when he informed him of the decision to supersede him.

At the time Hunt, however, considered that

when Auchinleck was in the Middle East he cast a very kindly eye on as weird and wonderful a collection of funnies* as was ever assembled in one spot during the war. At the time I thought he was being put on by a

---

* Military nickname for unorthodox thinkers and units.

gang of charlatans. It was to his credit in many ways to be so open-minded, and perhaps it didn't matter much, but I thought it was a shame.

I was most agreeably surprised to find that regular officers had such keen minds open to any ideas. Auchinleck, as an officer commissioned in the Indian Army, knew that he would be regarded as the archetypal Colonel Blimp; he was all the more ready to show he could put up with almost anything.

Hunt, among many others, felt that 'the Auk's' tolerance sometimes extended too far, and that the appointments of Corbett, Dorman-Smith, and Ritchie were examples of this. De Guingand, for instance, thought Corbett 'a complete fathead', and Brooke had serious misgivings about his appointment, saying, 'I did not know Corbett, nor did anybody I asked about him ... I might have advised the Auk to choose someone of higher calibre.' (This is not altogether to Brooke's credit – it is the duty of the CIGS to know his generals since he may at any time have to call upon them.) Of Dorman-Smith Brooke also wrote that he 'had a most fertile brain, continually producing new ideas, some of which (not many) were good, and the rest useless,' and he considered that Dorman-Smith had far too much influence over Auchinleck. Ritchie, steadfast as he had been during 'Crusader', with Auchinleck present to guide him, was too young and inexperienced to command a large army during a crisis; he had been over-confident at Gazala, and that, in the end, had proved disastrous. Ritchie, of course, was dismissed by Auchinleck; the other two were replaced at the same time as their C-in-C. The same view of this over-tolerance of subordinates was expressed by G. P. Smart, who had first met Auchinleck as his bank manager in Delhi in 1937, and had later served in the desert at the same time as the general. He said:

I never met him during my military service. In fact I only saw him once and that at a distance. That was on our return along the desert road to the Alamein Ridge after the disastrous retreat in July 1942. I felt better for the sight of him. His selection of Ritchie to take over from Cunningham was understandable as a temporary appointment, but to retain him will ever be a mystery to me. I believe Ritchie, who had certainly not inspired much confidence, was junior to his two Corps Commanders, which could not have made for easy relations.* I have wondered since if the Auk was handicapped to some extent by not having much experience of the personalities in the British Army. Did this make for difficulties in the selection of subordinate commanders, or was he not ruthless enough in this respect?

There were many in the Middle East at that time who thought along the same lines, and they came from all ranks. The soldiers appreciated the fact that Auchinleck was 'one of them', that he lived as hard as they did, that there should be no special privileges for the higher ranks. (This often did not seem to apply to those sybaritic officers in Cairo, but Auchinleck's eyes were on the desert, not Cairo.) His generalship was admired, and he could and did win battles – Lt-Gen. Sir Francis Tuker said of him that 'he was bred for the battlefield'. Unfortunately, it seems that his choice of subordinates *was* poor. It was not that they let him down, as he would have been the first to admit, it was that he had made the mistake of appointing men to jobs for which they were unsuited. When he realised his mistake, he was perfectly capable of dismissing a man, but here is the real reason for his failure to smash Rommel utterly in the fourteen months allotted to him. He replaced Cunningham in time to save the situation, but by the time he took over from Ritchie the Eighth Army was in very poor case, and the whole desert war appeared lost. Auchinleck was not afraid of Churchill, the War Cabinet or the Germans. His concern was simply to do the right and fair thing. When it was all over he realised it is sometimes necessary to be unfair occasionally for the general good.

* Ritchie technically was junior to both Norrie and Godwin-Austen – he was made up to Acting Lieutenant-General from Temporary Major-General when given command of Eighth Army. And, as we have seen, his argument with Godwin-Austen during the retreat to the Gazala line had caused the latter's resignation.

14
'A GOOD DAY'
INDIA ONCE MORE

In India, after a period of leave, Auchinleck began working on his dispatches,* a task which took him three months. At intervals he took his mind from past battles and looked at the situation around him. In the months that followed his enforced 'retirement', he pondered the developments in India in 1942 and 1943. There was clearly much to be done before victory could be ensured. The Japanese had been held on the India–Burma border, and were unable to cross the Indian Ocean to mount an attack further south. Wavell was still Commander-in-Chief and Lord Linlithgow the Viceroy; under their guidance India was producing munitions and sending excellent divisions to the front. Potentially, however, the country was like a rumbling volcano. Nehru, with the other Congress leaders, was in jail, and Gandhi under house arrest; there was a feeling abroad that all would soon change and not necessarily for the better. The fact that America was now in the war put the Indian situation in a new light. Americans, at that stage, were firmly pledged to the idea that they were not in the war to sustain imperialism, and the obvious imperialists in their eyes were the British, Dutch and French. India may not have been the brightest jewel in the British crown but it was a source of persistent disquiet to liberal-minded Americans. In later years they would take a second look at the so-called iniquities of the old colonial powers and secretly wish their successors were as benevolent.

In one sense India was a backwater. The real war against Japan was being fought by General MacArthur and Admiral Nimitz in the Pacific, where already Japanese domination of the ocean had been broken by the US

* Field-Marshal Sir Claude Auchinleck, *Despatch: Operations in the Middle East from 1st November 1941 to 15th August 1942*, London, 1948.

224

carrier fleets. Nobody was going to conquer Tokyo with an expedition launched from India. Even Churchill showed no particular interest; he did not like Wavell, whom he had already treated badly, and he doubted whether India's C-in-C could grasp new opportunities if he had them. Then his mood changed. Montgomery's success at Third Alamein (23 October–4 November 1942) had given the Prime Minister a taste for victory; now, in February 1943, and stirred by Amery, he suddenly visualised an impressive British thrust into Burma which would push the Japanese into confusion. Their communications were clearly overstretched, and Wingate's Chindit operations of mid-February had shown that they could be beaten on their own terms. Churchill realised that it would be a mistake to move Wavell out of India altogether, and instead decided that Linlithgow should return, Wavell become Viceroy and Auchinleck, the man on the spot with the appropriate experience, should be Commander-in-Chief with effect from 20 June.

Unknown to Auchinleck, there had already been suggestions that he should be given another command. In February 1942, following the Casablanca Conference of January, Churchill once more raised the question of Auchinleck as C-in-C of the Iraq–Persia command. The CIGS and others agreed, but on 8 February Churchill, having talked to Montgomery about the idea, was writing to Brooke expressing concern about 'the very strong line taken by General Montgomery upon his [Auchinleck's] work.' It is doubtful, however, whether Auchinleck would have accepted a command he had already once refused, but it is certain that Brooke and Churchill listened to Montgomery's advice and dropped the idea. The charges levelled by the junior man – based presumably upon his jaundiced and inaccurate view of the state of Eighth Army when he took over – had thus prevented Auchinleck from receiving an active posting. Later in February Wavell suggested Auchinleck as commander for the proposed offensive in Burma, scheduled for the autumn. On 2 March, however, Churchill wrote to Amery of this proposal: 'As a result of our conference with General Montgomery and reports received from him on the state of 8th Army, CIGS and I have both lost confidence in General Auchinleck as a military commander in the field.' Montgomery, miles away in Tunisia, and largely ignorant of conditions prevailing in the Far East, was still determined that his predecessor should have neither command nor credit; his interference had now lost Auchinleck his last chance of an active command.

The announcement of the changes in India was published on 18 June 1943, but there was a sting in the tail. Amery's statement added the following rider:

It is proposed to relieve the Commander-in-Chief in India of the responsibility for the conduct of operations against Japan and to set up a separate East Asia Command for that purpose.

The Secretary of State for India and Burma followed up the announcement with an explanatory letter to Auchinleck:

For some time past I have been increasingly convinced that no man could efficiently combine the preparation and conduct of operations in South-East Asia, which will increasingly, I hope, extend away from India's borders, and at the same time do full justice to the part which the Commander-in-Chief ought to play both in keeping the Council informed on all military issues, and also in perfecting the organisation and tuning up the morale of the immensely enlarged army which India has accumulated in the last two years. The Prime Minister indeed has become seriously, perhaps excessively, alarmed at the prospect of the Indian Army losing morale or even being sapped by disloyalty and feels we should certainly call a halt to further expansion and possibly even consider some reduction below the present target. Well, on that you can advise as soon as you have had time to get the reins in your hands and look around a bit.

That you will not yourself have the operational control of the South-East Asia operation should not be a disappointment to you. . . .

Although Auchinleck's job would be trimmed down when the new South-East Asia Command was set up, it would still remain enormous. Until that happened, he was still overall commander of the Burma theatre, and in addition he was C-in-C of the Army and the RAF in India, and of the Royal Indian Navy and the Royal Indian Air Force. His responsibility as C-in-C also extended to the administrative needs of Indian units serving overseas. He would have no field command, however – nor would he ever again.

Almost at once he was confronted with requests to perform tasks beyond the resources available at the time, requests stemming from the Allied conference held the previous January in Washington. One such called on him to arrange that Chinese efforts against the Japanese in Burma should be sustained by a massive air lift to Chungking, another insisted that there should be a British offensive into Northern Burma as soon as possible, backed by supporting operations along the west coast of Burma.

The first of these, which was American-inspired, seemed comparatively easy. The American sponsors of the idea, however, had at that time underrated 'the Hump', the mountain barrier between India and China which formed a major hazard to heavily laden aircraft. The second, the Burma offensive, required the establishment and maintenance of an adequate supply line from India or it would be starved and beaten. In any event the offensive would not be possible until 1944 at the earliest, and could not be staged at all if British efforts were fragmented in minor coastal operations. Auchinleck signalled these qualifications to the Chiefs of Staff on 2 July, and followed the message with an even less optimistic report on the 22nd. Churchill reacted angrily, and the old pattern of relationship seemed once more established.

Into the background of these plans came various natural disasters of the type for which India is all too well known, beginning in the summer of 1943. The Bengal famine, caused by the failure of the harvest, the loss of rice supplies from Burma, and Churchill's decision to switch a large part of supply shipping destined for the Indian Ocean to the Mediterranean theatre, killed more than a million people; while floods to the north-west of Calcutta, in part a cause of the famine, exacerbated the disaster by virtue of the fact that the waters washed away railways and roads along which relief might otherwise have arrived in time. The floods also greatly hampered construction vital to an offensive in Burma. There is never a disaster all over India at the same time, and one of the greatest achievements of British rule had been the establishment of an early-warning system of potential famine, and of the means to transport food supplies from other areas. By this system many a famine has been averted, but in 1943 the system did not function properly.

The resulting hardship and chaos made the planning of military operations more difficult than ever, but delays in the projected Burma offensive were not likely to be received very sympathetically by Churchill. He had been greatly impressed by Brigadier Orde Wingate's daring Chindit expedition of February–May 1943. This had taken seven battalions (described as '77 Brigade') into the jungle of Northern Burma and cut the Japanese supply lines, carrying out local attacks and demolitions, and thus creating great dislocation and havoc. It was a heart-warming feat, though in terms of material gains against the cost – 818 killed, wounded or captured – the credit balance was a narrow one. This type of intrepid and unorthodox raiding was warmly acclaimed by Churchill who had little enthusiasm for cautious, long-prepared, steam-roller tactics, and its effect on the morale of troops in Burma, who had suffered heavily since 1941, was considerable. The first Chindit expedition had been mounted under Wavell's auspices, before Auchinleck took over; Wingate, however, left a trail of disruption behind him in more places than one. He was possessed of a genius for this style of fighting, but throughout his career in Palestine and Ethiopia he had demonstrated a special gift for making enemies of potential friends. Yet, though he exasperated many people, he could win over others, and there were those in high places who felt that a few more Wingates would enable the Allies to win the war more efficiently and swiftly. These included Churchill, Mountbatten, Wavell and Slim. In August 1943, as we shall see,

Churchill took Wingate with him to the 'Quadrant' talks in Quebec, and was much impressed by the soldier's ideas on warfare in Burma, and also by his outspoken opinions of his seniors and of the Indian Army.

When Auchinleck took over his new post he found that Wingate had created almost as much dislocation behind his own lines as he had behind the Japanese. Richard Rhodes James, who was a cipher officer in the second Chindit expedition (March–June 1944), said of Wingate:

> He acted as if an order from him was sufficient to rule the world. Personal contact with Wingate was a bewildering experience. The untidy wispy beard, the atrocious hat, the harsh ungracious voice which sounded like the grating of stone against stone. I remember considering seriously with my brother officers the question Is he Mad?

For several reasons the war in the Far East had never caught the public imagination like the campaigns in other parts of the world (to this day Slim's victorious Fourteenth Army is often referred to as the 'Forgotten Army'). It was possible for the average newspaper reader to understand the dashes back and forth across the desert, the naval and convoy battles, the bombing offensive and even the campaign in Italy; the Far East war, however, occupied too large an area, and was too complicated, involving China, Indochina, Malaya, Burma, India, the East Indies and the oceans. Burma, where the Japanese had scored major successes demoralising to Britain, was not easy to find on a map and, even when the amateur strategist found it, the peculiar shape of the country made any military moves exceptionally difficult to understand. Then, suddenly, Wingate, a bizarre, piratical figure, had shown the world that he could not only beat the Japanese at their own game where, seemingly, others had failed, he could make fools of them too – or so it looked. Small wonder, then, that not only Churchill was dazzled by his appearance on the scene – others took up the cry for more of his type.

Wingate did not stop at military success, however. Despite having been given all the help and co-operation from

India he had asked for, he wrote a report in July 1943 which was highly critical of GHQ, India and of the Indian Army, and which suggested that Burma could be won by Chindit operations alone. Before any of its criticisms could be seen or commented on by those concerned he sent a copy to Amery, who disapproved of the report but passed it on to Churchill. Since it confirmed Churchill's suspicion that GHQ, India was at that time as overstaffed and lethargic as he considered Cairo to have been, and probably worse, he immediately decided that new blood was needed in the area. He suggested that Lt-Gen. Sir Oliver Leese, at that time in Sicily following the Anglo-American landings there of 9 July, should be the overall commander for the Burma theatre, and that Wingate should be Commander-in-Chief of the Burma Army:

There is no doubt [he wrote to Ismay on 24 July] that in the welter of inefficiency and lassitude which has characterised our operations on the Indian Front, this man, his force and his achievements, stand out and no more question of seniority must obstruct the advance of real personalities to their proper stations in war.

On the strength of this Wingate was summoned to London, and from there taken to attend the 'Quadrant' Conference in Quebec. Although nothing had been decided officially at this stage, Rear-Admiral Lord Louis Mountbatten, Chief of Combined Operations, also accompanied Churchill to Quebec. Wingate was now in the favourable position of being the chief authority on the Far East, and particularly on Burma; nobody with Far Eastern experience was present to modify the Wingate viewpoint before the Joint Planning Staff, the most senior commanders from Britain and the United States. He proposed an exciting strategy of Long Range Penetration Groups (eight were envisaged) which would enter enemy territory and live off their own resources and the land, and which would slice the Japanese opposition to ribbons. It was proposed, somewhat grudgingly, that conventional forces would follow them in, but chiefly the LRPGs would rely on supply from the air. They would, of course, require considerable numbers of men, mules and transport and, not least, aircraft to deliver and supply them. The general plan thus settled to the satisfaction of Churchill, the Chiefs of Staff and Wingate, it was communicated to Auchinleck for comment on any administrative problems on 14 August. Auchinleck, happily, was not aware at the time that in addressing the Combined Chiefs of Staff on the 17th Wingate had described the Indian Army as 'that system of outdoor relief'.

Not surprisingly, in his reply of 19 August Auchinleck pointed out that, whatever disruption and destruction the LRPGs might achieve, all would be nullified if there were no army to occupy the areas they had penetrated and then withdrawn from. But as the manpower and other requirements of the LRPGs on the proposed scale would be very great, the main army would be so depleted that it would be unable to perform its own task of occupying the required territory. Auchinleck was insistent that there must be an effective follow-up, for he realised – as many others did not – that any Burmese in the areas penetrated by the LRPGs would suffer severely from the Japanese if the latter re-occupied the former LRPG areas; reprisals would not be concerned with details such as proof. However, he could see considerable value in LRPG operations if they were on a realistically smaller scale. Eight columns could still be produced but adapted in size to logistical possibilities. Expansion could be made when the 81st and 82nd West African Divisions arrived; the first of these had already been trained for jungle warfare.

This reply, setting out Auchinleck's view, was delivered in Quebec at a moment when the conference was particularly testy. There were divergences of opinion about the strategy for Europe, but there at least the objectives were the same. When it came to the Far East, however, the situation was bedevilled by the American feeling that they had a special relationship with and responsibility for China (an illusion rudely shattered when China became Communist in 1948), and that they themselves were not in South-East Asia to restore moribund and illegal colonialism. The British, on the other hand, felt that a considerable effort must be made to restore their country's prestige in an area where formerly they had been so highly respected, while the Chinese were almost completely occupied with internal problems. The American leaders at the Conference thought that the Chinese might be able to send an expeditionary force to help in Burma. Auchinleck felt that this was highly unlikely; if, by a near-miracle, it did happen he doubted whether it would be effective.

Needless to say, Wingate, who by this time was the accepted authority on all strategy east of Suez, was asked for his reactions to Auchinleck's reply. Also needless to say, perhaps, he confirmed Churchill's view that Auchinleck was still playing the caution game: the fact that there were a million soldiers in India, of one sort or another, suggested that once more there was an unhealthy lack of offensive spirit.

As it happened, Auchinleck was in sympathy with the idea of Long Range Penetration Groups, providing they were properly organised and did not upset every other plan in the theatre. At this point, however, a change in the command arrangements meant that such operations would no longer be his responsibility. Although Wingate's ambitious plan was approved in principle, it would be conducted from HQ South-East Asia Command, not GHQ, India. On 24 August, during the 'Quadrant' Conference, SEAC came into being, under a Supreme Allied Commander, with responsibility for conducting operations in Burma, Thailand, Malaya and Sumatra, while the C-in-C, India's responsibilities would extend only to the administration of India in support of these operations. The Supreme Allied Commander would be British, and for this post Mountbatten was chosen. His Deputy was to be American and to this Lt-Gen. Joseph Stilwell, commanding the predominantly Chinese Army in North Burma, was appointed. Stilwell, whose disposition had earned him the nickname 'Vinegar Joe' from his compatriots, detested everyone and everything British, so the auguries did not appear too promising. (Indeed, within a year Stilwell had quarrelled with everyone except Auchinleck, whom he urged to visit him in America.)

In early September Auchinleck and Mountbatten, who

had met previously, exchanged cordial telegrams, each looking forward to a fruitful and co-operative association – later events would make that 'fruitful' appear very ironic.

Although Auchinleck's post was now some way removed from the active soldiering which he liked and at which he excelled – indeed, with the creation of SEAC his last chance of active service had disappeared – it had many agreeable compensations. His residence in New Delhi was outstandingly gracious and attractive (it is now the official residence of the Prime Minister of India), and GHQ, India was in the equally fine Secretariat Buildings. Auchinleck's Private Secretary was Lt-Col. Robin Ridgeway, his British ADC was Captain Ronald Hamilton, and he appointed as Indian ADC Captain Nawabzada Murtaza Ali Khan, the son of the Nawab of Rampur. With very few exceptions Auchinleck would only have on his staff officers who had been down-graded medically as being unfit for front-line service. Thus his personal medical officer was Major Christopher St Johnston, who had been taken off the Burma draft after severe recurrent malaria.

Within three months of taking up his appointment Auchinleck was writing to Brooke requesting that Indian units in the Middle East should now be returned to India, unlikely though it was that this wish would be met. His reason was that their experience was needed for training the new divisions in India, urgently needed for the campaign in Burma. He gave a survey of the resources of the Indian Army and pointed out that although on paper it included some two million men, only a quarter of that number was available for deployment in Burma and on the Frontier. This figure did not include those on active service in the Middle East, Persia, Iraq and Italy.

As expected, the C-in-C, India's responsibilities were mainly directed to supplying the needs of SEAC. Even so, Auchinleck found his task tremendously interesting and stimulating. He travelled extensively, in which he was helped considerably by the fact that he now had his own aeroplane. Wherever he went he impressed, and to this day people whom he met express the surprise they felt on realising how much he understood about them and the jobs they were doing. The fact that he was complete master of several languages never failed to astonish. He would have been a god-like figure to many had he not so clearly demonstrated that he was so approachable, so human. He found that the Indian Army, which had been considerably disturbed by Kitchener's changes during his own early period of service, had now settled down to the different organisation and seemed well pleased with it. He himself suggested that a few of the more cumbersome military titles should be shortened, and pressed for the Military Medal to be made available to the Indian Army, a suggestion approved in 1943, to his great satisfaction. (The Military Medal is an award for junior ranks for courage in face of the enemy; sergeants are awarded the Distinguished Conduct Medal, and warrant officers and officers the Military Cross on the same basis.)

But elsewhere the situation was not so happy. By the beginning of 1944 Churchill and the War Cabinet had decided that the danger of a Japanese invasion of India was now over, and thus that keeping a huge number of men under arms in India was an unnecessary expense. There was some truth in this view, but in so far as it underrated the contribution that India had made and would continue to make to the Fourteenth Army in Burma, as well as to the other theatres, it seemed a little premature. When, early in 1943, Slim had begun his fight back in Burma there were desperate shortages of everything from food to medical staff, and the result had been a series of defeats by inferior numbers. These failures had angered Churchill, and were one of the chief causes for the reorganisation of the High Command in South-East Asia. There were in addition very special problems connected with jungle warfare which were not appreciated at home – fortunately they were appreciated by Auchinleck. His experience in the First World War had taught him what disease and bad conditions can do to the fighting potential of an army. As many diseases are related to a poor or unsuitable diet, the improvement of rations was given immediate priority. (It is extraordinary how long the belief that men can remain fit on bully beef and biscuits has survived; throughout history army food has usually been chosen because it was portable rather than palatable.) Anti-malarial precautions were also given top priority, as were the treatment of other diseases and the care of the wounded. The best assessment of the situation obtaining when Auchinleck took over came from the receiving end. In *Defeat into Victory*, his war memoirs, Slim wrote:

My second great problem was health. In 1943 for every man evacuated with wounds we had one hundred and twenty evacuated sick. The annual malaria rate alone was 84 per cent per annum of the total strength of the army and still higher among the forward troops. Next to malaria came a high incidence of dysentery, followed in this gruesome order of precedence by skin diseases and a mounting tide of mite or jungle typhus, a peculiarly fatal disease. At this time the sick rate of men evacuated from their units rose to over twelve thousand a day. A simple calculation showed me that in a matter of months at this rate my army would have melted away. Indeed it was doing so under my eyes.

On the food supplies Slim said:

Something vigorous would have to be done to avoid disaster. Luckily, General Auchinleck was the man to do it. There was a considerable and prompt injection into the Indian administrative machine, military and civil. Even at the beginning of 1944 the results of Auchinleck's drive began to show. Gradually, with now and then a temporary setback, our rations and reserves climbed up and up. It was a good day for us when he took command of India, our main base, recruiting area, and training ground. The Fourteenth Army, from its birth to final victory, owed much to his unselfish support and never-failing understanding. Without him and what he and the army in India did for us we could not have existed, let alone conquered.

Slim considered that he himself had made tactical errors in March 1944 by 'mistiming the withdrawal of the

17th Division from Tiddim and underestimating the strength of the Japanese thrust at Kohima'. He went on to say: 'These errors would have been disastrous but for the way in which, supported by the Supreme Commander [Mountbatten] and General Auchinleck, General Giffard* sent so speedily to my rescue reinforcements from India.'

Morale, as everyone on the spot knew very well, was not helped by the fact that the soldiers of Slim's Fourteenth Army knew themselves as 'the Forgotten Army'. Rain, insects, heat and disease made life irksome enough, but the worst factor was the suspicion that everybody else in the war was better supplied, better equipped, better regarded at home and having a better time than the soldiers of 'the Forgotten Army'. One outstanding problem was the belief that wives and sweethearts were consoling themselves with Americans, Poles and Free French, or even with German and Italian prisoners of war, while erratic mail deliveries added to the frustration felt by soldiers who had been in Burma for three or four years with no home leave. When their plight was realised in Britain the official response was that long service overseas without home leave was due to the inefficiency of India Command. The British Government therefore decided to repatriate all soldiers who had been more than three years and eight months overseas, thus irretrievably weakening forces in the Far East. Auchinleck responded briskly to this, and to the slander, in a letter to the Viceroy, Wavell, written in December 1944. He accused the Secretary of State for War (Sir James Grigg) and the Adjutant-General of blaming India Command unfairly for matters which were not within its control:

> I know this is a serious accusation to make, and I would not make it did I not think that something must be done to check this tendency, which promises to make my own situation as C-in-C extremely difficult if not impossible. . . .

* General Sir George Giffard, C-in-C Eleventh Army Group in South-East Asia, 1943–4.

236

If it is necessary for this purpose to retain officers and men beyond the period fixed by the War Office for their repatriation, then this must be done and HMG must accept the necessity, or acquiesce, in the retardation of operations against the enemy and the probable prolongation of the war. They cannot have it both ways and the responsibility is theirs, not yours or mine, or the Supreme Allied Commander's.

It was an invidious position. If men were withdrawn from operational units the drive would inevitably slow down. If they were not, the Home Government and the War Office would blame India Command. SEAC, although just as closely concerned, seemed to escape criticism.

Auchinleck put the situation forcibly:

It is, I think, imperative that the public in the United Kingdom should be authoritatively informed with the least possible delay of the true situation, which, to put it briefly, is that war cannot be carried on without men and that trained leaders and soldiers cannot be taken away without proper replacement from formations engaged with the enemy without jeopardising the success of the operation in progress.

Having one's actions and motives misunderstood by those in Britain was no new experience for Auchinleck, but it became no easier with repetition. Fortunately Mountbatten appreciated the position and said so. He referred constantly to the enormous debt SEAC owed to India Command and on more than one occasion criticised the Home Government for its attitude towards India.

By now the end of the war was, it seemed, in sight, although, as most people appreciated, there could be delays and setbacks – as indeed occurred in December 1944 in the European theatre, with the German counterattack in the Ardennes. But whatever happened in Europe, where a successful conclusion looked likely within the next year, it was obvious to all in the Far East that much long and bitter fighting would be involved before the Japanese surrendered. Fourteenth Army opened a new offensive in December 1944 and by 7 March 1945 had captured Mandalay. On 1 April the Americans began invading Okinawa, an island only some 400 miles from Japan itself. These were encouraging events, but there was nothing in them to lead anyone to believe that the conquest of Japan would still not require a costly fight, probably lasting another year. During that time SEAC would be launching an invasion of Malaya, while the Americans would invade Japan itself. Subsequently, after the surrender of Japan on 14 August, the invasion of Malaya was carried out as planned, but as a military exercise and without opposition. Those who took part were extremely relieved that the 'invasion' had not taken place in wartime, as the cost would have been high. With the European war over, the pressure to employ newly trained arrivals rather than battle-hardened troops in such an invasion would have been hard to resist, and in consequence the casualty rates would have been appalling. The Japanese had mined every important road and bridge and would have defended each key point with kamikaze-minded troops – if Malaya was thus defended the cost of finally defeating Japan in such battles may be imagined. Fortunately, it never happened that way and the war, which would probably have caused a further million Allied casualties, ended after atomic bombs were dropped on Hiroshima and Nagasaki on 6 and 9 August respectively. Horrifying though those were, the total number killed was many, many times less than would have died had the war been fought to a finish with an invasion of the Japanese mainland.

General Sir Claude Auchinleck, GCB, GCIE, CSI, DSO, OBE, Commander-in-Chief in India, ended the war a victor, if a neglected one. His direction and energy had channelled the resources of India to achieve a striking success against a tenacious, brave and at times fanatical enemy; he would now turn back to that continent in a task that would bring him little joy. He had commanded fearlessly and well in Norway in an impossible situation; his forces in North Africa had been badly defeated between Gazala and Mersa Matruh and, for his choice of subordinates and his failure to interfere in the battle early enough, he had been blamed for these defeats. But between November 1941 and January 1942 he drove the legendary Rommel back out of Cyrenaica with considerable speed, and in July 1942, when Egypt, the Canal, and the only effective British army in existence all seemed lost, he stopped Rommel cold, brought the will to resist back to an exhausted and demoralised army, and laid the foundations for a decisive victory which would not be his.

Auchinleck was careful of his men's lives, obstinate where his strategic sense told him to be so, and largely uncaring of the opinions of others. These qualities had cost him two battles, one against a great politician bearing an almost intolerable burden, the other, unknowingly, against a gifted soldier whose reputation owes much to Auchinleck's generalship. It seems a poor reward for distinguished service, though, typically, he would never complain of it.

15

A CHANGED WORLD

During 1945 it was clear that whatever happened elsewhere there would be ferment in India with the approach of independence (it had been decided that, after the war, India would be granted Dominion status). Not least of the subjects of pressing importance was the future of the Indian Army under whatever new constitution might be provided for India, and a problem which had to be settled at an early stage was the position of the Gurkhas. The Gurkhas had always been included in the Indian Army, although they have a special status as Nepal is not, of course, a part of India. The question was whether the Gurkhas should continue with the Indian Army or whether they should be taken out of it altogether, to serve as part of the British Army establishment. To the Indians Nepal is a foreign country and the Gurkhas foreigners. On the other hand, any future Indian government would hope to remain on terms of the closest friendship and co-operation with the Gurkhas.

Auchinleck set out the pros and cons in a lengthy document in March 1945, and was summoned to Whitehall to discuss it in April. It was a time of flux in Britain and for many the German surrender on 7 May, signifying the end of the war in Europe, was taken as the end of the entire war. A general election was to be held on 5 July, although Churchill had proposed to the Labour members of the coalition that it should be postponed until the Japanese had been defeated. On 14 June Wavell, as Viceroy, published the proposals for constitutional changes in India.

The importance of the Army in Indian life meant that the Commander-in-Chief would be involved in the constitutional changes as much as the Viceroy. It was a new and delicate area and not one for which Auchinleck had much liking. And it was not the best possible moment for a man to be losing his wife, though that was what was now happening. Almost incredibly, it does not seem to have affected his judgement. We shall return to this later.

The political problems of India were made the more intractable by the fact that they were fundamentally religious. The majority of the population – over 400 million people – was Hindu, but there was also a powerful Muslim element, at the time numbering in the region of 76 million. In accordance with the accepted principles of assisting constitutional development in the countries of the British Empire, there had in the past been a series of conferences to decide the future of the Indian sub-continent. These extended back to 1773, when Lord North's Regulating Act had established that British rule in India, administered by the East India Company, should be carried on in the name of the Crown. North's Act had followed the acquittal of Robert Clive on charges of corruption and had preceded that of Warren Hastings, Governor-General of India from 1774 to 1785, who, though arbitrary in method, had devoted much of his energies to trying to implement the justice which he was accused of defying. In the early days there had been considerable doubt about the political activities of the commercial East India Company.

Although subsequent legislation had been passed to ensure that India was governed fairly, the British had been considerably surprised by the Mutiny of 1857. It was not perhaps realised that this had been limited to a rising of the sepoys of the Bengal Army and that the Madras and Bombay Armies had remained loyal, as had the Sikhs, but savagery on both sides had left a legacy of resentment and mistrust. The consequent India Act of 1858 established a Secretary of State for India in London, and a Viceroy in Delhi to represent the Crown in India, and thus transferred administrative power from the Company to the British Government. To be appointed Viceroy a man had to be of high rank and great capacity.

There had been numerous benefits from British rule in India: the progress against disease, barbaric practices, famine, had all been associated with better medicine and hygiene, better education, and better irrigation and transport. But attempts to unify India had run into considerable difficulties from such matters as religion, language, caste, and the position of the Princes.* Even so, by 1935 a promising and workable Government of India Act had been passed, giving India a federal constitution to which the Princely States would be subject. The outbreak of the Second World War had suspended constitutional development, but India and its resources had clearly played a major part in the Allied victory.

'India' was a concept difficult to grasp; those who did not know the country suspected that it was a place where pompous British subjects with an overstretched idea of their own importance lorded over a naive and poverty-stricken people; those who did know India were passionately fond of it yet slightly frightened by its complexity, dangers and intractability. Life in India for these last was congenial and often elegant, and they despised the views of those ignorant of the country and its problems. Few people realised the enormous size of the sub-continent, which is roughly equivalent to an area from mid-Atlantic to Moscow and the Arctic Circle to the Mediterranean. In addition, India was a country where violence of one sort or another always seemed near the surface, where the most peaceful scene might easily obscure imminent danger. There had been examples in the past of how quickly trouble could suddenly erupt, and in 1945, although, despite a certain amount of unrest, there seemed to be nothing particularly dangerous in the offing, those who knew the country felt that unless some political progress was seen to be made, India could be the centre of great trouble. The fact that, in the past, India had been governed by an absurdly small body of officials, backed by a similarly small army, was no reason to suppose that the process could continue indefinitely.

Yet there were grounds for optimism. Hindu and Muslim had learned to live side by side and in friendship.

---

* The Princely States (sometimes Native States) were semi-autonomous states with their own ruler, usually a prince or maharajah, and with which Britain had treaties, unlike the Provinces, which were administered by a British Governor. In practice, most of the Princely States had a British Resident *in situ*, to advise and, if necessary, to mitigate some of the Princes' more feudal methods. Even after Partition and Independence, the Princes could wield considerable power.

Given time, an Indian Government might see members of the two religions working together in harmony. The Sikh faith contained elements of both Hindu and Muslim religions; it remained to be seen whether that would make them tolerant. The best augury for the future was the army, in whose regiments members of different tribes and different religions worked and fought in harmony. Clearly the army would have a vital stabilising part to play in the new India; it would serve as an example, and as an important peace-keeper.

The Indian National Congress had originally, in 1885, been formed primarily as an association to educate Indians for government posts, and became almost an unofficial parliament. It was not initially anti-British, but opposition from Curzon made it a centre for the ventilation of grievances against the imperial power. At first the Muslims had opposed Congress but in 1916 the Muslim League, originally a religious and cultural movement founded in 1906, agreed to work with it. In 1920 Congress was completely dominated by Gandhi, and continued to be even after he officially retired from both Congress and politics in 1934. As early as November 1939 there were active protests that the British had failed to define their war aims adequately, and the Viceroy's declaration in August 1940 that as soon as the war was over the British government intended to bring in a constitution formed by Indians did not have the effect hoped for. A month after this declaration Gandhi had launched a Civil Disobedience campaign, suggesting that certain individuals, selected by him, should repeat anti-war slogans in public. This, however, proved ineffective. In March 1942 Sir Stafford Cripps had gone out to India (after visiting Auchinleck in Cairo on the way, as has been mentioned) and had taken with him firm proposals for the programming of the new legislation. These measures had been rejected by Congress, which had then sanctioned a non-violent protest. Non-violent protests (which Gandhi had used to some effect in 1919) had, in 1942, led to riots in which some 600 people were killed, and for a time Gandhi himself was imprisoned. Subsequently he suspended the *Satyagraha* (literally 'soul force') campaign of passive resistance, but the damage had been done. All this was happening when India was in danger of being invaded by the Japanese, whose armies had crossed Burma and whose fleet had a menacing presence in the Indian Ocean.

Subsequently there was a considerable strengthening of the Muslim League, which had been led since 1934 by the active and uncompromising Mohammed Ali Jinnah. It had had three years, from 1942–5, to extend its influence when the Congress leaders had been imprisoned for refusal to support British authority over India's entry into the war, since Indian opinion had not been consulted, and following the Civil Disobedience and 'Quit India' campaigns they had instituted. Jinnah had vastly increased his standing by adopting a pro-British stance during the war; now his rallying cry was for Muslim separation and independence – for a new Muslim state. This was to be Pakistan, a six-province country comprising the chiefly Muslim areas, and including the North-West Frontier and Bengal.

When Wavell brought back the proposals for Indian Dominion status, to take effect when the war ended, it soon became obvious that Jinnah would remain inflexible in his demands. The concept of Dominion status had been used effectively since the British North America Act gave Canada conditional self-governing status in 1867. There it had been designed to protect a minority, and also to allow for modification in the future. Subsequently, Dominion status had been granted to Australia, New Zealand and South Africa – 'The Crown', it was said, 'was the Keystone of the Arch of Empire.' Clearly it was not going to be a concept which Jinnah would accept, as he showed to the All-Party Conference in June 1945. But while, in July, the Conference was in a state of deadlock, the results of the election in Britain were declared. The Labour Party came into power, with Clement Attlee as Prime Minister. Attlee had been a member of the Indian Statutory Commission sent out to India in 1927 under the chairmanship of Sir John Simon; its brief was to examine the workings of the 1919 Government of India Act and make suitable recommendations. He was hardly likely to have forgotten the bitter resentment caused by the fact that there had been no Indians on the commission. In the new British government Cripps, who had worked hard to solve India's problems, was not immediately concerned with them, though now, as President of the Board of Trade, he was likely to be made aware of them. The new Secretary of State for India and Burma, replacing Amery, was F. W. Pethick-Lawrence, an Old Etonian; he was promptly made a baron. His socialist convictions were in no doubt (he had been sentenced to imprisonment in 1912 for his part in a Suffragette demonstration), but his abilities as an administrator and diplomat seemed open to question.

It seemed reasonably clear, in view of the philosophy of the current British government, that democratic constitutions for former colonies would be arranged as soon as possible, although it was perhaps not widely realised at the time that this would mean that within three years India and Pakistan would be separated, Ceylon become a Dominion, and Burma leave the Commonwealth altogether.

Auchinleck's immediate concern was, however, more practical than that of the parliamentary theorists. On 26 July 1945 he had written to Wavell pointing out the possible sequence of evils when demobilisation began to discharge large numbers of soldiers who had become used to good administration, a higher standard of living than they had known before joining the army, and a critical attitude towards civil management. The fact that corruption in civil administration was widespread was not likely to pass without comment by the soldiers, or even action. Auchinleck could see great possibilities for good if those who had learnt to take responsibility in the army were able to continue to do so once they returned to civil life; if they could not and they felt that their standard of living was being kept unnecessarily low by the lethargy, incompetence and even corruption of government officials then there was bound to be trouble. He suggested that these problems should be examined for long-term solutions rather than short-term expedients.

On 22 August he followed this with a further letter to

the Viceroy in which he considered the possible future of a British Army in India. He felt that there could be no justification for the retention of purely British units on Indian soil. In the past this had been necessary, but times had changed; the only reason for such units to be there at all would be when they were engaged in joint activities with the Indian Army.

But the question of British personnel serving with Indian Army units was a different matter, even though in the long term these British soldiers might well also go.

But even while these moderate statements were being made, a new and highly emotional turn was about to be given to concepts about the Indian Army, arising from what was known as the Indian National Army.

In February 1942, when the Japanese captured Singapore, nearly 60,000 Indians became prisoners of war. Many had been separated from their original units, or had had officers or NCOs killed, and thus went into captivity lacking any guidance of what to expect, and how to behave. They were completely bewildered by this outcome, being totally unlike the 33,000 Allied personnel who had been surrendered at Tobruk and the 250,000 Germans and Italians who would later become prisoners of war in Tunisia. The Japanese promptly separated the Indian troops from their officers and mixed up the units; most then found themselves among other Indians to whom they were strangers and could well be hostile. Even so, over half then put up with everything the Japanese inflicted on them in the way of beatings, starvation, untreated disease, humiliation, and blandishment. The fact that they were Indians – subjects of the hated Imperialists – did not make them less susceptible to the rigours of captivity by the Japanese. Some 25,000, however, were deceived by their captors into believing that if they joined the Japanese they would be assisting in the Co-Prosperity Sphere for South-East Asia, from which India would obtain almost unlimited benefits. They therefore agreed to serve with what was called by the Japanese 'The Indian National Army'. Their first leader was a Sikh officer, Mohan Singh, but when he realised that the Japanese had no intention of keeping their promises he resigned, being replaced by a Cambridge-educated Bengali, Subhas Chandra Bose. Bose was a man of some spirit and attainment; he had quarrelled with Gandhi on the policy of non-violence, believed that a decisive, uncompromising approach was needed for the future of India, and had visited Moscow, Berlin and Tokyo. In October 1943, under Japanese aegis, he had set up the Government of Free India (Azad Hind) in Tokyo, with himself in the leading roles as Head of State, Commander-in-Chief and Foreign Minister. He appointed a Cabinet, declared war upon Britain and the United States, and distributed ambassadors to Germany, Italy, Japan and countries under their control. The Japanese, however, would not allow him to have more than 16,000 soldiers in the INA; the rest were discharged to be prisoners of war again. A further 4000 had resigned with Mohan Singh, but fresh volunteers were found from Indians living in Malaya and Singapore. Eventually about 15,000 were embodied in one division and sent to Burma and Assam, but as the Japanese allowed them nothing but rifles to fight with, their potential usefulness was heavily restricted. Their record was inglorious: they won no battles, 750 were killed (of which only three were officers), 5000 deserted, 1500 died of disease and the remainder were captured.

The Japanese attempted to make the maximum propaganda out of these oppressed Indians striving to liberate their country, but as their existence was scarcely known in India this merely caused scepticism. Bose was killed in an air crash on Formosa (Taiwan) on 18 August 1945, while on his way to Tokyo after the Japanese surrender, but his death gave events an unexpected turn. This leaderless rabble, as they now were, could be used as a symbol by an astute politician, whereas had Bose still been alive this would not have been possible. The ex-soldiers of the INA, many of them now imprisoned, soon found a champion in Nehru, himself only recently released from prison along with the other Congress leaders. Although the Government announced that the INA leaders only would stand trial, the rest going free, Congress decided to give passionate support to the principle that there should be no recriminations against those who had worked for 'the freedom of India'. The Congress view was not, of course, shared by the Indian Army, all of whose members regarded the INA with contempt, dislike or pity. When it was announced that initially three INA officers would be court martialled, Nehru and Congress came out in indignant condemnation of the idea. There was, in fact, no reason for exonerating the three officers concerned, for they all held the King's Commission, in other words, British commissions instead of Viceroy's Commissions. (Viceroy Commissioned Officers [VCOs] were of a lower status, and were not entitled to be saluted by British soldiers as KCOs were.) Not least of the offences of which the three men were accused was that of using brutal methods to try to persuade other Indians to join the INA. Despite this, however, an INA Defence Committee quickly came into being, and in February 1946 there was considerable rioting in Calcutta in favour of the release of imprisoned INA soldiers.

Auchinleck's attitude was that, while he very much regretted that the Japanese had been able to suborn any members of the Indian Army, their fate was one for their own countrymen to decide. He therefore urged that their courts martial should be postponed until after the next elections – a matter of some six months: then the Indians themselves would have full responsibility in the matter.

However, the Government decided to proceed, and the trials began on 5 November 1945 at the Red Fort in Delhi. The defence alleged that the officers were entirely correct in their actions, which were motivated by a desire for the liberation of India. Extremists noted that this 'persecution' of patriotic Indians was a golden opportunity for making anti-British propaganda, and swept to one side the counter-argument that the INA had acted against loyal Indians. Obviously, if the three officers were found guilty and executed they would be the matrys for whom the extremists were looking; their value would be incalculable.

In the event, the three were found guilty and sentenced to transportation for life, to being cashiered, and to forfeiture of pay and allowance due for the time they had served with the Japanese. The judgements were passed to the Commander-in-Chief for confirmation. On 1 January 1946 he remitted the sentence of transportation and confirmed the other judgements, and later trials gave lesser offenders prison sentences. It was a difficult decision, for whatever he decided to do would be considered wrong by many, and would be twisted by others to make anti-British propaganda. Some interpreted it as showing that the Raj was on trial, perhaps was itself guilty, but others felt that Auchinleck had shown that mixture of wisdom and clemency which is usually described as statesmanship. The C-in-C went on to set out his views and reasons in a memorandum circulated to the army commanders throughout South-East Asia. He pointed out that the shock of the fall of Singapore had had a great effect on the average Indian soldier, that the removal of the officers to whom he looked for guidance had bewildered him, and that he had been subjected to skilful and persuasive arguments. Auchinleck felt, with one eye on future INA trials, that to have confirmed the sentence of 'transportation for life' might have led to widespread riots and uprisings; besides he considered that the faults did not lie entirely with the Indians. He said:

> There is no excuse for the regular officers who went over, beyond the fact that the early stages of 'Indianisation' [a policy which Auchinleck had first met as DCGS in India in 1936] from its inception to the beginning of the late war were badly mismanaged by the British Government of India and this prepared the ground for disloyalty when the opportunity came.
>
> There is little doubt that 'Indianisation' was at its inception looked upon as a political expedient which was bound to fail militarily. There is no doubt also that many senior British officers believed and even hoped it would fail.
>
> The policy of segregation of Indian officers into separate units, the differential treatment in respect of pay and terms of service as compared with the British officer and the prejudice and lack of manners by some – by no means all – British officers and their wives, all went to produce a very deep and bitter feeling of racial

discrimination in the minds of the most intelligent and progressive of the Indian officers, who were naturally Nationalists, keen to see India standing on her own legs and not to be ruled by Whitehall for ever.

It is no use shutting one's eyes to the fact that any Indian officer worth his salt is a Nationalist though this does not mean, as I have said before, that he is necessarily anti-British. If he is anti-British this is as often as not due to his faulty handling and treatment by his British officer comrades.

It is essential for the preservation of future unity that this fact should be fully understood by all British officers.

No Indian officer must be regarded as suspect and disloyal merely because he is what is called a 'Nationalist', or in other words, a good Indian.

The letter, Auchinleck ordered, was not to be quoted as the official statement of the Commander-in-Chief, but its contents could be made known. His concluding words were:

Finally let me again state the object; it is to maintain the reliability, stability and efficiency of the Indian Army for the future, whatever government may be set up in India.

In the end fourteen other ex-members of the INA were sent for trial in April, before the C-in-C discontinued further proceedings. In May 1946 Nehru, President of Congress, wrote to Auchinleck commenting on the INA issue. He exculpated himself from exploiting the INA trials for political reasons, and hoped that the Indian Army would not itself suffer from the recent events. He said:

I suppose everyone who has given thought to the matter realises that it is a dangerous and risky business to break the discipline of an army. It would obviously be harmful to do any injury to a fine instrument like the Indian Army and yet at every step until major changes take place converting it into a real national army we have to face the political issue which governs every aspect of Indian life today. Risks have to be taken sometimes, more especially when existing conditions are felt to be intolerable . . .

Auchinleck's reactions to this letter are not recorded, but may be imagined.

16

THE END OF AN ERA

In the Indian general elections of 1945–6 the Muslim League was strikingly successful, winning almost every seat in the Muslim areas; the results were a personal triumph for Jinnah. His rallying cry was separation from Hindu domination and the creation of a separate state of Pakistan,* comprising Baluchistan, Sind, the Punjab, Bengal, Assam and the North-West Frontier. He rejected proposals for a Pakistan without most of Assam, the Punjab and Bengal – claiming that this would be a 'maimed and moth-eaten' country. At the same time, it became noticeable that the whole country was now keener than ever to see the end of British rule. In January 1946 a British all-party parliamentary delegation had toured India and departed in no doubt of India's desire for independence at the earliest date. This visit was followed in April by a Cabinet Mission to India, led by Pethick-Lawrence, and including Cripps and A. V. Alexander, the Minister of Defence, which had as its brief the task of assisting the Viceroy in finding a solution, and taking part in discussions with him and the Indian leaders on how power could now be transferred quickly and peacefully.

Already there were signs that any form of disorder could quickly become unmanageable. In mid-January there had been strikes (not violent enough to deserve the name of mutinies) at various RAF stations, not only in India but also at other foreign stations. The causes of grievance were ostensibly slowness in demobilisation, but the origin of many seemed to lie with the British National Servicemen who, now the war was over, found themselves

* A name originally coined in 1933 by the idealist Chaudhri Rahmat Ali at Cambridge, and with which he inspired a group of young Muslims. The first four initials stand for the states sought for the Muslims: Punjab, Afghans (i.e. the Frontier Province), Kashmir, and Sind; the 'tan' stands for Baluchistan, and the whole name is said to mean 'Land of the Pure'.

engaged in apparently meaningless routine. Almost any diversion was welcome, if only as a change, to servicemen, and there was a feeling among them that now that there was a Labour government in power it would see that nobody was punished for breaches in discipline. One of the most unfortunate effects was that units which had won a high reputation during the war were now disgraced by the activities of an influx of newcomers who had no genuine motivation and no sense of responsibility. The fact that many units were in a state of constant change, caused by repatriation and new arrivals, made the situation easier for the disaffected to exploit. When, early in 1946, these troubles spread to the Royal Indian Air Force, the situation became even more emotional since the strikers declared themselves to be in sympathy with the disgraced INA.

On 18 February the mutiny spread to the Royal Indian Navy at Bombay; here the events were not merely limited to refusing to work or to parade, but included attacking officers and British soldiers as well as commandeering naval lorries. It seemed that unless swift action was taken in Bombay there would be similar outbreaks in Calcutta and Madras. Prompt measures by Lt-Gen. Sir Rob Lockhart, GOC, Southern Command, India, who used a battalion of the Mahrattas for the purpose, soon had the 3000 mutinous Indian sailors back in their quarters. The next day, however, the mutineers tried to break out and there was sharp fighting in which both sides used rifles and grenades. Lockhart had a squadron of RAF Mosquitoes fly over the scene, to show that he meant business, but the 22nd showed no improvement in the situation, and the mutineers were by now in control of the ships in the harbour and had their guns trained on the city. Lockhart thereupon trained army guns on the ships, leaving no doubt in anyone's mind as to how the situation could develop. An appeal by Admiral John Godfrey, Flag Officer Commanding, Royal Indian Navy, to the mutineers that they should surrender was rejected, but pleas by Nehru, Jinnah and Patel (a prominent Congress politician) produced a surrender on 23 February. Meanwhile, there had been a brief but bloody outbreak in

Karachi which was suppressed by force. Inevitably, civil riots and disorder followed and lasted several days. In the generally uncertain political situation the trials of the leading mutineers were lethargically pursued, and the punishments accorded them derisory.

As the army had been severely shaken by the INA issue, and as the Royal Indian Air Force and Royal Indian Navy had mutinied, it was desirable to obtain some clarification of the role expected of the services in the future of India. At this time it seemed essential to receive some declaration of intent on the future of the armed forces in India. Would British forces still be required and, if so, what conditions were the Indian Government prepared to offer? Would India agree to help elsewhere in the Commonwealth, if forces from other Commonwealth countries would agree to help in the defence of India? These and other matters needed to be resolved very soon if the armed forces were to continue without over-much disruption.

The Cabinet Mission was well aware of the urgency of the situation and in May suggested a compromise solution of a central government dealing with Foreign Affairs, Communications and Defence, and two provincial groupings, one mainly Muslim, the other mainly Hindu. The aim was, however, to preserve a united India while in some way appeasing Muslim opinion; the position of the Indian Princely States could then be negotiated separately at a later date. An Interim Government of India was proposed, to handle the running of India and what would become Pakistan until the transfer of power.

On 17 May both Wavell and Auchinleck broadcast an explanation of this plan for self-government to the nation. They appealed for patience, co-operation and stability. Meanwhile Congress pondered the proposals.

On 1 June Auchinleck was promoted Field-Marshal:

The King has been graciously pleased to approve the promotion to the rank of Field-Marshal of General Sir Claude John Eyre Auchinleck, GCB, GCIE, CSI, DSO, OBE, Indian Army, Colonel 4th Royal Inniskilling Fusiliers, Colonel 4th Bombay Grenadiers,

Aide-de-Camp General to the King, with effect from June 1, 1946.

Among the congratulations and expressions of approval, few put the situation more clearly than *The Times*:

> No appointment could have been more welcome or better merited than that of Sir Claude Auchinleck to the rank of Field-Marshal. He is acknowledged on all hands to have been one of the **greatest** Commanders-in-Chief in India in the history of that office. His period of command in the field was one in which the British forces were still inadequately equipped, but the forces under his command nevertheless managed to snatch victory at Sidi Rezegh and, though defeated in the next campaign, succeeded in barring the road to Egypt against all expectations.

There were many others. Auchinleck had reached the highest possible rank, and it was deserved. (Montgomery had been promoted Field-Marshal on 1 September 1944.) Sadly it came when there was no one who could really share his pleasure. His wife had left him for another man, he was childless, and it was all too clear that the army – the Indian Army – to which his life had been devoted was now to become the plaything of politicians. Even then, he probably did not imagine how unwelcome would be the task over which he would preside. And whatever his successes and whatever his disappointments, he would face them, as always, as a man alone.

Meanwhile Jinnah was not resting on his laurels. He accepted the Cabinet Mission's proposals on the basis that, since they included a measure of deference to Muslim autonomy, they were merely a step towards the establishment of the state of Pakistan, but within weeks rejected the proposals as unsatisfactory for Muslims. He suspected that unless the Muslim League achieved its ambition, the creation of a separate state, it would soon be put in an inferior position, and nothing Nehru said allayed Jinnah's suspicion of Hindu intentions. The Muslims were, of course, outnumbered by approximately five to one, so there was perhaps some reason for Jinnah's attitude; on the other hand, it may be remembered that his bargaining technique was the time-honoured oriental method of asking for at least half as much again as one expects to get. The Labour Government was inclined to brush to one side British experience gained from centuries of diplomatic and commercial contacts with eastern peoples, assuming that a straightforward working man's approach of putting all the cards on the table would produce a similar response – an assumption soon to prove illusory. (Just as western peoples love to think they are getting a bargain, eastern peoples enjoy the subtleties of obtaining the best price; a quick sale is as much of a disappointment to the seller, or buyer, as an easy victory at, say, tennis.) The Hindus, of course, thought Jinnah was bluffing; Jinnah knew what the Hindus thought; but those British experienced in Indian ways of thought were considered to be tainted with obsolete ideas and felt snubbed by their own officials. At any moment, in the lack of any form of progress, India could suddenly be swept by riot and massacre.

In July 1946 Auchinleck, still cherishing the hope that Partition, the splitting of a Muslim state – Pakistan – from India, could be avoided and that the Indian Army could be preserved in being as a force for law and order, as well as a strong defence against outside aggressors, produced a report summarising proposals and ideas he had received from his subordinates and combining with them thoughts of his own. The substance of it was that the development of nuclear weapons, guided missiles, chemical warfare and rapidly developing air power would make 1946 concepts of armies obsolete within a few years. This would mean the end of large bases and depots; they would be replaced by smaller ones for forces of increased mobility. Logistics would be largely a matter of air supply. For India it would be necessary to have some compact divisions, each equipped with tanks, motorised infantry, artillery and engineers; in addition there should be an airborne division. There should, he said, be a screen of Defence Groups which could hold key areas, including if necessary some in enemy territory and, in addition,

Frontier Groups which could safeguard the frontiers and take the first assaults by any enemy. Internal security would be provided by the Defence Groups except in wartime, when that function could probably be taken over by the militia. All forces except the last should be highly mobile so that they could move rapidly in and out of battle areas: 'While in action they must live hard and strike hard – otherwise they will fail and probably perish.'

At a time when many people were looking back with satisfaction at the military organisation of the Second World War and seeing it as reasonably suitable for the future, Auchinleck's paper was almost revolutionary in its thought. Many of its concepts would, however, be adopted and become commonplace over the next thirty years. Perhaps the most unfortunate effect of Auchinleck's enforced retirement from the mainstream of Allied military policy-making was that his assessment of future military needs was not appreciated enough at the time. But the splitting of India into two antagonistic countries would make his overall plan impossible. Although his ideas could have applied elsewhere, too many ambitious staff officers were sitting in conference and drawing up their own plans for them to adopt the ideas of a field-marshal who had been commissioned over half a century before.

Meanwhile, events in India were moving faster than had been anticipated. Jinnah declared that 16 August would be 'Direct Action Day', the theory being that this would be the day when the Muslim League would express its dissatisfaction with, and rejection of, the Cabinet Mission's proposals. 'Direct Action Day' was interpreted somewhat differently by the most dangerous mob elements, and Calcutta saw four days of unrestrained killing and burning. The exact death toll is not known, but undoubtedly ran into thousands, and the rioting unfortunately soon spread to other cities, notably in East Bengal and the United Provinces. The fighting was, inevitably, Muslim versus Hindu, and both groups suffered heavily, but the Indian Army, which included members of both religions working side by side, joined with British regiments to clear the corpses off the streets and helped to restore order. It was a symbol of hope for the future that the Indian Army, with its many mixed elements, could act impartially and efficiently as a civil police force in a situation so charged with emotion.

Montgomery, who had been appointed CIGS earlier in the year, and was thus now Auchinleck's senior, visited India at this time and made various comments and observations which appear in his memoirs:

> The major military problem in India was dependent on future political decisions. Wavell told me he was convinced the British would have to hand over the country to the Indians; there had been no recruitment into the civil service and we could not continue to govern it much longer. He wanted to do it gradually beginning in the south; the British Government wanted it done quickly ... I was concerned with the military repercussions of whatever plan was finally adopted. If developments resulted in civil disturbance then the military would be faced with the task of safeguarding British lives and interest; in this connection the attitude of the Indian Army would be a factor of the greatest importance.

He went on to say that he himself was very anxious to withdraw British troops from India as soon as possible so that they could be deployed elsewhere, but that Maulana Azad, the then leader of the Congress Party, since Nenru was now Vice-President of the Interim Government, was most unwilling for this to happen. After a conversation with Jinnah, Montgomery reported him as saying 'he would never tolerate Hindu rule over Muslim'. When Montgomery asked why this must be so, he said, 'How can the two lie down together, the Hindu worships the cow, I eat it.' Jinnah also said that civil war was inevitable if British troops were withdrawn.

Montgomery had 'long talks' with the Viceroy and Auchinleck, and said:

> I myself was uneasy in my mind at the treatment British troops would receive in India if and when a purely Indian government took over the reins. It seemed to me

that Auchinleck was wrapped up entirely in the Indian Army and appeared to be paying little heed to the welfare of the British soldiers in India.

It was not Montgomery's last word on India, nor on Auchinleck, for that matter. He returned to India on 23 June 1947, by which time the Partition plans had been agreed. He wrote later:

I was intensely interested in the personalities of the leaders of the two parties, Hindu and Muslim. Nehru I had not met before. He was calm and self-confident, had a marked sense of humour and was easy to deal with. We became very good friends and it was impossible not to like him. Jinnah was totally different. He was keyed up to a high state of tension; he openly expressed his deadly hatred of the Hindus, saying he would have nothing to do with them. He was deeply suspicious of being asked to share anything with the Indian Union and was determined that Pakistan should stand alone. He expressed his intense distrust of Auchinleck, and his hatred of Mountbatten [by then the Viceroy] who, he said, was 'in the pocket of Nehru'.

In his biography of Jinnah* Hector Bolitho quotes Auchinleck on the Muslim leader: 'I admired him; his tenacity and tremendous personality – his inexorable determination.' Interviewed by David Dimbleby years later, Auchinleck said of Jinnah: 'He was a definite leader ... a leader of a minority ... and therefore at a disadvantage ... Jinnah could be difficult at times. Once or twice he nearly brought about a war between India and Pakistan.'

As far as possible Auchinleck tried, as he had always tried, to keep himself clear of political matters, but it was not easy. With the knowledge that before much longer British officers would be leaving India, he encouraged subordinate commanders to pass on as much of their acquired knowledge as possible to those they surmised would succeed them. His next hurdle, in late 1946 and early 1947, was the request by the Indian government,

* *Jinnah, Creator of Pakistan* (London, 1954).

inspired by Nehru, for the release of members of the INA who were serving their sentences; this implied an amnesty not only for the INA but also for the other mutineers. He objected, as those concerned had received their sentences for various acts of brutality, including murder. In January 1947 his firm and reasoned replies, backed by Wavell, checked the demand for the time being, though the issue would rise again.

The long-awaited date for the transfer of power in India was announced by Attlee to the Commons on 20 February 1947 – 'a date not later than June 1948'. On the same day Attlee also announced that Mountbatten would now succeed Wavell as Viceroy, and would be responsible for a smooth hand-over to Indian government. Wavell's tenure of the post of Viceroy was described in the announcement as 'a wartime appointment'; it seemed a gratuitous insult in view of his distinguished service to India and to that country's struggles in war and peace.

Mountbatten's account of the arrangements for his appointment were recorded in a series of filmed interviews which were not released until after his death by terrorist action in 1979. In them he emphasised his reluctance to leave the Navy, even for a short time, and said, somewhat surprisingly, that King George VI had told him that he himself had originated the idea of his becoming Viceroy. The King, Mountbatten reported, was very worried about the position of the Indian Princes who had made treaties with him as the King-Emperor; it would therefore be a relief for the King to feel that a member of his own family would be there to keep an eye on their interests.

In March 1947 Mountbatten was given his instructions by Attlee. He was told to work for an agreement of a unitary government of India, but was also informed that if no solution had been reached by 1 October 1947 he should report on the steps which should be taken for handing over power on the due date. He was further told to impress on the Indian leaders the great importance of avoiding any breach in the continuity of the Indian Army, and of maintaining the organisation of defence on an all Indian basis. Secondly you will point out the need for continued collaboration in the security of the Indian Ocean area for which provision might be made in an agreement between the two countries. At a suitable date His Majesty's Government would be ready to send military and other experts to India to assist in discussing the terms of such an agreement.

In the proposed date for Independence Jinnah foresaw his Muslim victory, saying 'the Muslim League will not yield an inch in its demand for Pakistan' – the combination of a British government desperate to quit India and a political vacuum, backed by potential violence would, he knew, be irresistible. The coming of the Labour government, and its appointment of Mountbatten, made Partition virtually inevitable, and Jinnah sensed this.

Mountbatten, wrote to Auchinleck on 14 March:

My Dear Claude,

God knows I did everything in my power to be allowed to go back to sea. Since however the King overruled me and I am to come to India I would like you to know that the feeling I have such a true and wise friend in you makes all the difference to me.

I hope we shall see lots of each other.

Looking forward to seeing you

Dickie

Further signs of what was in store for India came in the same month. Lahore, Multan, Amritsar and Rawalpindi all saw a flare-up of violence, in which over 2000 people were killed and five times as many wounded by the time the Army had restored order. The Sikhs, who, for reasons of religious and political differences, had taken a major part in these disturbances, were clearly going to be a force to be reckoned with; their aims were stated to be the complete elimination of India by partition. Undoubtedly Jinnah's party seemed to be doing nothing to allay fears, for at this time a Muslim member of Congress again put forward a resolution that all INA prisoners should be released forthwith, and that all their lost pay and allowances should be restored; the effect of passing such a resolution would be immediate trouble in the Army.

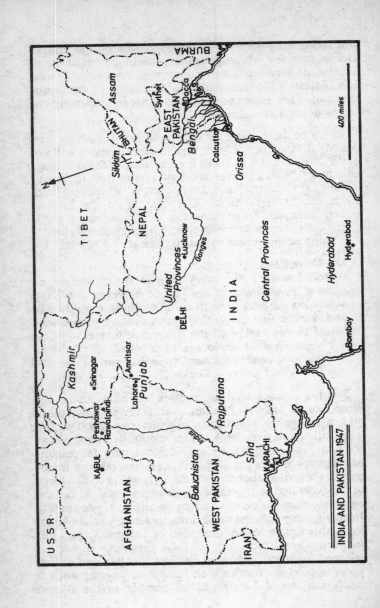

INDIA AND PAKISTAN 1947

400 miles

Fortunately Nehru made a statesmanlike speech against the resolution, which was withdrawn.

A new pressure upon the C-in-C then came from Liaquat Ali Khan, the Finance Minister of the Interim Government, who said that as Muslims were inadequately represented in the armed forces some arrangements should be made so that the balance would be more even. Auchinleck promptly responded to this with the statement that:

> The Armed Forces of India, as they now stand, cannot be split up into two parts each of which will form a self-contained armed force.
>
> Any such drastic reorganisation would have to be carried out in stages over a period of several years, and during this period there would be no cohesive Armed Force capable of dealing with any serious defensive operations on the North-West Frontier.
>
> As it is likely that any rumour concerning a proposal to divide the Armed Forces would have an immediate and unsettling effect on the morale of the Muslim soldiers, ratings and airmen, it is urged that this matter should not be discussed except on the highest level.
>
> I wish to stress that in the present state of communal unrest in India any publication of such discussions might well be disastrous to the continued morale and efficiency of the Armed Forces.

However, the replacement of Wavell by Mountbatten had put an entirely different complexion on matters. Mountbatten's private assessment of the situation – after talks with Indian leaders – was that there was no hope of keeping India united even with a federal government; he considered the alternatives to be Partition or anarchy. He therefore began to work on what became known as the Mountbatten Plan, which would divide India and its armed forces, as Jinnah wished, into two separate states and armies. He asked Auchinleck what sort of an army Pakistan would possess if Partition became a reality. The reply was that to provide Pakistan with armed forces would be difficult and expensive, 'and that no guarantee of success could be given'. Nevertheless, the Partition plan was now the only possible solution, and indeed was being pressed ahead both by the Muslims, perhaps understandably, and, with less reason, by Mountbatten. And in spite of the importance of keeping secret the question of the armed forces being split until some agreement was reached privately, Mountbatten brought it into the agenda of the Defence Committee, India, which met at the end of April. One of the issues was the 'nationalising' of the armed forces (that is, making them completely Indian), the other was the problem of separating them. Mountbatten thought that either of these objectives might be accomplished by 1 June 1948. But he pointed out that any premature moves might lead to disaster:

I bear personal responsibility for law and order. I must carry this on until such time as I can hand it over to one or more responsible authorities. While I bear that responsibility I have, in the last resort, the use of British troops to fall back on. After 1 June 1948 there will be no more British troops. But the need for reliable and impartial armed forces may still exist. By unduly hastening the process of separation we may defeat our own ends and produce a situation in which the Armed Forces may be semi-organised and not reliable. Much as I should like to see the separation completed I must emphasise my own doubts as to the possibility of achieving this in the time available without weakening the Armed Forces. This I cannot possibly accept while I am responsible for law and order.

With the prospect of fifteen months to overcome such problems the situation appeared difficult although not entirely impossible. The Committee decided that the armed forces should not be separated until Partition had been decided, if such a decision were to be made, but Auchinleck, as Commander-in-Chief, was instructed to set up committees to consider the problems likely to arise from any separation of the armed forces.

The problem of Partition, as the recent riots had shown, was that once Muslims and Hindus realised they had different allegiances, and once those allegiances were crystallised in the founding of new countries, racial and religious differences would lead to violence. Hindus and Muslims were closely intermingled: in some areas there was a majority of one religion; in others a majority of the other. There were many Hindus in what would become Pakistan, and many Muslims in India. People who had lived and worked amicably together for generations were now becoming conscious of their differences, and of new grievances. Certain areas would have to be divided; thousands, if not millions, of people would have to move. There were, for instance, very small Muslim majorities in Bengal and the Punjab, while Kashmir was a Muslim area but with a Hindu Maharajah who wished to join his state to India. (This was to lead to bitter fighting later; Nehru's grandfather had been a Kashmiri Brahmin, a fact which influenced him in his desire to join Kashmir to India.)

Gandhi, whose long-held belief in independence for India had been a major factor in bringing it to reality, was resolutely against Partition but his influence, though great, was no longer great enough to prevent it. Nehru was doubtful about it; Jinnah was firmly in favour. Feeling was now running so high in India – and risking becoming so regular and widespread – that most of the British there felt that the country was on the verge of civil war. Reluctantly Auchinleck accepted the fact that with Partition division of the forces was inevitable. Politically, it was hoped that if India separated, both new countries would remain as Dominions within the British Commonwealth. But as the term 'British Commonwealth' preserved memories of the original (and now changed) British Empire, it was decided that this largely voluntary association would be better described by the term 'The Commonwealth of Nations'. (There were problems over this too, since Australia was already designated 'The Commonwealth of Australia'.) In theory, the 1931 Statute of Westminster, by which Commonwealth was defined as 'autonomous communities ... equal in status, in no way subordinate to one another in their domestic and external affairs, though united by a common allegiance to the Crown and freely associated as members of the British

Commonwealth of Nations' should have satisfied everyone. There were, however, fears that it might not, and those fears proved to be correct. In addition, there were forebodings about what might happen if one country decided to retain Commonwealth allegiance but the other to renounce it.

Within two weeks Mountbatten had changed his mind completely about the date for the transfer of power, although there were admittedly reasons for him to do so. The vacillations of the leaders of Congress produced an atmosphere of unrest and uncertainty, which created an admirable opportunity for lawless mobs to murder, burn and loot under the guise of seeking political freedom. The British Government, advised by Mountbatten and feeling that the situation was rapidly becoming uncontrollable, and thus endangering the lives of British subjects, believed that the only way to restore law and order would be through elected Indian and Pakistan governments, though many people were still against Partition, at least in so short a time. 31 December 1947 was now chosen as the date for the transfer of power – a full five months before the date mentioned at the Defence Committee discussion, and before the British Government's avowed date of 'not later than June 1948'. So, far from delaying Partition, Mountbatten was now urging the Labour Government to put the necessary legislation through the House of Commons as speedily as possible. But a political decree was one thing; the partition of the Indian Army was another. The fact that it must now be divided dismayed many who felt that undivided it was the one means of ensuring a smooth transfer of power in conditions of stability and order. Nehru's suggestion at this time that India should be regarded as the successor to the British Government and Pakistan as a country which had seceded did not make would-be Pakistanis more amenable to reason.

On 4 June Mountbatten, after talks in London, announced that the date for the transfer had now been advanced to 15 August. This statement was made at a Press Conference to some 300 journalists in the Legislative Assembly in New Delhi, but hardly were the words

266

out of his mouth than someone pointed out that the astrologers did not favour 15 August for such an event (the date had been chosen because it was the second anniversary of the Allied victory over Japan). A diplomatic solution was quickly found, however – the transfer would be effective from 15 August, but would take place at midnight on the 14th, a propitious date; and, subject to voting, with Independence would come Partition, agreed on 7 June.

Suddenly the Indian leaders realised that they had achieved what they had set out to do, and upon which they had for so long set their hearts. They were less pleased than stunned. It is, perhaps, a great psychological shock to those who have campaigned through a lifetime for the replacement of their alleged oppressor suddenly to find that they themselves have replaced him.

At the end of June Bengal and the Punjab voted for the partition of their own states, West Punjab and East Bengal seceding from India; Sind voted to join Pakistan, and Sylhet, part of Assam, voted to join the now-Pakistani East Bengal. Pakistan, in essence two states separated by some 1100 miles of India, would now come into being at the same time as Indian Independence, though Kashmir and the Frontier Province had not yet decided. Auchinleck was therefore now faced with the distasteful task of tearing apart all those links which he had spent his life creating or enhancing. Given time, he could probably have found a way of avoiding some of the disasters which would now fall on the Indian Army, but with the proposed time-scale, that would prove impossible. Nevertheless, on 11 June he addressed a note to General Ismay, who had arrived in March as Chief of Staff to the Viceroy, in which he said:

I cannot stress too strongly my conviction that the success of any plan for the division of the Indian Armed Forces depends on the willing co-operation of the British officers now serving with them, the great majority of whom it will be essential to retain during the process of reconstitution.

He went on to say that he thought that this was more likely to be achieved if the future governments of the two countries 'openly state that the services of the British officers are essential to the success of reconstitution, notwithstanding the "Quit India" cry of the past'. One point, which everyone but Auchinleck himself realised, was that if he asked these officers to help the new governments they would do it, but it would be for the respect they had for him, and not out of any respect for the Indian leaders.

With a fine sense of timing Montgomery now paid a flying visit to India (23 June), and made the remarks noted earlier concerning the characters of Jinnah and Nehru. He was in the country for three days only, but his presence cannot have eased Auchinleck's worries. These would clearly become worse as each day passed, as when, for instance, some Sikh troops expressed anxiety about their deployment in such troubled times, thinking that they should be at home guarding their wives and children.

But chief of his problems was that during the next six weeks a formula had to be found to divide the Indian Army. Auchinleck envisaged a situation in which a Muslim might wish to continue to serve with his former regiment, even though it was now in the army of India, or a Hindu willing to be in a Pakistani regiment. Clearly this could not be permitted, for it could only lead to trouble.

Committees were set up to deal with the new arrangements as a matter of urgency. Even as they began work further changes occurred and ominous signs of dangerous unrest began to show. And at this moment Nehru decided once more to bring up the issue of the INA prisoners. On 19 July he wrote Mountbatten a letter containing several dubious hypotheses, among them the possibility that many would think it inequitable that 'political prisoners' should be kept in prison after independence and that Pakistan might release the prisoners in her care, which could raise an outcry in India for similar action. He concluded with the words: 'It is thus far better to keep the initiative with ourselves than to be compelled by circumstances to take action.'

The letter was sent on to Auchinleck who, of course, in replying to the Viceroy's Private Secretary on the 21st, made the point that the INA detainees were not political prisoners but people convicted of 'murder and brutal conduct'. He added: 'I cannot agree to take independent action for the summary release of these men on the grounds of purely political expediency.' Auchinleck knew how bad for the morale and discipline of the Indian Army the release of these ex-soldiers would be.

In Britain, the Indian Independence Bill was pushed through Parliament so fast that it became law by 18 July. As the appointment of 'Commander-in-Chief, India' now had come to an end, new Commanders-in-Chief were appointed for India and Pakistan, respectively Lockhart and General Sir Frank Messervy. Both armies would, however, be within the overall jurisdiction of Auchinleck, now appointed Supreme Commander. His responsibilities in India had not quite finished. He officially informed the two new Cs-in-C, both of whom were old friends and comrades in arms:

I, as Supreme Commander, have been made responsible by His Majesty's Government in the United Kingdom for the Command and administration of all British forces staying in India after August 15th. I have been empowered to report direct to the Chiefs of Staff in the United Kingdom on all matters concerning this responsibility through the GOC British troops in Indian and Pakistan, and the AOC-in-C at Supreme Commander's Headquarters ...

... We shall, I hope, have no difficulty in achieving our common object which is to reconstitute the Armed Forces of India with the minimum of disturbance and delay and the maximum of efficiency in the equal interest of both Dominions.

At midnight on 14 August an independent India and a separate Pakistan officially came into being. The observations of the two leaders who had campaigned are not without interest. Nehru said:

Long years ago we made a tryst with destiny, and now the time comes when we shall redeem our pledge, not wholly or in full measure but very substantially. At the stroke of the midnight hour, when the world sleeps, India will awake to life and freedom.

Jinnah said, 'Do you know, I never expected to see Pakistan in my lifetime. We have to be very grateful to God for what we have achieved.'

In contrast, Auchinleck's final command read:

SPECIAL INDIAN ARMY ORDER
by
His Excellency Field-Marshal Sir Claude J. E. Auchinleck,
GCB, GCIE, CSI, DSO, OBE
Commander-in-Chief in India
New Delhi 14 August 1947
SIAO 79/S/47 Discontinuance of India Army Orders
This is the last Army Order
R. A. Savory, Lieutenant-General
Adjutant-General in India.

17

A NEW WORLD

Jinnah's comment that he never expected to see Pakistan in his lifetime (though his lifetime would only last another thirteen months) shows how completely he misled Mountbatten: from the moment the British Government announced the date for the transfer of power Jinnah guessed that an autonomous Muslim state lay within his grasp, and invariably presented to the Viceroy the impression that there was no other solution, nor even possibility of delays. Jinnah's own very great doubts, expressed in his comment, were never allowed to show, and Mountbatten was taken in by his confidence and his adamant refusal to compromise in even the smallest detail. In fact, listening to Mountbatten's comments on the negotiations leading up to the transfer in 1947, it is difficult to decide which is the greater, his naivety or his self-esteem. Even after he knew the results of the headlong transfer of power – religious and political differences, a country in two separate 'wings' hundreds of miles apart, a confused army, and so on – for which he bears considerable responsibility, there was no trace of genuine remorse in his utterances. To him everybody was wonderful: Krishna Menon was one of his greatest friends, he admired Gandhi and was deeply grieved at his death* – the deaths of millions of other inhabitants of the Indian sub-continent were received resignedly.

Mountbatten emphasised that he was by no means an enemy of Jinnah, although he agreed that the Muslim leader was 'very difficult, very awkward to deal with'. He had met Jinnah for the first time in April 1947 and found him disdainful and frigid. It took two hours to make Jinnah joke with him, but by the evening of the following day they were firm friends. (It is not always clear what Mountbatten

* On 30 January 1948 Gandhi was assassinated by a Hindu fanatic before a crowd of followers in New Delhi.

meant by the word 'friend'. Jinnah, who brushed the Viceroy to one side, was a 'friend'; so too was Auchinleck, many of whose problems he largely either ignored or increased.) Just before his death in 1948 Jinnah said, 'The only man I have been impressed with all my life is Lord Mountbatten.' In 1947 (Mountbatten said) Jinnah claimed that the Viceroy possessed *nur*, 'divine radiance'. Asked why, if this were so, Jinnah's subordinates constantly attacked Mountbatten in newspaper articles, he replied: 'They must have someone to attack and Lord Mountbatten is big enough not to mind.'

Mountbatten firmly stated that he could not have partitioned India any more slowly, and added, 'History will prove me right.' And Jinnah was not to be moved from Partition (in spite of that friendship); he was fanatical in his desire to build a Muslim state. In addition he was determined to retain East Bengal (which became East Pakistan), rich in jute and tea, and suggested that if necessary the two portions of Pakistan should be linked by a land corridor; it is easy to see why the new India would not agree to such a corridor through more than 1000 miles of Indian land. Jinnah usually got his way, according to Mountbatten, by saying 'No, no, no' to every sensible suggestion. The only consolation Mountbatten could give himself was to predict that within twenty-five years the State of Pakistan, as two separate pieces, would finally be found unviable and would break apart. The fact that East Pakistan seceded, becoming Bangladesh, in twenty-five years almost to the day, was apparently a great satisfaction.

The history of Auchinleck's dislike of Partition – or, more particularly, too swift a partition – dates back to before Mountbatten's arrival as Viceroy. During these years (1946–7) Lt-Gen. Frank Simpson* was Vice-Chief of the Imperial General Staff, a post he was already holding when, in 1946, Montgomery became CIGS. The latter had taken a long time to settle in, for he did not get on at all well with the other two Chiefs of Staff (Naval and Air), and thus usually allowed Simpson to go to Chiefs of Staff

* Later General Sir Frank Simpson.

meetings rather than attend himself. The other two Chiefs, Admiral Sir John Cunningham and Marshal of the RAF Lord Tedder, liked Simpson and were as helpful as they could be, for though there were, as he put it, 'many rows', all would become amicable later over a drink in the evening. (As the other two were both older and senior to Simpson in rank, it was not easy for him to argue for his own Service, though he tried.) In November 1946 Montgomery decided to tour the Commonwealth looking at British military installations. The other Services did not care for this idea but, since Montgomery had obtained the Prime Minister's (Attlee's) approval, there was little they could do about it. Just when the CIGS was about to leave, however, it was realised that Tedder had recently set off for a visit to Japan. There was immediately a tremendous row; Montgomery flew into a temper and 'was going to raise hell' with the Prime Minister, and the Vice-Chief of the Air Staff mentioned privately to Simpson that if matters continued like this there would be a rift between the Army and Air Staffs which would not be healed for years. Simpson succeeded in calming Montgomery down, but the fact remained that Attlee had ordered that two of the three Chiefs of Staff could not be out of action at the same time. Simpson, incidentally, had been told by the Vice-Chief of the Air Staff that Tedder had only gone because Lady Tedder had said she wanted to see Japan. When he told Montgomery that this, and not a more serious reason, was the cause of the impasse, Montgomery laughed, became good-humoured, and told Simpson that he must go in his place to the Far East.

Simpson flew out to India in a Lancaster bomber, and visited Karachi, Rawalpindi, and Delhi. Auchinleck invited him to stay in his house in Delhi and arranged for him to see anyone he liked. Before setting out, Simpson had been told by Montgomery that it was obvious there was going to be a real mess in India and that Simpson should therefore try to find out as much as he could while he was there. Simpson already knew India well, and as a young officer had served for eleven years with the Bombay Sappers and Miners.

Auchinleck gave a number of dinner parties for the

VCIGS, and on his last evening Simpson asked Auchinleck for a private discussion. After dinner, 'with a couple of large drinks', they went off into the conservatory to talk. Simpson was aware that there was some trouble between the then Viceroy (Wavell) and the Home Government, and that Wavell had already flown home once for discussions. The Chiefs of Staff were not getting any of the telegrams passing between the Viceroy and the India Office; Attlee had given strict instructions that they were not to see those telegrams because 'he felt they would make trouble'. Wavell had been accompanied on his visit home by Auchinleck's Chief of Staff, and former CGS in Cairo, Sir Arthur Smith, a man of great rectitude and personal charm. In London, Simpson, guessing that something was very wrong, had asked Smith to outline the problem. Smith had the option of rudely refusing to tell him, of telling him a lie, or telling him the truth. He chose to do the last, in accordance with his character. Wavell was apparently completely frustrated by his inability to get a decision from the British Cabinet on what he should tell the Indian leaders about future British policy for India. He felt that the British should leave India completely by August 1948, about eighteen months after making the announcement of the decision. The Cabinet had refused, however, to give either a decision or a firm date. Simpson gave a résumé of all this to Auchinleck during their private discussion. Auchinleck said he entirely agreed with Smith's view that Wavell was 'selling the pass'; he himself thought that it would be dangerous to leave India as quickly as was proposed. He did not say Britain should not leave, but he was emphatic that the transitional period should be three years, five years, or even longer. Auchinleck told Simpson that the Indian Army was virtually non-communal, with different castes mixing together, and that there would be no trouble amongst them if they were given the task of keeping order in the country. He went on to say that, though he was probably being disloyal to Wavell himself, he felt that the Viceroy had given up hope of producing any other solution. Simpson did not entirely agree with Auchinleck's view, for he felt that Wavell was not so much selling the pass as trying to force the British Government to declare its policy and timing. He then asked Auchinleck what the Governors of the Provinces of British India* thought about it at all, to which the C-in-C replied that the Provincial Governors, all extremely able and experienced members of the Indian Civil Service, considered that the country was not yet ready for independence, and were themselves becoming distinctly agitated at the prospect. Auchinleck felt that there were, however, three governors who could be relied on to cope with any emergency: Sir Francis Moody in the Punjab, Sir Frederick Burrows (a former railway porter) in Bengal, and Lt-Gen. Sir Archibald Nye in Madras (who as, VCIGS, had accompanied Cripps to Cairo in April 1942).

Auchinleck said that the Indian Army, numbering at that time about two million men, was so non-communal in its outlook because of the way that he had handled it. He saw the whole of his patient work being torn to pieces if India was going to be divided up between Hindu and Muslim; Simpson noted that the thought of this happening distressed the senior man greatly. Auchinleck went on to say that if Britain pulled out of India too soon there was liable to be severe civil war, with its attendant looting, murder, plunder and rape, on a very large scale indeed – Simpson registered his exact words very carefully. This, said the C-in-C, was not merely his own opinion but one shared by several of the Governors; and if Simpson were to ask his principal staff officers, such as Lt-Gen. Reginald Savory, the Adjutant-General, Lt-Gen. Cyril Burnford, the Quartermaster-General, and others, he would find that they had all arrived independently at the same conclusion. He had not pressed his views upon them.

The conversation, reported briefly here, lasted for a long time, and left a deep impression on Simpson. The following morning he talked to several of the principal staff officers individually, and found that their views were exactly as Auchinleck had said. Later that day, on the aircraft bound for Burma, Simpson drafted a telegram for Montgomery, using a private cipher, giving the gist of

---

* That is, all the Indian states except those ruled by Princes.

Auchinleck's views; however, he allowed the five other generals travelling with him in the aircraft to read it through before coding it. They too had the same impression of the potential dangers to India and its army, and agreed with Auchinleck's questioning of Wavell's actions.

After arriving back in London just before New Year's Day, Simpson asked Montgomery what he had done about the message. The CIGS said he had taken it to Ernest Bevin, the Foreign Secretary, but that Bevin had told him not to worry as the Government was determined not to do what the Viceroy wanted. 'It would upset,' said Montgomery, 'the whole of my plans for the Middle East if the Viceroy annoyed the Arabs.'*

Montgomery departed for a holiday in Switzerland in February 1947, leaving Simpson in charge in London. On 19 February (the day before the official announcement of the transfer of power) the Chiefs of Staff were suddenly ordered to call a special meeting at which they would be addressed by A. V. Alexander, the Minister of Defence. Alexander, who had been a member of the Cabinet Mission to India in April 1946, handed round a telegram which had just been received from the Governor of Bengal, Sir Frederick Burrows. It had been sent direct to the India Office with a copy to the Viceroy.

The Governor of Bengal had heard that an announcement was going to be made the next day that there was going to be a withdrawal from India in the middle of 1948. Burrows felt that it would be extremely dangerous to fix a date and mentioned that there were very few British troops available for security duties. He predicted all sorts of dire disasters if the statement was made. This news, and the opinions given, were completely fresh to the other Chiefs of Staff, and so Simpson felt that he must now relate what Auchinleck had told him, though he had considerable misgivings since he had originally stated that he would tell no one except Montgomery. Plainly, however, the import of his message to the CIGS had not penetrated to the Government. His audience was apparently aghast

---

* A reference to the need not to offend Muslim opinion in general, since Britain still had many Defence commitments in the Middle East.

both at what he told them and at the seriousness of its implications. Tedder urged that the Chiefs of Staff should at once put their views of the matter on paper for Alexander to take with him when he went to see Attlee. Simpson was asked how many British troops might be available to deal with any crisis in India, to which the answer was fifteen to sixteen battalions in all, in five brigade groups. There were ten to twelve Indian battalions but most of the Indian troops were still on garrison duties overseas.

Simpson then went to the India Office to see the Military Secretary there, General Sir Geoffry Scoones, to tell him that he had breached the confidence of the Commander-in-Chief. Scoones told him not to worry, for he had that very morning received a telegram from the Viceroy expressing the opinion of the Commander-in-Chief, and using exactly the words Simpson had noted. The Prime Minister called a meeting at 5 pm that day – a sort of Staff Conference – of the Chiefs of Staff, the Foreign Secretary, the Minister of Defence and the Secretary of State for India, Lord Pethick-Lawrence (who was always known in the War Office as 'Pathetic Lawrence' since he invariably shook his head whatever he had to say).

Attlee opened the meeting by turning to Simpson and saying that he understood the VCIGS to have given a very alarmist report that morning to the Chiefs of Staff about what Auchinleck thought; a report, the Prime Minister added, which he simply refused to believe. Simpson swallowed his annoyance and said firmly, 'Prime Minister, I have quoted the opinion of the Commander-in-Chief in the very words he spoke to me.' He suggested that Attlee should compare the 'alarmist words' with the words in the telegram just received by the India Office; he would then find them to be the same. Attlee replied, 'I still don't believe it. If there is a telegram in the India Office, get it at once.' Scoones was reluctant to deliver the telegram, but eventually agreed to do so. While they were waiting for him to bring it over, the Prime Minister's Private Secretary turned to Simpson and said, 'That telegram is already in the file which the Prime Minister has in front of him at the moment, but he has so many papers he doesn't have time to read them all.'

The telegram was handed round, and Ernest Bevin growled, 'Prime Minister, what did I tell you? There will be real trouble in India.' (Alexander was speechless – which was not unusual.) Attlee then said, 'I think we had better postpone making the statement [of the proposed date for the transfer of power] in Parliament until we have had talks with the Viceroy;' at which Pethick-Lawrence shook his head even more and answered, 'Prime Minister, you cannot postpone the statement. You have already got me to authorise Lord Wavell to tell Nehru and Jinnah this afternoon that the statement will be made and what it will contain.' Attlee shrugged his shoulders and said 'So be it.' The minutes of this meeting have disappeared from the files at the Public Record Office; they have obviously been 'weeded' as being too sensitive by some over-zealous civil servant.

Simpson noted that Attlee said nothing to him, although he had more or less called him a liar in public. A few days later, however, Attlee brought him in on another matter, and, when the meeting was over, apologised to Simpson for saying he had not believed him. From that moment their friendship was established. And when, later, Simpson told Auchinleck that he had broken the latter's confidence, he received the answer, 'You were quite right to quote me. I am only sorry it did not work' – referring to a postponement or delay of the transfer of power.

Wavell, whose views had precipitated these alarms in India and Britain, did not know that Mountbatten had been offered the appointment of Viceroy as early as the previous December, but he did know that the Labour Government was anxious to settle the Indian problem as soon as possible. Attlee had informed Wavell on 31 January that he would be replaced towards the end of March. The Prime Minister's curt letter clearly indicates that he himself felt ashamed of the shabby treatment he was meeting out to the Viceroy.

Mountbatten and his entourage arrived in New Delhi on 22 March, and from that moment a hasty Partition was probably inevitable. 'The Auk', said Simpson, 'gritted his teeth and did his best, but he was rushed off his feet when Mountbatten arrived.' The exact figure of those killed on the borders of the new countries was estimated at about four million by the Joint Intelligence Committee – Auchinleck felt that it need never have happened.

Simpson believed that Mountbatten never understood the problem at all. 'He was always master of the slick solution. He had tremendous magnetism. If he went and addressed troops in Burma they all listened to him.' It is, however, clear that, magnetic or not, 'Pretty Dickie' (as Auchinleck used to call him) was one of the most extraordinary appointments of the war. As Chief of Combined Operations his championing of the Dieppe raid caused severe casualties and, arguably, set back the invasion of Europe; as Supreme Commander, SEAC he had frequently sent home ill-informed or irrelevant telegrams which infuriated Brooke and the other Chiefs of Staff; and at his headquarters in the Far East the conferences were so elaborately stage-managed, with the 'principal boy of the pantomime' presiding in immaculate uniform over what were known as the 'Dickie Birds' (his staff officers), that it was difficult to believe they could achieve anything useful at all. He had been promoted to Combined Operations with little experience of staff work or planning, and while still relatively junior – in itself an extraordinary appointment. But the most dangerous decision of all was the choice of Mountbatten to solve the India problem. Solve it he did, but at considerable cost.

The question which obviously springs to mind is why Auchinleck did not make a stronger stand for what he knew to be right. The man who had defied Churchill and was dismissed for it now took no other steps than saying in confidence to the visiting VCIGS that he thought that early independence would lead to a catastrophe. There seem to be two possible answers to this question.

The first is that in February Auchinleck did not believe that the Cabinet would act so hastily, and his comments to Simpson were therefore in the nature of a warning which he hoped might be heard in the right quarter. He would be aware that Simpson was the one person who could probably bring Montgomery – the only person to whom the VCIGS could confide Auchinleck's views – on to the side of delay. Although his own personal relations with Montgomery had clearly shown that Auchinleck himself could have no influence, there was a strong possibility that Simpson, as an experienced military diplomat, might sway his chief.

The second reason why he did not resign, or in some other way demonstrate his worries, when Mountbatten was pushing independence along hard was that he probably felt that it would not do any good, that it might in fact make the inevitable chaos in India worse, given Auchinleck's strong influence on the Indian Army. It was not through lack of moral courage. Unlike many army officers, Auchinleck had plenty of moral courage. Physical courage is abundant in the Services and men will often face certain death much more willingly than they will risk unpopularity through going against current opinion. (This particular weakness among servicemen was recognised by Hitler, who exploited it perfectly; when at last the Generals tried to assassinate him they were so muddled and incompetent that they themselves finished up by being hanged with wire from hooks.) Auchinleck at this stage had nothing to lose, indeed everything he cherished was lost, but he perhaps realised that to make a gesture – and resignation could have been no more than that – would have no impact on the Labour Cabinet, Montgomery, or the Indian leaders. He would simply be replaced by someone less able to do his job.

What he did appear to lack was not moral courage but the assurance to tackle Mountbatten and, if needs be, intimidate him. Major Alexander Greenwood, who was Auchinleck's ADC in India and who saw a lot of him subsequently, says that Auchinleck was curiously shy with the aristocracy. Wartime leaders like Brooke or Wavell did not count in his mind as aristocrats, but holders of older titles did. Mountbatten's royal connection made him a formidable figure; it was virtually impossible for Auchinleck to demand an audience, or to thump the table if such an audience was granted. Equally he would have been at a loss if he personally had tried to impress on the Labour Cabinet the folly of hastening independence. Attlee might have understood, and Ernest Bevin undoubtedly would have done so, but the other leading Labour politicians of the time – Aneurin Bevan, Cripps, Dalton, among others – would almost certainly have dismissed Auchinleck's views as either intellectually unsound, or out of touch with enlightened working-class opinion. (Cripps had been educated at Winchester and London University, and Dalton at Eton and King's, Cambridge, but their patrician backgrounds did not inhibit their confidence as barometers of honest, proletarian common sense.)

Perhaps, at the age of sixty-three, Auchinleck felt that he had learned the hopelessness of trying to convince dedicated politicians. Had his experience of being harassed by Churchill been unique he might have felt that it was worth a final try at taking on the politicians of the Labour Government. But he knew that Alexander and Montgomery had also been pressed to do the impossible by Churchill when he himself had left the European scene, and he saw no reason why the 'prodding' of soldiers by politicians would cease with a change of government. Above this, he knew that world opinion was strongly in favour of making former colonies independent at the earliest possible moment; it was not merely his own government which was pledged to this idea. As has been said, America, on whose financial aid most post-war reconstruction depended, was actively hostile to the idea of former colonial powers occupying and retaining their erstwhile colonies. Thus the French were urged to pull out of Indochina and the Dutch from the East Indies: America herself set the pace in the Philippines. Auchinleck was able to see these events as clearly as anyone else; with Mountbatten as Viceroy he probably realised that this was a battle he could never win, though he would do all in his power to alleviate any crises.

18

THE LAST OF THE INDIAN ARMY

Partition did not, as the idealists had imagined, mean the end of dissension: in fact it made the divisions sharper. Auchinleck was now left in an impossible position, for, besides the maintaining of order, he was expected to continue the orderly division of the former Indian Army into the armies of the new states, and at the same time he was responsible for all British military personnel serving in the two countries. When Partition had occurred all British officers were automatically transferred back to British service; however, any who wished to stay on during the period of transition could do so, but would still be the responsibility of the Supreme Commander.

The first signs of major trouble appeared almost immediately, notably in the Punjab and Bengal. In July 1947 two Boundary Commissions had been appointed, made up of Hindus and Muslims and under the chairmanship of Sir Cyril Radcliffe, a distinguished lawyer. Muslims, Hindus and Sikhs all agreed in principle to the Commissions, whose task would be to define the borders of the new states – the partitioned Punjab and Bengal – and to settle any disputes arising over territory. In practice, however, once the Commissions began their work directly after Independence it became obvious that, however hard they strove to be fair, their decisions only aroused greater rancour in an already highly-charged situation. Trouble in Bengal was occasioned by the exclusion of Calcutta from East Pakistan, though this died down relatively swiftly, but not without considerable loss of life. The Punjab was a different matter: that the state was to be partitioned was itself a source of conflict, but on top of this such division would divide the entire Sikh population between two countries, one Muslim and the other Hindu. And, most ominously, the Indian police in Lahore (which was now in West Pakistan) had deserted on a large scale;

it was impossible to introduce martial law since there were not enough troops to enforce it. The results were the Punjab massacres of August–September, fundamentally a Sikh-versus-Muslim and Muslim-versus-Hindu war but with other factors involved, in which at least half a million died and a further ten million or so of both sides fled as refugees. Muslims poured into Pakistan and Hindus into India, spreading violence and racial and religious hatred as they did so.

The Sikhs were particularly active. In Amritsar on Independence Day they drove a number of naked Muslim women through the streets, raped them, chopped the more fortunate ones to death and burnt them all. Before nightfall Muslims had taken what they considered appropriate revenge on the Sikhs in Lahore. Whatever law and order existed was preserved by a portion of the Indian Army known as the Punjab Boundary Force, a body of some 50,000 Indian soldiers under Maj.-Gen. T. W. ('Pete') Rees hastily assembled in July at Mountbatten's instigation as a counter to the terrifying situation developing. The Force worked under Auchinleck's direct orders 'to maintain law and order in the disputed area'. Nehru refused to allow British troops to be used, with the result that the Force was too involved to be very effective; and needless to say its efforts to preserve life and stability were vilified in the Delhi press. The solution was obvious: the Boundary Force must be abandoned and the two new Dominions must settle the matter themselves. Since they appeared almost certain to do this in their own way very soon there was little point in keeping the much maligned and greatly overworked Boundary Force in being, and orders were given by the two Governors-General, Mountbatten and Jinnah, to disband it on 29 August. With it went the last real chance of stemming the rising flood of anarchy, for as soon as the Boundary Force broke up, fighting, looting and murder began on an even more professional scale, and late in August Delhi itself suffered its own civil war. For a time the central government was threatened, but by late September the fighting began to die down, though the enormous refugee problem remained, and would do so for a long time. (The person who emerges as well as anyone from this period is Mount-batten's wife, Edwina, who toured the centres of conflict, visited hospitals and refugee camps, and spoke with offi-cials, in the hope that something might be done to alleviate the plight of the terrified and homeless.)

The dissolution of the Boundary Force meant that the old Indian Army had ceased to exist. All that remained to be done now was the physical distribution of assets, and the safe withdrawal of British personnel. But newly in-dependent nations do not care to be reminded of an imperial past, however distinguished, and frequently seek to throw off every last reminder of that past. The Indian Army could no longer be the object of vituperation from politicians, demagogues and trouble-makers, but they would find themselves a new target. Mountbatten could scarcely be a subject for attack, since he was an accepted figurehead; there was, however, one last relic of the old regime – Field-Marshal Sir Claude Auchinleck. That he was getting on quietly and efficiently with his job – the dissolution of an old army and its reconstruction as two new ones – was not enough; the last sacrifice must be demanded and granted. The continuation of the post of Supreme Commander, higher in rank than the Com-manders-in-Chief of the new Dominions, rankled with the politicians of both India and Pakistan, though not of course with the holders of those posts. In addition, many Indians considered Auchinleck to be biased towards Paki-stanis, though there was no very real foundation for this charge. Any hint of bias, however, merely added fuel to the emotional fire.

In this particular instance, Mountbatten, only too well aware of the hostility that was building up in the govern-ment circles of both Dominions towards Auchinleck, acted responsibly and sensibly. He decided to advise Auchinleck to resign, and to that end wrote a long letter on 26 September, explaining the view of the Joint De-fence Council that the continuation of the post of Supreme Commander would lead to trouble, and adding that reasonable arguments that Auchinleck's rank and prestige did not give him power, merely responsibility, were totally unavailing. He himself felt appalled that Auchinleck, a man who had given so much to India, should now be dragged into this undignified argument:

> You have often and often told me with characteristic unselfishness that you would willingly and indeed gladly fade out of the picture if I were at any time to tell you that this would help me personally or the general situation in this country. Bitter though it is for me to say so I sincerely believe that the moment has arrived for me to take advantage of your selfless offer and my suggestion is that you should yourself write a letter ... proposing the winding up of Supreme Headquarters ...

Mountbatten went on to explain that he had discussed the matter with the Secretary of State for India (the Earl of Listowel had replaced Pethick-Lawrence in April, and held the post until it ceased with Independence) on his recent visit, and had informed him that 'a position might be reached when the feeling of nationalism and the desire to be masters in their own house would reach a point at which it was impossible for any living Englishman to retain title of Supreme Commander'. The date suggested for the closure of Supreme HQ was 1 April 1948.

He mentioned that he had already recommended Auchinleck for a peerage in the first Indian Honours List he had submitted on 14 August, and that the King had approved this honour. He said that Attlee wished to know if Auchinleck would be willing to accept a barony, and he urged him to accept because it would give so much pleasure to the officers of the former Indian Army, and to others.

Auchinleck saw at once the sense of the Viceroy's suggestion, however painful it might be to him personally. But he felt that to receive a peerage for presiding over the destruction of the army to which he had given his life was totally unfitting, and refused it. The offer had come at a point when he was busy drafting a long report on the Indian situation for the British Prime Minister and the Chiefs of Staff. In the report, dated 28 September, he suggested the withdrawal of British officers from Indian units, as feeling between India and Pakistan was now running so high that they were likely to be involved in war:

> Those who volunteered did so in the general desire to help in a fair and efficient division of the Armed Forces. Out of a rough total of some 8000 officers of the Indian Army some 2800 have volunteered. Those officers are now asking to be released from their contracts under the three months' notice clause in ever increasing numbers. One of the chief reasons for this is because they hold that they volunteered to help in Reconstruction and not to help the new Governments keep law and order in their own territories. The conditions of massacre and bestiality of the worst kind in which many of these British officers have been working continuously for many weeks have sickened them. They have lost faith in their cloth and in their men, of whom they were so proud a short two months back.

He followed this with more details of the massacres, in which some officers had already been killed while trying to prevent them. His concern, as ever, was for his men, but the spectacle of his beloved Indian Army in such disarray must have been a bitter blow to him.

On 5 October he wrote to Scoones, saying that, although the Government of India wanted an earlier date, he felt that 31 December would be an appropriate time for closing down his headquarters. He mentioned that there was great hostility in India to 'any form of joint activity which may help secure anything for Pakistan at the expense of India'. Auchinleck went on: 'We are quite willing and indeed anxious to go as you will readily understand; but we cannot quit leaving all the British officers out here without a head or without an organisation to look after them and their families.'

He then wrote more fully to Mountbatten, noting that 1 April 1948 had been the date *originally* mentioned for the closing of the Supreme Commander's headquarters. He was aware, however, of the pressure from India (though not Pakistan) for the closing of the headquarters at an early date, and therefore suggested that it could be closed on 30 November provided it was replaced by a Command for British Forces, India and Pakistan. This would be responsible for all British officers, other ranks, and their families in India, and would in turn be closed on 31 December 1947. This, and his report of 28 September and comments to Scoones, would seem to give the lie to Montgomery's view, based on a very brief visit but nevertheless published in his memoirs, that Auchinleck had little or no concern for the British soldiers in India, though undoubtedly his chief preoccupation was with the Indian Army.

Even on this compromise proposal there was bickering between the two Dominions. Auchinleck therefore decided to go ahead with it without further discussion, and on 21 October informed Scoones that the headquarters would be closed on 30 November. He suggested that General Smith should have the post of Commander, British Forces until that organisation was also wound up. Auchinleck warned Scoones that the Indian Government was certain to object, even if, as was likely, Pakistan agreed. But, he continued, 'I am entirely against bowing to the wishes and prejudice of the Indian Government in the matter. They are the people who have made the present position impossible and they are the people who would like to get control over the British officers and other ranks who will still remain after I go.' The British Government supported the proposal for the winding up of Supreme HQ, though they took more than a fortnight to make up their minds. On 30 November 1948, after forty-five years of service under arms, Field-Marshal Auchinleck would cease to command in India – or indeed to have a command at all.

But he had one final card to play. On Partition the Princely States had all been asked to declare to which Dominion they wished to join themselves, since Britain had renounced all her treaty rights with these states. (There numbered in India at this time some 362 Princes, ruling anything from large estates to areas like Hyderabad with a population of seventeen million.) The Maharajah of Kashmir, Sir Hari Singh, was, as has been mentioned, a Hindu, though ruling a predominantly Muslim state. He was, therefore, in a difficult position, as he knew that his subjects wished to be Pakistani even though he himself wished to accede to Hindu India, an outcome to which Nehru also aspired, for historical and personal reasons, but to which Jinnah, not unexpectedly, objected. For a time after independence the Maharajah stalled and refused to declare himself, until some of his subjects then decided to make up his mind for him. In late August those nearest to Pakistan, in a district called Poonch, declared themselves the Free Kashmir Government. Since their 'government' looked distinctly frail, they were joined on 24 October by 5000 Pathan tribesmen from Pakistan, who would certainly have captured the Kashmir capital had they not stopped to loot a lesser town on the way. On the 26th the Maharajah, panic-stricken by these developments, announced that he had at last made up his mind and would accede to India; he asked for Indian troops to assist in security. India promptly flew in a battalion to defend the capital, Srinagar, and the invasion was halted. The actual orders to fly in troops had been given perfectly legitimately by the C-in-C of the Indian Armed Forces, General Lockhart, whose position gave him a place in the Indian Government.

Auchinleck promptly flew to Lahore. Here General Sir Douglas Gracey (deputising for Messervy, C-in-C of the Pakistan Armed Forces, who was on leave) informed him that he had been told by Jinnah to send troops to Kashmir for various missions, including that of capturing Srinagar – obviously Pakistan's Governor-General would not let Kashmir go willingly. Auchinleck stated very clearly to Jinnah that what he was proposing to do was quite irregular, for Kashmir had now legally become part of India. He quietly pointed out that if Jinnah tried to proceed he himself would order all British officers to withdraw from Pakistan's army, a threat which infuriated but at the same time checked Jinnah. Auchinleck then suggested that Jinnah should meet Nehru, Mountbatten, the Maharajah of Kashmir and his Prime Minister in a conference, to which the Muslim leader had no choice but to agree. In the event Nehru was ill and was unable to go, though it was agreed in principle that a plebiscite would be called to determine the real feeling in Kashmir. The crisis died down as quickly as it had begun, though the 'Kashmir question' would recur over the years, eventually involving the United Nations. But Auchinleck, who had spent a lifetime preparing men for war, had now prevented one.

As the closure of Supreme Headquarters, and retirement, approached, Auchinleck began to receive messages from all quarters. Among them was this tribute from Mountbatten:

> No one could have done more for India over an entire life's career devoted to her army and nobody contributed more to help find a peaceful and acceptable solution. I hope you will not let the fact that impartiality is no longer respected by many Indians make you feel that you have somehow failed – history will show very much the reverse.
>
> ... Finally may I tell you again how deeply I appreciate your friendship, loyalty and help throughout this very difficult time. You are a very great man, Claude, and I'm proud to have worked with you.
>
> Yours ever
Dickie

His last official function in India was to inspect a farewell Guard of Honour of the Royal Scots Fusiliers outside the C-in-C's house in Delhi, and, six days later, on 30 November, as he had proposed, Supreme HQ ceased to exist, and with it the post of Supreme Commander. Auchinleck left India on 1 December 1948 and went to Italy. Later in December Attlee wrote to him:

> I must convey to you in writing what I should have liked to express in person, namely the sincere gratitude of the Government and, I am sure, of informed opinion throughout the country, for the way in which you have accomplished the thankless task which was set you as Supreme Commander. All of us who have intimate knowledge of Indian officers realise that, in the last

twelve months, your influence has been of incalculable weight and value, not only on the military side, but even more in the wider political sphere, into which you have so often found yourself dragged.

Attlee was not given to overstatement – of his own experiences at Gallipoli he had merely remarked that they were 'interesting' – but he had sensitivity.

You may feel that your job ended in little but frustration; but the fact that the Army held together as well as it did, that reconstitution went through so smoothly, and that both India and Pakistan now have disciplined Armed Forces at their command is clear proof of the real and lasting success of the work you did.

Auchinleck must have liked that.

19

A LONG SUNSET

Retirement, at the age of sixty-three, began in Santa Margherita, near Rapallo in Italy. Auchinleck did not stay there long, however, and – in spite of his earlier disinclination to live in England – he went to London, where he lived until, in 1960, he moved to Beccles in Suffolk.

Peter Smart, who was his bank manager before and after the war, saw a fair amount of Auchinleck during the Field-Marshal's last days in India, and writes of him:

He was of a frugal nature but a generous host. I met him first when he called occasionally at the bank [Grindlay's] in 1937–8 . . . I really got to know him after the war in 1947 at the time of Partition. I was once again with the bank in New Dehli. It was a sad time, especially for him as he loved the Indian Army, and to preside over its division must have been heart-breaking. By July he had nothing to do except make plans for his future. He was determined not to live in England and I arranged the necessary formalities for him to settle in Italy – exchange regulations were involved.

At this time he dropped in frequently to my office, ostensibly about his financial affairs, but these did not really need his attention. He was just killing time. Delhi during that summer was a pretty rugged experience, as were many other parts of India. The most ghastly atrocities were being perpetrated at one's doorstep. One day he told me that he still had one British battalion under his hand and that if things got any worse I would be welcome at Command House. I can't remember what we talked about. It was certainly not about the war. I enjoyed these visits and knew I was greatly privileged to have them, even in such circumstances.

The Italian project cannot have worked out. In 1949–50, when I had been moved to Bombay, he joined the bank's board and made at least one visit to us. The work probably gave him some satisfaction, since his numerous connections in both India and Pakistan must have been of great benefit to us. However, India decided he was too pro-Pakistan, and there was one ridiculous situation when he decided it would not be tactful to land in Bombay as he was on his way to Karachi. So the manager visited him on the boat. He had other business interests, including a carpet business in Lahore. I don't think these were a success and I was told that people had used him for his name.

The early years of retirement in England were not a very happy time for Auchinleck. The period after being a serving field-marshal and a commander-in-chief – with the memory of his last, sad task, that of overseeing the breaking-up of his beloved Indian Army, only too fresh in his mind – was certain to be a depressing time as he adjusted himself to being an ordinary citizen again. He had no roots anywhere else, and few enough in Britain. The man who had been immediately recognised wherever he travelled in India, now passed unnoticed in England. This was, in some ways, an advantage: if he had retired to Camberley or Cheltenham he would constantly have been asked to recall his experiences in the Middle East, or to comment on India after Partition. The simplest solution was to live comparatively anonymously in London; there was then less likelihood that he would be bothered by people whose attention he did not want but whom his natural courtesy prevented him from freezing off.

London was not a very inspiring place in the early post-war years. Wartime austerity seemed to have settled like a grey cloud over everything; there was the inevitable balance of payments crisis; there were shortages of many goods, which today are classed as necessities and were then regarded as luxuries. It was as good a place to live as any, particularly as petrol was very strictly rationed, but it was not a place to raise one's spirits. Londoners had sustained six years of war, suffering incendiaries, land mines, V1s and V2s and endless queueing for everything, from a place in an air-raid shelter to a pound of potatoes; subsequently they had been told that they were leading the way in post-war reconstruction and it would be morally wrong for the British to enjoy themselves more than those in other countries.

Auchinleck lived alone in a flat in Down Street, Mayfair, but downcast as he may have been, he did not retire into obscurity. He had friends in England, and although an individual in any form of contest, he enjoyed company, loving to share his pleasures – soldiering was his first love, but he had many other interests – whether they were art, wine or food. (It is reported that he used to roam around London looking for new Indian restaurants: 'I think I've found something really good this time,' he would write to his friends.)

He took up a number of appointments on various boards: from 1946 to 1959 he was a Governor of his old school, Wellington College; he was Vice-President of the Forces Help Society and Lord Roberts' Workshops, and in 1956 he was President of the National Small-bore Rifle Association. Of especial interest to him, however, was the London Federation of Boys' Clubs, of which he was President from 1949 to 1955. Its work and 'Outward Bound' courses were not unlike the activities of the Boys' Companies in India which Auchinleck himself had founded. The initial aim of his establishments had been to train future leaders and specialists for the Indian Army, with the emphasis on all-round development of character, determination, initiative and imagination. Physical fitness was given high priority, of course, but there was a substantial allotment of time for general education, and hobbies were encouraged. By 1946 – shortly before the disbandment of the Indian Army – there had been 10,000 boys participating. Obviously the British scheme was in many ways different from the Indian, but there were similarities, and the aim of the London Federation was one with which Auchinleck sympathised.

There were, too, the business interests mentioned by Auchinleck's former bank manager, Peter Smart – though none of them particularly profitable to the Field-Marshal. He was Chairman of Dowsett Holdings Ltd; and he was also Chairman of the Murrayfield Real Estate Company, based in Birmingham, for a while. In 1963 Murrayfields completed a £1¼-million office and shopping centre at Five Ways, Birmingham, which was named **Auchinleck House**. A bronze statue of Auchinleck, in desert boots, shorts and bush shirt, but with no hat or stockings, stands in the precinct. The artist was Miss Fiore de Henriques, who had sculpted figures of Princess Margaret and Adlai Stevenson among others, and was described in the local paper as 'an unconventional, cheroot-smoking Italian who lived in America'. It would be interesting to know what Auchinleck thought of it. He was always an extremely modest man; he never expected any sort of tribute, and was always grateful when paid one. In 1962 a classroom in his old school was converted into the Auchinleck Room: 'At Wellington I had to open a sort of reading-cum-museum room which they have been good enough to name after me, which makes me feel very unworthy but very proud.'

During these years Auchinleck was able to pursue his interest in painting, and in 1950 he was Chairman of the Army Art Society (now the Armed Forces Art Society); he also exhibited a few paintings at all their annual exhibitions (in 1964 opened by Mountbatten). In 1955 the Trafford Gallery, in Mount Street, London W1, owned by Mr Charles Harding, held an exhibition in aid of Toch H.* It was called 'Painting is a Pleasure'. Auchinleck, who exhibited several paintings there, was quoted in the catalogue as saying, 'I know no better way of "escaping" the nuisances of every day than settling down to paint a picture or catch a fish.' The painter Michael Noakes considered that if Auchinleck had been able to devote time to developing his talent, his paintings would have been greatly improved; in the circumstances they were much better than the art world expected, though one comment is that they were 'low-keyed and subdued in tone and colour'. They were quickly snapped up when offered for sale, but Auchinleck dismissed that airily by

---

* Toch H: from the morse pronunciation of the initials of Talbot House, founded in 1915 as a rest and recreation centre for British troops, which developed into an interdenominational association for Christian social service.

saying, 'It's only because I'm a field-marshal and you don't expect field-marshals to paint.' Whatever the reason, his watercolours fetch a high price.

Auchinleck was given considerable help and encouragement in his painting by the painter Edward Seago, who had been his camouflage officer in 1940 and had remained a good friend. A portrait of Auchinleck by Seago hangs in the Indian Army Memorial Room at the RMA, Sandhurst. In 1964 it was suggested that the Field-Marshal should be painted in his official robes; Auchinleck's reply is typical of his modesty and healthy lack of reverence for ostentatious trappings: 'I am afraid the last thing I want to be painted in is the Mantle of the Bath. It would certainly make a very luxurious dressing gown. I don't own it, they hire them out. Ted [Seago] has already done six pictures of me and he says he is fed up with it. I don't blame him!'

By 1960 Seago had settled in Suffolk, and, urged by him, Auchinleck that year bought Oswald House, a very fine Queen Anne House in Beccles. He lived there for some seven years and then, at the age of eighty-four, took the somewhat surprising step of going to Morocco to settle down in Marrakech. This meant leaving not only friends, but his sisters Cherry Jackson and Ruth Chenevix Baldwin. Entirely different in manner and outlook, they were a close-knit family – indeed, Cherry had joined her brother in India to act as his hostess when Jessie Auchinleck left him in 1945 – nevertheless it is not unreasonable to suppose that one of the reasons which helped Auchinleck to make up his mind to emigrate was the self-effacing thought that the alternative would mean eventually imposing upon his relatives. He chose Marrakech for three reasons: the scenery reminded him of the hills of India, the climate suited him, and the cost of living was lower than in England.

Just before leaving England Auchinleck gave his personal papers to Manchester University. Asked why he had chosen Manchester, he replied, 'I think it is a good thing to spread these things around a bit. I'm all for these younger universities taking their place.' Manchester University was, in fact, founded in 1851, but it was a kindly thought! The Auchinleck Papers are excellently kept and catalogued there.

For many years Auchinleck revisited England regularly, attending regimental dinners and the annual garden party of the Association of British Officers of the Former Indian Army at Roehampton. He was Patron of this association which had been founded by the late Lt-Col. J. P. Lawford and Major W. E. Catto, now its Secretary. On 23 June 1971 he attended a ceremony in St Paul's Cathedral when HM Queen Elizabeth II unveiled the tablet to the former Indian Army. The tablet commemorated 201 years of service by British, Indian and Gurkha soldiers, first in the service of the East India Company, and after 1858 under the Crown. It recorded that their first overseas expedition was in 1762; and that in the First World War the Indian Army sent a million men overseas, and in the Second, two million more on active service.

Fond as he was of his sisters, Auchinleck, on these visits to England, like many other people found it easier to stay with friends and visit his relatives, rather than stay with relatives and visit friends. When in London he stayed at the United Services Club (the Senior) until it closed down; he then became a member of the Naval and Military Club (the 'In and Out') in Piccadilly.

Among his greatest friends were Christopher St Johnston and his wife Margot. St Johnston, as a major, had been Surgeon to the Commander-in-Chief in India during Auchinleck's second term in that office. Auchinleck often stayed with them at their house in Edgbaston, and they often visited him in Marrakech. He wrote literally hundreds of letters to them and there can be little doubt that his friendship with the St Johnstons, and his constant correspondence with them, was a source of great interest and solace to him, particularly after he had gone to Marrakech. Every time he wrote of some attractive feature of life in Morocco – a picnic in the Atlas Mountains, corn growing in the fields, summer weather – he would say, 'Wish you had been here to enjoy it!'

Among other good friends were Hubert Wilson-Fox and Sydney Cooper. Wilson-Fox took Auchinleck on several fishing trips to Norway where he had a beat, and where they caught several salmon and many trout. Cooper, who was an ardent traveller, often visited Auchinleck in Marrakech. They used to play piquet, a game which suited Auchinleck – as Mrs Chenevix Baldwin said of her brother, 'He does not like partner games like bridge, but always prefers the games where he battles alone.'

It was a simple but comfortable life in Marrakech and satisfying, if sometimes rather solitary. Auchinleck's health continued to be astonishingly good – he had had his appendix removed at Millbank Hospital in 1957 but had recovered very quickly – although he eventually became rather deaf and during his last years his memory began to fail. Until then, however, he was alert to past and present, reading, talking to guests, writing regularly to his friends. His routine was to get up early, walk to the Renaissance Café, drink some beer and read a newspaper, often an American one. He was always pleased to see visitors particularly if they had military connections – but he was suspicious of journalists and slow to thaw towards them, feeling that in the past he had often been misrepresented by them. He was not an easy man to interview, remaining wary even in extreme old age, and those who tried found him cautious and unenthusiastic at first. As he got to know them, however, he relaxed and his natural courtesy made him try to be helpful.

For many years Auchinleck was looked after by a Moroccan named Bashir, an excellent cook and valet, who spoke and wrote good French. Bashir was suspected by many to be lining his own nest, and thus keeping his employer permanently hard up. They were probably quite correct in their suspicions: Auchinleck gave him a free hand financially, and, as bills were in French or Arabic, he ended up giving Bashir many times their amount – and Bashir was well known as a frequent visitor to the local betting shop. It is likely, too, that in later years Bashir helped himself to more and more of his employer's money, for the ageing Field-Marshal became forgetful and he would often have absolutely no idea how much money he had had in his pockets the previous day. Auchinleck knew most of the ways in which servants have traditionally robbed their masters – but Bashir looked after him well, and he would have probably been hard put to it to find an equally good servant who was honest into the bargain.

The Moroccan was probably something of an autocrat, too – for instance he never allowed his master into the kitchen, where, it is said, he kept pigeons, but Auchinleck had nothing but praise for him. Bashir kept the flat and Auchinleck's clothes immaculate, he planned meals of imagination and variety, and respectfully teased his distinguished employer. Auchinleck became very fond of his servant, and it especially pleased him when Bashir took to his visitors. One of the ways the servant showed his liking for them was to put on one or more of his masks for their entertainment. A visitor might, therefore, be somewhat surprised to see General de Gaulle, complete with képi, appearing round the door with a tray of drinks – or perhaps it would be Churchill, or even Charlie Chaplin.

Bashir was not the only one to cheat Auchinleck – the buying of petrol offered similar opportunities to his chauffeur. Auchinleck owned a Volkswagen, which he used for excursions, often up into the Atlas Mountains, and he became very attached to it. Eventually, however, it gave too much trouble and had to be replaced. Auchinleck wrote:

Have been busy and a bit anxious this week getting rid of the VW which hurts me a little as I got very fond of it. (Dotty old fool!) But it's nearly four years old and if anything does go wrong with the gears they cannot deal with them. I have bought a Renault. Bashir does not approve of it, probably because he was not consulted.

The climate and scenery of Morocco suited Auchinleck very well and, in general, he found life there greatly preferable to that in Britain. Not long after moving to Marrakech he wrote, during a visit to England:

I just cannot go on living in this state of affairs knowing that I can do nothing to help, so I am getting out. It is no use staying here and getting more and more frustrated. I hate leaving my friends but I must preserve if I can my peace of mind and my sanity if I have any. I need to be able to relax – to have space and air and mountains and *sunshine*. Selfish, if you like, but I do not wish to become an ill-tempered, crotchety, censorious old man, especially as I am a very old man already – although I don't feel it.

(He had said much the same when he sold Oswald House and emigrated.)

That same year – back in Marrakech – he was writing: 'I feel better after Bashir's lunch of tomato and onion salad and four (small ones) red mullet, topped up with fine dates. I am sure it is a meal of which my medic would approve.' Clearly, he was keenly appreciative of these simple pleasures, as he was of the changing countryside, and of visits. In 1971 he wrote:

Yesterday with two military attachés from the Embassy in Rabat to pass the time of day with thirty 'Tommies' from the Fusiliers in Gibraltar learning to ski under Moroccan instructors. Delightful for me to meet young soldiers off duty and full of life. They are really no different from the 'Tommy' of yesterday, more open, perhaps, and full of intelligence, beautifully mannered and friendly as the British soldier always was until he was roused by bad manners or cruelty – very rarely.

Later that year, in June, at the age of eighty-seven, he was back in England and revisited Sandhurst:

Yesterday went well at Sandhurst – a fine parade but a bit of a strain — nervous rather than physical as it is a long time since I had to stand at attention for a salute and a march past. The new memorial windows in the Old Chapel to the men of the Indian Army are, I think, very good and splendid. I am so glad that at last we have been able to do something to make people remember them.

As Auchinleck entered his nineties, he found himself less and less inclined to visit England. Each year seemed to make him more disillusioned with that country, and more sharply aware of the joys of Morocco:

When politics become a profession as far as money is concerned they are sure to deteriorate. Of course I realise that in the old days money and dishonesty came into it but most of them did not depend on politics for a living.

Glorious weather here and wonderful views of all the high Atlas under heavy snow. The narcissus and mimosa just starting to flower but all the walnut, silver birches, poplars still bare of leaves or with their autumn colouring still there. [It was January.] *Very* lovely.

He also had fewer surviving friends to visit in England. Hubert Wilson-Fox died in 1972; Seago died in 1974. And in 1975 Auchinleck's sister Ruth died: 'It has been a great shock to me,' he wrote, 'and I feel very depressed. We used to have our fights but we loved each other I think in a queer hard way. Her husband was my oldest friend.' That same year he was writing:

The days of colonies and overseas empires seem to be over, and also, I think, the days of European supremacy in the other continents. But that's the way the world goes. Queen Elizabeth I's ambassadors approached the Great Mogul in Delhi(?) on their hands and knees ... I do not think Spain can hang on much longer to Spanish Morocco. The days of European colonisation seem to be over. Perhaps the next generation may see the reverse – Asia and Africa flooding over into Europe. After all the Moors were in Spain for 400 years.

A note of wistfulness for days gone by seems to have crept into Auchinleck's letters – but always countered by a cheerful reasonableness. At the end of 1975 he commented in a letter:

I am rather sad to see on your postage stamps that they (whoever 'They' are) are to prevent the people round the world knowing that we have a Queen still on her throne by having a tiny silhouette tucked away in a corner. I wonder if the great Victoria in whose reign I was born would have put up with this sort of treatment.

Bashir is in his usual form bullying me but seeing I am well fed and kept out of mischief. Old Mahjoob is just the same – old humbug – but he does keep the car well. I am lucky as I seem to keep fit and can walk three miles a day without effort. No boasting.

Earlier he had spoken of going to England that year, but: 'Travel gets more and more expensive and so far as I know they have not given Field-Marshals on half pay a rise.' (Earlier he had mentioned that a pay increase amounted to £46 a year.)

His lack of money seems from his letters to have become a matter of some concern to Auchinleck – though one cannot help wondering how much he really wanted to revisit Britain. Certainly money was short, owing partly to Auchinleck's misplaced trust in Bashir; however generous throughout his life as he was, Auchinleck seems never to have had any money of his own, nor more than a few very small investments. From his prestigious positions in the business world nothing seems to have emerged for him – while others made fortunes. He had probably remained content with a small director's fee and had made no effort to acquire shares in the booming concerns with which he was associated. A less modest man might have made a better bargain.

The following year, 1976, Auchinleck again felt that he would not be able to visit England:

I am really very sorry that I may not get to England this summer. You see fares and prices go up and up while my half pay as a FM on the ACTIVE LIST (FMs never retire but go on HALF PAY) remains stationary. I'm not grumbling. I'm very comfortable and well-looked-after here and am lucky to have a car.

That year a ceremony was held at St Paul's Cathedral to unveil a memorial to those field-marshals of the Second World War who had commanded a theatre of operations, of whom Auchinleck was the sole survivor. As he was unable to attend, his family represented him at the service.

Although content to lead a quieter and less mobile life than previously, Auchinleck, as always, received many visitors. Among them were an American couple, Donald and Marion Brownlow, whom he had known for a number of years; indeed, in the early years of their acquaintance, Auchinleck had gone to Pennsylvania and stayed with them for three weeks. They visited him frequently in Marrakech and always expressed much solicitude for his welfare. Donald Brownlow wrote a book on the First Battle of Alamein – *Checkmate at Ruweisat: Auchinleck's Finest Hour* – which was published in the USA in 1977.

An unexpected visitor was General Sir Peter Hunt, recently Chief of the General Staff. (He had declined the rank of field-marshal, saying that he had enough to live on, and that as the Defence Budget was being restricted it would be quite wrong for him to accept a rank carrying more pay when it was unnecessary.) General Hunt appeared at the door of the flat in Marrakech. Auchinleck opened it: 'Good Heavens! Whatever are you doing here, Peter?'

'Well,' replied the General, 'I've really come to discuss with you the sort of funeral you should have when the time comes.'

'Funeral,' said Auchinleck, 'I don't want a funeral. When I die just dig a hole in the ground and pop me in it.'

'Ah, no,' said the General, 'We couldn't do that with a field-marshal. The Queen wouldn't like it, you know.'

'Oh, wouldn't she? Well, that's different – we'd better talk about it.'

There would, of course, have been other subjects they might have talked about. They had both been at Wellington; both were Scots; both were distinguished; and of both it has often been said they were 'too nice to get to the top'. In many ways they were remarkably alike.

In 1977 Bashir died, which greatly saddened Auchin-leck:

Bashir's sad death after a very short illness has been a great blow to me and I feel really lonely without his cheerful criticising sallies and his very efficient care of me over seven years. I know Kipling says, 'Never give your heart to a dog to tear' but I had a great affection for Bashir and his ways of bullying me. He was a staunch friend and a wise counsellor who saved me a lot of expense and made life easy. I miss his very pungent ideas of people and things. Stupid to have become so dependent and so fond of Bashir. However, life goes on and the youth is not a bad cook and keeps the flat fairly well ... It has been a shock to me and I have had thoughts of closing down and returning to England or rather the UK. I do not want to leave here and there is no doubt the climate is almost perfect for me ... I hope to get to England next year if I am still on my feet perhaps to celebrate my 94th birthday. 21st June 1884 was birthday at Aldershot, where my father was a captain or major in the Gunners. How long ago!

In that year Auchinleck's memory faded almost completely, a circumstance possibly hastened by Bashir's death. He did not revisit England the following year, although he did remain in good health. For a time after Bashir's death he was not well looked after; then he received a visit from A. R. Hall, Organising Secretary for the Society of Protection of Animals in North Africa – who as a young RAF officer in 1941 had once met, and been much impressed by, Auchinleck. Seeing how unsatisfactory the Field-Marshal's arrangements were, Robert Hall approached the British Embassy and suggested they might wish to take steps. This they did, and arranged for the British Army Lance-Corporal Millward and his Moroccan wife to move into the flat above Auchinleck's and look after him. This seems to have worked very well. In addition to them, during his last years the Field-Marshal had many people quietly keeping an eye on his welfare, foremost among them his cousin Lt-Col.

Clive Auchinleck, his nearest relative bearing the name.

Never having been in the habit of brooding over the past, Auchinleck remained interested in the world and the people around him up to his death, and this seems to have kept him young in spirit. His decision to retire to Marrakech has often been criticised, but it seems that he knew what he needed and what was good for him. As he was still able to enjoy living at the age of ninety-six, that alone seems a reasonable answer to his critics. Auchinleck died in his Marrakech home during the night of 23 March 1981.

20

THE DIMBLEBY INTERVIEWS

In 1974 when David Dimbleby, the distinguished broad-
caster and writer, was on holiday in Marrakech, he was
introduced to Auchinleck. He was surprised to find the
eighty-nine-year-old Field-Marshal so fit and alert, and
asked him if he would agree to being interviewed for a
television film. Somewhat reluctantly Auchinleck agreed.
Dimbleby was astonished at the way in which the elderly
Field-Marshal stood up to hour after hour of television
interviewing. The results of these interviews were in-
corporated in a film entitled *The Auk at 90* which was
shown on BBC Television. Auchinleck's comment on it
was: 'People of my age should not appear on television!'

Two years later Dimbleby went to Morocco again for
a further series of interviews. These were to be the basis
of a book to be published by Leo Cooper, but Dimbleby
had too many other commitments to find the time to write
the book and, very kindly, he and Leo Cooper agreed that
the transcripts should be made available to be used here.

Dimbleby was greatly impressed by the fair-mindedness,
generosity and imperturbability of Auchinleck, who
stressed his admiration for Churchill, even though the
latter had not really understood the problems of desert
warfare, could see Montgomery's good points although
Montgomery had been less than generous to him, and
could even speak sympathetically of Rommel's problems.

The conversations had begun with Dimbleby asking
whether Auchinleck had ever thought of being anything
else except a soldier. He had not, but never regretted the
fact, even in his less comfortable moments. He recalled
that early life had been a time when money was always
short, but that this had not mattered when he joined the
Indian Army for there an officer could live on his pay. He
certainly did not regret not being able to be in the British
Army; nobody wanted to leave the Indian Army when

once in it. Nor did anyone in the Indian Army feel inferior because he had less private money than his British counterpart, for all, British and Indian Army officers, came from the same background. India had been delightful from the beginning. From India he had gone to Suez for the First World War, then to an uncomfortable time in Mesopotamia. He agreed that he was ambitious but certainly never expected to become a field-marshal.

Was he more professional in his attitude to soldiering than other officers serving in the Indian Army? he was asked.

'Perhaps yes. Not to be a snob about it. But I think soldiering was in my blood and I really cared for nothing else ... I mean, I played games and went in for shooting birds, and sport and that sort of thing but soldiering was what I cared about always.' This he felt most strongly when he commanded his battalion. Later 'the responsibilities got greater and greater and one became lonelier and lonelier.'

At the start of the Second World War he found himself in a very different world, that of England, commanding a British corps. The corps front ran from Bognor to Bristol, and most of his men were from untrained Territorial divisions. The Regular Army had been reorganised and was no better than the Territorials. But 'they were all right, they came through.'

'Was it very alarming, holding a line from Bognor to Bristol ...?'

'No good being alarmed ... One sometimes wondered what would happen if the Germans did land, because there were very few troops there, really.'

'What do you think would have happened?'

'I think we should have held them. But I don't know. Very difficult to say, really ... I don't think one had any doubts of holding them somehow, eventually.'

The conversation changed to the Middle East. Asked about his relationship with Churchill: 'Oh, I had a great respect for him. Very great respect. But I'm not sure he realised what difficulties the army was working under at that time. But of course his job was to instil into everybody the certainty of winning. And the necessity of fighting. Which he did do.'

Wasn't Churchill very quick to accuse Auchinleck 'of stiffness or unbendingness or delay or whatever it was'?

'Yes, but his job was to give me a job to do and let me do it in my own way, not do it in his way. Any soldier will tell you that. Any commander who tries to make his subordinates think the way he's thinking, and they don't want to think like that, is wrong. He ought to give them a job and let them do it in their own way. If he doesn't think they can do it, then he can remove them. But it's fatal to try and suggest things to a chap who's already made up his mind, I think. That may sound to you obstinate but you can't change plans in an operation of that size ... You can only make minor alterations.'

'How much of your energies were spent fighting London rather than fighting the enemy?'

'Very little, really. Chiefs of Staff couldn't have been better. Churchill was all right. But his habit of trying to interfere was fatal, really; one just had to disregard it.'

Did Auchinleck feel a very strong urge to take over command in the field?

'Oh, yes,' came the answer, but he couldn't do both his jobs.

'Twice during that year you had to remove commanders, Cunningham and Ritchie. What was it like to take that decision?'

'Oh, it was very unpleasant, of course, because they were old friends. But still it had to be done. Cunningham certainly realised it, and I think Ritchie did too.'

'People said afterwards – with hindsight – that it was one of the difficulties of coming from India straight into the desert that you didn't know people well enough to make good appointments of the people under you. Is there any truth in that, do you think?'

'Well, I think I knew ... because one had met a good many of the British Army in India – but it was difficult afterwards, in a way. But one could always consult the Chief of the General Staff. One wasn't absolutely on one's own, you see.'

'What was Rommel like as an opponent?'

'Oh, very agile. Very agile. Very dangerous too. He had his troubles, of course. The German troops were very good ... The Italians were not so good. And the bulk of his army was Italian, really. He was a first-class commander; you couldn't go to sleep when he was about ... [But] you could tell – more or less – what he was likely to do in certain circumstances ... I was afraid [he might have a kind of hold over British troops]. That's why I sent out a certain message* that he wasn't God Almighty ... The British are rather ... inclined to idolise their opponents.'
Rommel's weak points were, in Auchinleck's opinion, over-confidence and an underestimation of what the British Army could do.

'Do you think that London understood what had happened in the desert and what you'd achieved up to the point you reached Alamein?'

'I think so ... [But Churchill] was desperately searching after results, to keep the morale in England up, and to keep the war going.'

'... Is is true that Montgomery used your plan for his battle of Alamein?'

'I don't think there's much difference between them, really. No, I think it was his plan. Mind you, it took place a long time after I left. And things had changed in the interval; I mean reinforcements had arrived ...'

'Why was it, do you think, that both Churchill in his way and Montgomery much more strongly gave the impression there was an air of defeat in the desert when he arrived?'

'I can't tell you. But there certainly wasn't an air of defeat. Because, after all, the Australians had carried out a very successful counter-offensive in the north and the New Zealanders had done one in the south too. I found no signs of depression among the troops at all. In the front line.'

Did Churchill seem irritable or prickly when he flew out to Cairo on 3 August 1942 to see Auchinleck?

'No, he was perfectly all right. Didn't say much.'

* March 1942: 'There is a real danger that our friend Rommel will turn into a bogeyman ... He is not superhuman – energetic and capable as he is ...'

'Did you have any idea at all that he might be on the verge of firing you?'

'I think I had a suspicion, but it came as a shock. No, I think I expected it. ... I think he'd made up his mind before he came. I'm sure he had.'

'Would you have respected him more if he'd told you face to face?'

'I respected him a great deal. I always have ...'

'Were you hurt?'

'Possibly slightly humiliated, but not hurt. A change of commander by a politician is a very different thing to a change of commander by a higher commander.'

Auchinleck was asked what he felt about Tobruk, whose loss probably contributed greatly to his removal. He regarded it as unimportant. It was valuable as a port if the army was moving forward, but as a besieged city it was quite useless. Its defence meant a great deal to Churchill but not to him.

'Why did [Montgomery] claim that you had planned a retreat to the Nile and beyond?'

'Absolute rubbish. I did plan that if we were driven away from the Alamein position certain operations would take place. We would retire up the Nile as an army in existence ... To prevent the enemy advancing into Egypt certain demolitions ... were to take place. We were pretty thin on the ground ... It was a plan if the worst came to the worst and we had to get out of Alamein; we would retreat into Egypt and if necessary turn southward up the Nile remaining as an army, not allow ourselves to be defeated in detail.'

'I'm curious that you never chose to join in the argument or to defend yourself directly.'

'Well, I think history defends oneself, really. I don't think as a soldier it's one's duty to defend oneself.' History does that accurately, Auchinleck believed.

Dimbleby asked the Field-Marshal why he and Montgomery did not seem to have been able to get on together. 'I suppose we looked on things differently, quite differently ... Montgomery had his methods and I'm sure they were very good, very successful. But they weren't my methods of dealing with men or commanding; ... I didn't approve of [his methods] and he didn't approve of me. Of my methods.'

Which generals or heroes did Auchinleck particularly admire? 'Well, the Duke of Wellington [and,] I think, Lord Roberts.'

Dimbleby went on to ask the Field-Marshal about the beginning of his military career, in Tibet in 1906–7. Auchinleck recalled that they had lived in an old Tibetan fort, where the routine was to rise at 7 am and engage in pre-breakfast drill or musketry training. Breakfast would be followed by more instructional periods, and then riding on small Tibetan ponies before lunch. Twenty-five of his men were what is known as 'mounted infantry' – they used horses to reach their objectives, and would then dismount to fight on foot. After lunch there would be more training followed by hockey and football. Nobody was allowed to go far from camp, but it was permissible to visit the nearby city where there were huge monasteries. Later, in India, there was the same sort of routine but it was also possible to go trekking in the Himalayan foothills at the weekends. He was very seldom bored, although he agreed that ordinary soldiering could be boring at times. His regiment was made up of Hindus, Sikhs, Pathans and Punjabis, but, of course, it was divided later on Partition. When it was split the different races wept on each other's shoulders – it had existed as a regiment for 150 years. All the men in the 62nd (later 1/1st) Punjabis were volunteers. Each man's father must own a piece of land, perhaps only two acres, but landowning was essential, since it gave status and stability to the recruits, and a common language shared by men from different areas and of different religions.

In view of the long history of the different peoples living together the massacres at the time of Partition were a shock. Asked whether the army could have been used more effectively to prevent them Auchinleck said that he doubted it, in view of the fact that it was itself split up at the time. Had it remained intact that would have been a different matter. The outbreaks of violence were too scattered, too widespread for the army to be able – at that time – to restore order quickly.

He had no regrets over insisting that the INA trials should take place in the Red Fort in Delhi. People had suggested that the venue was provocative and that trials should take place discreetly elsewhere, but Auchinleck felt that though this might be discreet politically it would be wrong morally. 'While we were still there,' he said, 'it seemed to me completely wrong to allow these people to walk about free when they'd broken their oath of allegiance and, in fact, committed a treachery.' He was being fair to those who had remained faithful.

His saddest memory was the break-up of the Indian Army. Up to the last, the entitity and discipline of the army had been maintained; better, for instance, than the Indian navy which had mutinied and had had its mutiny put down by the army.

What was the worst time in his career? he was asked.

It was the period he spent in India from August 1942 to June 1943 between being C-in-C, Middle East and his appointment as C-in-C, India – a time of doing virtually nothing.

Did he approve of Britain today? No, he didn't – 'But it'll come round all right. It always has. A lot of common sense at the bottom.' He thought he had been wise to move to Marrakech because it was cheap and pleasant to live in. He did not brood on the past.

'Are you a religious person?'

'No ... never have been, really ... I'm not irreligious, but I'm not religious, really. One's knocked about too much for that. Seen too many religions, too. They all breed priests and priests are all the same everywhere.'

When, two years later, Auchinleck was asked again about his relationship with Churchill he reverted to the point that Churchill's view was probably understandable in the light of his need for a quick victory. But it was not correct for Churchill to try to force Auchinleck along further than he wished to proceed; if Churchill wished for a faster pace he must find a different man for the job.

Dimbleby raised the point of Wavell's relationship with Churchill. 'Some people say that Wavell fought the "Battleaxe" campaign earlier than he thought right and that as a result "Battleaxe" was a failure . . . Dill told you [that it was his opinion], didn't he?'

'Yes, that's right. That's quite true. That was an indication to me of what was likely to happen.'

'But if that's true it would mean that Churchill caused the failure of "Battleaxe".'

'Yes, he did undoubtedly, I think.'

But if he had waited longer, 'Battleaxe' could have been successful and the whole war ended two years earlier than it did, Dimbleby suggested.

Auchinleck avoided making any comment on that, but later, when discussing warfare in general terms, said: 'For a man in command to start a major offensive with what he thought was inadequate means was little short of murder, really, and the general had to consider the men under his command first, before he considered anything else, really. There are occasions when he has to ask them to do the impossible because he is forced to do so by the enemy.'

Auchinleck had always considered that, in general, for an offensive in the desert to succeed, you need to be twice as strong as the enemy: 'You see, the desert was completely different from Europe. Europe became static very quickly. The desert always had an open flank and movement around the desert was possible anywhere practically . . . provided you can find water and transport.'

'If you met on equal terms does that mean there could never be a winner?'

'If you meet on equal terms . . . [it becomes] a question of mobility of your forces. You hold your enemy with the minimum that you think necessary to hold him in position and you try to manoeuvre round him. Well, that opens up all sorts of possibilities on both sides. I was always anxious that Rommel would try to turn my southern flank and I expect he thought the same.'

David Dimbleby asked the Field-Marshal if he had liked that form of warfare, and if he thought it was, as some claimed, the 'purest form of warfare'. Auchinleck was cautious: yes, but 'within limits'.

When pressed about his reasons for appointing Cunningham, whom he had not known before meeting him in the Middle East, he said: '. . . I put him in command because I thought he had the idea of mobile warfare . . . and I was rather impressed by what he had done in Central Africa on a small scale, and I put him in command for that reason, and I think he did very well. His health cracked up eventually – that's why I had to remove him.'

Dimbleby expressed surprise that Auchinleck had not been 'broken' by losing the Middle East command: 'How did you manage to remain so calm about what happened to you?'

'Well, it was no good fussing about it anyway. No good fussing. No, no, no . . . A soldier accepts that sort of thing.'

And many people would have been broken had they been in his position as C-in-C, India during Partition and the division of the Indian Army, but Auchinleck did not seem to have been, Dimbleby commented. The Field-Marshal replied: 'Well, that's nothing to bother about if one has done one's best, that's all. One didn't like it very much . . .'

What about life in Cairo? he was asked.

'I didn't go to Cairo much. I didn't take part in any social life there. You had to go to a dinner now and again or give a dinner party but in the desert they didn't have any social life, really, and I kept away from it as much as I could. I hadn't got the time for it. Cairo was a handicap, really . . . I should have thought so myself, but then I'm different. Some people like society and that sort of thing. It was very difficult to get a wartime atmosphere into Cairo.'

'But can the work of command, which is intellectual work, be done as efficiently out in the heat of the desert as it can in proper offices in Cairo, do you think?'

'Much more so, I think . . . There were all the maps and things you wanted. You had all the people you wanted, you had your own brain. For me, anyway, much better. I should never have been happy in Cairo. I wasn't happy there, anyway.'

Asked about the conditions he had lived in: 'I slept on the ground . . . I don't like living in comparative luxury while the troops are living very simply. It always affects me like that. I think it affects them, too. They may think you are a bloody fool or take advantage of you, and that sort of thing, but otherwise they may think it is a good thing to have you nearby. I may be quite wrong.'

'Are you an austere sort of person really?'

'No, no, I like comfort. I like my good meals. I like my drink but I don't like being separated in comparative luxury from troops who are living hard.'

Dimbleby then returned to the subject of Tobruk, and asked if the siege had affected Auchinleck's plan.

'From my point of view it was a bloody nuisance because I would have much preferred to use the forces that I had in a very wide strike to the south instead of plugging forward to relieve Tobruk ... But Tobruk was sort of engraved on Churchill's heart, I think.'

'Can you tell me a bit about Rommel and your view of Rommel?'

'He was a very dangerous enemy, there's no doubt of that ... He used his resources such as they were to the very best ends, really.'

'How did you yourself learn this new kind of warfare?'

'Oh, one knew about the desert already. We had studied war in the desert long before the first war started, and exercises ... In India you had vast spaces ... [and you were not] tied to roads. Movement wasn't possible everywhere – where there were sand hills and dunes – but compared with a European country there were no roads.'

'Was Rommel cleverer than we were?'

'Do you mean was he cleverer than I was, or what? ... I don't know, we beat him in the end, didn't we? ... He depended on his Germans mostly and there weren't a hell of a lot of Germans ... His Italians ... were all right in defence. The Italian isn't a bad soldier ... but I don't think that Rommel relied on them very much compared with his Germans ... I don't think their leaders were very good.'

Dimbleby pressed him hard once more on his relationship with Churchill. 'I was not afraid of Churchill,' he said. 'Some people were ... [But his interference] was a disturbing influence on a chap like myself who the whole day and night was concentrating on one thing and determined to get the best out of it.' He did not need encouraging to beat the enemy, the Field-Marshal continued; 'I was glad to get encouraged if things went well, but I didn't want any encouragement to put everything I had into beating the Germans.'

It was the nearest he ever came to criticising Churchill's treatment of him, and even then it was only because the interference impeded his work. At no time did he make a personal criticism.

21

SOME ASSESSMENTS

Unlike many soldiers of distinction, Auchinleck never wrote a book about his experiences, not because he was bitter about them, but simply because he felt no special wish to do so. History, he believed, would relate the facts, and he saw no reason to speak of himself nor justify his own actions – history, he was sure, would be his judge. So far, it would seem that his faith in its impartiality and accuracy was somewhat naive.

When John Connell published his long, comprehensive biography of Auchinleck in 1959 it was admired for its skilful handling of an enormous quantity of material but criticised because it was said 'to have too much sympathy with him, too little with his detractors' and to be 'twice as long as it should be'. Nevertheless it was praised for revealing 'the noble character of Auchinleck and his most incalculable services to Britain and the Commonwealth over those most testing years from 1940–7'. Some of the critics stressed what they felt was Auchinleck's inability to choose the right subordinates, many felt that he was an unlucky general, but all agreed that, to use Ismay's words, 'he was a most impressive figure; dignified, commanding and apparently self-confident'. But Ismay went on to say: 'Only those who knew him well realised that he was shy and sensitive. He was as much an introvert as his political chief was an extrovert, and there were likely to be misunderstandings unless they got to know each other.'

Connell's respect for the subject of his book is easily understood. Auchinleck was a man who merits high esteem on three main counts. He was a general who demonstrated great skill in commanding inadequately equipped forces against a very determined and skilful opponent; he was a man of great understanding and compassion; and he was a person of complete integrity. There is no record of any chicanery or dishonesty at any stage in his life; he was, perhaps, too honest for his own good.

Connell, it should be remembered, was no novice at assessment or biography. An exhibitioner at Balliol College, Oxford, he became a successful novelist and biographer – he was awarded the James Tait Black Memorial Prize for his biography of W. E. Henley – and was a leader writer on the *Evening News*, and, in 1944, Chief Military Press Censor in India (he had been commissioned into the Royal Artillery). He died of a heart attack at the age of fifty-six while engaged on a biography of Field-Marshal Lord Wavell.

A subsequent, much shorter, biography, written by Roger Parkinson, *The Auk: Victor at Alamein*, was published in 1977. In the preface Parkinson wrote:

Auchinleck has still to be given full credit for his achievements, and if this biography results in any move in this direction then it will have achieved its purpose ... I feel so strongly about the ill-treatment which I believe Auchinleck received both at the time and by history. As I said to him: 'I feel angry even if you don't.' He chuckled again and finally admitted: 'Oh well, I felt a bit angry too as a matter of fact!'

Parkinson, who died of cancer at the age of thirty-seven, felt that Connell's defence of – and admiration for – Auchinleck had been justified by the documents in the War Cabinet files which had not been available before 1970. Parkinson's own study of the Field-Marshal is lucid and interesting, and he too had an impressive record as a writer and biographer.

In later years fresh light has been thrown on the events in which Auchinleck was involved by the publication of information about Ultra. Ultra was in fact of little value to Auchinleck: it was not sufficiently developed to be of use in the Norway campaign, and in the desert it tended to put him at a disadvantage, since Churchill received Ultra information before he did. What was worse was the fact that Churchill implicitly believed the information from Ultra relating to Rommel, although few others did. (During a battle Ultra information about tactical developments was never decoded and distributed to commanders in time to be effective.) Most damaging of all was that Churchill believed the accounts, intercepted through the Ultra system, that Rommel sent to his higher command lamenting the inadequacies of his equipment and supplies. It seemed obvious to Churchill that if Rommel was as weak as he said he was Auchinleck should attack and secure victory at once. But Rommel was not nicknamed 'the Desert Fox' for nothing, and he was as adept at beguiling his own superiors as he was the enemy. Thus assessments of what Auchinleck might have done are only valid if balanced against the real strength of the Axis forces in North Africa, not against wartime estimates, even if those estimates derived from Ultra.

There have, of course, been many references to Auchinleck in other books, including Montgomery's memoirs, mentioned earlier. Auchinleck did not allow Montgomery's libel about the plan to retreat up the Nile to pass without comment. When extracts from the book were published in the *Sunday Times* he sent several very firm letters, including one to Montgomery, pointing out that the latter's account of their conversation in the desert was pure fantasy. The knowledge that the statement had already appeared in copies of the book and the newspaper which had been widely distributed was particularly annoying. Even if Montgomery apologised and withdrew that statement – neither of which seemed a likely possibility – there would be (and indeed are) numerous copies of the book on library shelves and in private hands which would still carry that damaging account. There is, of course, another factor: Montgomery's reputation is, rightly, very great, and his views can be a powerful influence upon succeeding historians; thus a considerable injustice could be perpetrated for a very long time, if not for ever. In later years, when discussing his actions in the desert Auchinleck would occasionally say, 'History will prove me right'. He made this remark very firmly when talking to R. B. Goodall during a visit to the National Army Museum in 1971, and again in the Dimbleby interviews. Sadly, he never wrote a book; Montgomery did.

There will always be arguments as to who was the

greater soldier, futile as these may be. Perhaps the most interesting aspect of Auchinleck as a general is that he is most often presented as the only true rival to Montgomery, something which the latter sensed. For all their many and obvious virtues Wavell, Alexander, Patton, Bradley, Rommel, Guderian and others are but rarely rated as better than Montgomery *in the field* – Auchinleck is the only true exception. Arguments are clouded by the enormous esteem in which both men are held; if Montgomery is considered to be the more professional and effective, then Auchinleck's is held to be the truer spirit. There can never be a satisfactory resolution to these debates, and it is as pointless to decry Montgomery's military genius by citing his treatment of Auchinleck as it is to bolster that genius by citing Auchinleck's apparent failure in the Western Desert.

One thing, however, remains: Auchinleck is undoubtedly the hurdle between Montgomery and his supporters' vision of him as 'the greatest military commander since Wellington'. That hurdle is founded not only on Montgomery's disgraceful behaviour towards his predecessor – great men often display a truly staggering pettiness and spite, as both Churchill and Wellington demonstrated. But beneath the surface appears to lie a genuine belief that Auchinleck *was* the better general: Montgomery's defenders make considerable efforts to disprove it; Auchinleck's supporters flounder among the 'if onlys'; Montgomery himself (who devoted much time to making sure that his version of history would prove him right) undoubtedly felt it. It is interesting, therefore, to compare the views of other writers, laying aside any question of Auchinleck's treatment at the hands of Churchill or Montgomery.

Nigel Hamilton says of Auchinleck that he 'had a presence which automatically evoked respect', and that others ascribed 'a bigness of character, of spirit, to him which might pass for greatness', qualities with which Montgomery was not 'naturally gifted'. This is faint praise, however, for Mr Hamilton also says that Auchinleck 'frittered away every advantage and happily permitted subsequent historians to invent every conceivable excuse to distract attention from the real problem', Auchinleck's failure to smash Rommel. He also describes 'Crusader' as 'ill-starred', and views the successes at First Alamein as the results of 'a series of German miscalculations'. A commander's ability to cause his enemy to miscalculate is, one would have thought, a prime military virtue; nevertheless, luck, the RAF and artillery are given as the causes of the Axis reversal. 'Auchinleck later acknowledged that he had no confidence, in the last days of June, that Rommel could in fact be held' – yet, as Norman Clark relates (see Appendix D), as early 13 June Auchinleck intended to draw Rommel on to the Alamein position, 'bring him on to our anvil and use the sledgehammer'. This demonstrates considerable aggressive intent during disastrous times, not lack of confidence. The proof is that the plan worked, Rommel was not only 'held', but beaten to a standstill.

Norman Clark's evidence also disputes Brigadier C. E. Lucas Phillips's assertion that First Alamein was the 'concluding phase of the Battle of Gazala'. It was indeed the 'aftermath of that rough harvest', but it was fought, and had been prepared, as an offensive battle, not as a desperate, hurried attempt to save the Delta. Perhaps the sincerest compliment to Auchinleck's inspiration in drawing Rommel on to the Alamein line was paid by Montgomery, who fought and won two battles on those same positions. Brigadier Lucas Phillips also quotes one of Rommel's staff officers, von Mellenthin, on 'the "complete lack of co-ordination and control" by the British'; Rommel, meanwhile, was writing 'the enemy are rounding up our Italian formations one by one. Our German units will be far too weak to stand by themselves. It makes me weep!' And Ronald Lewin writes of 'Auchinleck's defeat of Rommel in the First Battle of Alamein', going on to say that 'Neither Parliament, nor the nation, nor, in particular, the Prime Minister had grasped its profound significance.' There is a considerable irony in a victory admitted as such by the enemy, yet denied by those for whom it was gained.

The Cinderella at this particular ball is 'Crusader', that confusing series of battles (November 1941–January

942) which saw the relief of Tobruk and the recapture
of Benghazi and which proved – to both sides – that
Rommel could be beaten. Even John Terraine, describing
Auchinleck, rightly, as 'the first British general to defeat
a German general in battle in that war', gives the defeat
as First Alamein, not 'Crusader'. Brigadier Desmond
Young wrote of the operation: '. . . With a bare numerical
superiority of ill-armed, ill-armoured, unreliable tanks;
with a far inferior system of tank recovery; compelled, for
lack of anti-tank guns, to use 25-pounders to hold off the
panzers; with one division untrained to the desert; with
a total strength little more than that of the enemy, the
Eighth Army had defeated Rommel and driven him out
of Cyrenaica.' Rommel is reported to have shouted at his
Italian commanders that he would withdraw his forces to
Tripoli and have himself interned in neutral Tunisia –
'We haven't won the battle, so now there is nothing for
it but to retreat.' Here was a victory in which even
Churchill could believe; 'I rejoice in your continued
victorious exchanges and pursuit', he signalled Auchinleck on 20 December 1941. Within a few months, however, the pride of victory would be ashes in Auchinleck's
mouth.

'It is certainly doubtful if Montgomery was a better
general than Auchinleck, who possessed every military
virtue', wrote Sir Maurice Dean, and that is perhaps as
far as the debate can go – doubt. If Auchinleck has his
Gazala, Tobruk and Mersa Matruh, Montgomery has his
Dieppe, the delays in Normandy, and Arnhem. Yet the
latter is more often judged by his successes, Auchinleck
by his failures, for there can be no question that the ability
to publicise victory and conceal defeat is now a part
of modern generalship. Auchinleck's later commands,
not being in the field, brought him praise without
glory, where his efforts were noticed: stability in wartime
India, the armies of India and Pakistan, an unbiased and
moderating force in the midst of anarchy, his contribution
to victory in Burma, these achievements do not have the
popular appeal of even so costly a disaster as Arnhem.
Auchinleck may not have been a better general than
Montgomery but, had the chances been his, he would

undoubtedly have run him a very close second. The arguments can never be resolved, though they will rage for many years to come – not that they would have bothered Auchinleck. As John Connell wrote of him, quoting Stevenson, 'On he went up the great, bare staircase of his duty, uncheered and undepressed.'

David Dimbleby, who was greatly impressed by Auchinleck's ability to recall long-past events, received the impression that Auchinleck could see some reason behind Churchill's decision to relieve him of his command. Auchinleck felt that Wavell's removal had been reasonable because he was very tired. But Churchill's correct course of action should not have been to prod and probe at a commander to take the offensive but, if he felt that commander to be lethargic, to remove him – to that extent Auchinleck must have felt, on being dismissed himself, that Churchill was right. However, Churchill's inability to appreciate the basic military requirement of allowing adequate time to train reinforcements under desert conditions, made his action unjust. Auchinleck also felt strongly that Churchill should have dismissed him personally, not delegated the task to a junior man bearing a letter. This was not the 'soldier's way'.

It seems that Auchinleck, quite unconsciously, was guilty of the sort of Service arrogance which can be extremely galling to those encountering it. From the first moment of joining the recruit is taught – if he does not already believe – that the regular services are a breed apart. They have chosen a way of life and taken an oath binding them to its tenets. They will defend their civilian countrymen, but they cannot help but feel superior to them. Churchill knew this: he had once been part of the system, and as First Lord of the Admiralty in the early days of the First World War he had had ample opportunity of observing the way the Navy looked upon civilians, particularly politicians. He therefore came to the Second World War very conscious of the fact that, given half a chance, the Service chiefs would brush his ideas to one side. Determined not to let this happen, he harried them. In London the rules of this power game were well understood, but to Auchinleck it was a game of which he had no experience. He did not realise (though Ismay tried to warn him) that Churchill needed to be pampered. 'Pampering' meant giving Churchill the reassurance and help he badly needed; what he did not need was a series of entirely reasonable explanations of why what he thought vital was not possible. Still less did he appreciate that Auchinleck's refusal to return to London for talks was not military arrogance, the refusal to treat with politicians, but a reasoned assumption that nothing would be gained and much perhaps lost if he did return. Auchinleck did not seem to realise that he had been appointed to Middle East Command because he was thought to be a thrusting general, a man of drive and decision, a man who would waste no time. Once in his post he appeared to Churchill to be even more stubborn and cautious than Wavell. He seemed also to be making mistakes: the reversal after 'Crusader', the 'Gazala Gallop', the loss of Tobruk, the sackings of Cunningham and Ritchie. It was not the success story which had been hoped for.

Auchinleck seems to have been unaware of the need not only to pamper Churchill, but also to keep him reasonably happy. His answers about training and equipment were altogether too defensive; if he had replied by asking why it was impossible to produce more efficient tanks and better trained troops from England, Churchill might have growled, but he would have appreciated the spirit of it. Churchill admired dashing, flamboyant performances, even though he should have learnt his lesson more than forty years earlier from the disastrous charge at Omdurman, in which he had taken part. Churchill gave the impression that he felt that if he could harry his Service chiefs enough they would produce the results he wanted, without regard to practicalities. It is interesting in this light to recall the entry in Lord Hankey's Diary for 19 November 1941:

This morning announced the replacement of Dill (CIGS) by Alan Brooke and Pownall (VCIGS) by Nye. I wrote to both. I told Dill that the people who ought to be replaced were quite different, meaning

Churchill and Beaverbrook. Dill is furious with Churchill who took it on himself as Minister of Defence to make the changes. Dill told me that Tedder was kept in his command by Auchinleck (C-in-C, Middle East) who insisted he must stay. They have sent two Churchill tanks to take part in the push in Libya, which began yesterday. But, in order to try to make them go they have had their internal arrangements altered *by hand* by super-experts, so that they are not the actual machine being produced by mass production, which are duds. If they go they will say what wonderful tanks they are. The reason for the 3 weeks' delay in the 'push' is that they felt that even the useful Cruiser tanks were unreliable in the desert and strengthened their driving shafts . . .

Clearly Auchinleck was not the only one under pressure.

Sir David Hunt believes that Auchinleck quickly summed up Rommel's strength and weakness. He assessed his opponent as a daring but over-rash general who was not quite the genius he was made out to be. Rommel was brilliant at gaining a local tactical advantage but could go badly astray in more important matters. He made an enormous strategic mistake by pressing on after the Gazala victories, only to be checked by Auchinleck's defences at Alamein. What he should have done at that point was to abandon his dash for Cairo and concentrate instead on an attack on Malta. He chose the wrong objective, and this largely contributed to the ultimate German defeat in the desert.

Professor Michael Howard, Regius Professor of Modern History at Oxford and former Chichele Professor of the History of War, once suggested to Auchinleck that he saw the defence of the Middle East primarily in terms of the defence of India, and had his eye so firmly fixed on the German threat from the Caucasus that he did not give the Western Desert the sustained attention it needed until it was almost too late. Auchinleck did not dissent, but neither did he confirm the view.

Everyone (except perhaps Montgomery) seems to have

admired Auchinleck as a man and as a soldier, but some express doubts about his abilities at the highest level. Brigadier Frederick de Butts, GSO2 (Intelligence) with XIII Corps in North Africa, felt that Auchinleck was no match for Rommel at tank warfare, and furthermore could not pick the right subordinates to help him; in these respects he had much more confidence in Montgomery. Lt-Gen. Sir Terence Airey, who served under Auchinleck in the desert, considered that changes were needed when Alexander replaced Auchinleck and Montgomery took over the Eighth Army. Asked whether he felt that Auchinleck would have been a better commander of the Normandy battles, he answered that he believed that 'Montgomery was the only possible choice for the Normandy invasion', but he doubted that Auchinleck would have involved Britain in the Arnhem episode.

The supreme accolade of the Second World War was, of course, to have command of the Normandy landings and the advance into Germany. Auchinleck certainly had the skill, which would have been sharpened had he been kept in an active command – perhaps Italy – after the Middle East. Whether, however, he would have chosen the right people to support him seems more open to question. Montgomery never excused what he thought might be interpreted as failure in others; Auchinleck, seems to have been prone to do so, though not invariably. In spite of his rank and fame he was a humble man. Field-Marshal Lord Slim said of him: 'In all the time I served with him I never heard him speak ill of anyone – and, by God, he had reason to. Nor would he believe evil of anyone and this may have been a chink in his armour.' In some ways Auchinleck made life more difficult for himself. But then he had been taught from a very early age not to choose for himself the easiest path.

A former officer in the Black Watch, R. T. MacFarlane, met the Field-Marshal in Marrakech in 1978 and asked him if he had preferred the early carefree days as a subaltern to the later period as Commander-in-Chief. The answer was no; he had preferred the posts of great responsibility and power, though he had told Dimbleby that increasing rank brought greater loneliness. He certainly never abused that power, but he enjoyed using it occasionally to help people or causes he thought worthy. One of these was Major Norman Price, who became his Press and Public Relations Officer in India in 1945. Owing to rapid and erratic postings Major Price received no pay for several months. At the end of his resources, he mentioned the matter to Auchinleck. A letter from the Commander-in-Chief to the Paymaster-General was immediately dispatched and Price received his due pay with all arrears. It had not, however, been an unpleasant letter.

Admiral Sir Rowland Jerram, who, as mentioned earlier, had been a member of the Charfield Commission on the Defence of India in 1938, travelled widely with Auchinleck at that period and had ample opportunity to observe him. He noted the enormous affection the Indians had for Auchinleck, then a major-general, who seemed like a loved and respected father to them. He remembered that the Committee meetings often produced some sharp conflict of opinion between Air-Marshal Sir Philip Joubert de la Ferté, commanding the RAF in India, and Auchinleck. Joubert believed that the RAF could control the North-West Frontier by bombing alone, and he had supporters in London who shared his view. The Committee was not convinced, however. Bombing could not hold ground, as infantry could, and its effect on the Frontier areas was to change what had been a series of virtually ritualised skirmishes – conducted almost as a game – into a campaign of sullen hatred. This is not to say that Frontier warfare was not a very dangerous activity for those taking part; such warfare is, however, a very different matter when the entire countryside is imbued with resentment and hatred. Jerram felt that Auchinleck was put under considerable strain by Joubert; in those days there was substantial faith in the idea that a few well-placed bombs would calm tribal turbulence, and in some areas they did. Subsequent campaigns, such as Vietnam, have thrown doubt on the belief.

Jerram considered that Auchinleck was admirably suited for the post of C-in-C, India (an appointment which, of course, he held twice, though under rather different conditions) and that his personality and prestige did much to maintain stability. The Admiral shared, however, the general doubt about Auchinleck's ability to choose the right staff officers: he thought that Dorman-Smith, whom Auchinleck regarded as a right-hand man, was clever but quite unsound. He had no doubt that, of the two field-marshals, Montgomery was better suited to supreme command and that his ability in choosing the right subordinates and giving absolutely clear instructions, combined with ruthlessness in discarding those he felt were failures, were qualities which Auchinleck did not possess to the same, necessary, degree.

Jerram's experience of assessing people's ability extended over a long period. He had joined the Navy in 1907, had fought at the battle of Jutland in the First World War and had seen plenty of action in the Second. In his view Auchinleck was entirely admirable as a person, and undoubtedly of very great ability, but for the highest posts, and in dealing with politicians, he was too much of a gentleman and too compassionate.

Auchinleck had a great respect for intelligent soldiers but some of his favourites, such as Corbett and Dorman-Smith, seem to have been what is aptly known as 'brilliant but unsound'. Dill was clearly a hero and a model. A remark which Auchinleck often made was 'You must either trust your general or sack him.' In 1941 Dill had written to Auchinleck: 'Churchill lost confidence in Wavell. I maintain that in war you must either trust your general or sack him.' Amery too had a great influence on Auchinleck, and the idea of the 'enemy section' or 'German cell' in the Middle East was based on a message sent by Amery to Auchinleck on 25 June 1941. Amery had edited *The Times History of the War* and noted that in 1918 General Sir Henry Wilson had told his intelligence officers to 'wear their hats back to front and look at the situation as the enemy might see it'. Wilson also instructed his staff to 'aim at the impossible and if it proved unattainable to modify their plans'. Some of Wilson's own surmises about enemy intentions proved inaccurate: nevertheless the principle seemed a good one, so Amery recommended it and Auchinleck with his 'German cell' put it into practice. Soon, however, Auchinleck did not need a 'German cell' to guess what the Germans were thinking. He had Ultra information to give him the facts.

The most puzzling of Auchinleck's actions is the dismissal of Trappes-Lomax in Norway. Auchinleck thought highly of Brigadier Gubbins, an opinion, in the reigning confusion, not always shared by the Scots Guards. As the Scots Guards withdrew along narrow valleys from Mo to Bodø they were constantly observed and harassed by enemy aircraft and occasionally outflanked by German troops trained to move in such terrain. On 21 May 1940 Colonel A. A. B. Dowler (later Major-General), one of Auchinleck's staff officers, visited Bodø and reported of the Scots Guards:

This battalion undoubtedly feels the Germans are superior in skill. It does not understand nor is it trained for fighting in the kind of country in which it now finds itself. The impression I get is that it fails to secure its flanks by occupying the high ground on either side of the valley. As this is a matter of commonsense one is forced to the conclusion that leadership has as much to answer for as lack of training.

How Dowler expected the Guardsmen, unequipped and untrained for such work, to scale hills of soft snow, he does not explain. His statements, however, clearly influenced Auchinleck to relieve Trappes-Lomax. On the day this happened – 23 May, two days after Dowler's report – Gubbins himself ordered the Scots Guards to withdraw from the Storfjord position between Mo and Bodø which he (Gubbins) had planned to hold for three days. He reported: 'The reason for the withdrawal was that the flanks of the position were being turned and the force was being subjected to attack by low-flying aircraft.'

To Auchinleck, with Frontier training and knowledge, but with no experience of Norway, the apparent inability to make a proper tactical withdrawal would be sufficient justification for his action. But a Scots Guards comment was: 'Frontier tribes do not usually possess modern automatic weapons and complete air superiority.'

Subsequently Auchinleck must have realised that an unfortunate decision had been made because he himself had not been able to survey the ground. Later he probably spent too much time 'having a look for himself' in other theatres, and it is possible, as has been said, that the unfair dismissal of Trappes-Lomax made him more tolerant of the mistakes of juniors in later years.

In 1942 he seems to have acted unwisely by retaining Ritchie when he already had doubts about the latter's ability. His lack of confidence in Ritchie (who later commanded XII Corps in the D-Day landings) made him reluctant to leave his Middle Eastern post even for a short time to confer with Churchill at home. Churchill gave him an ominous hint on 15 March 1942 – 'It would give me the greatest pain to feel that mutual understanding has ceased.' What the Prime Minister was implying was 'What are you doing with these extraordinary appointments: Cunningham, Ritchie, Shearer, Corbett, Dorman-Smith?'

So Auchinleck was dismissed the following August. The official history says of the August changes that the War Cabinet was not happy at the idea of dividing the Middle East Command and thought that the command proposed for Auchinleck – Iraq and Persia – would suggest that he had been down-graded by being appointed to a less active theatre. It did appear so to Auchinleck, but he did not refuse it for reasons of pride, as he explained to Churchill in their subsequent interview, but because he felt that the new command would lack confidence through feeling it was receiving a 'failed' general. On this occasion Churchill stoutly defended Auchinleck who, he said, had done very well and should not 'be ruined and cast aside as unfit to render any further service.' But it was a grave setback to Auchinleck's career, for he was an ambitious man who wanted to be successful – now the victories for which he had laid the foundations were to go to a rival who would be unlikely to share any triumph with their original architect.

Colonel Jeff Alexander, who was on Auchinleck's staff as Military Assistant during 1941, believes Auchinleck was probably the finest field commander of the war, and that his understanding of desert warfare was better than anyone else's at the time, certainly better than Montgomery's. 'The soldiers loved him,' he said, 'because he was such an honest-to-God soldier.' However, Alexander too had doubts about Auchinleck's ability to choose Staff officers, and instanced Corbett. Corbett, he felt, was a man of considerable talent, but, like Dorman-Smith one who would create intricate plans which were too complex to be administered by anyone except himself. Alexander knew that his C-in-C was aware of the general opinion of Corbett, but said this made no difference to Auchinleck's decision to employ Corbett at a high level. Undoubtedly Auchinleck's suggestion of Corbett as a temporary replacement for Ritchie weakened his standing with Churchill and Brooke.

Alexander also commented that Auchinleck seemed so anxious to avoid being 'blimpish' or limited in outlook that he tended to tolerate ideas and idiosyncrasies that others might have thought unrealistic. Believing in drive and innovation, Auchinleck was always hoping to find it in others. One of his great contributions to the war was the stimulus he gave to recruiting in India – where all service was voluntary – for he recruited successfully in areas like southern India which had not previously been used as recruiting areas.

Not least of Auchinleck's characteristics was his coolness in the face of danger. Alexander, as Military Assistant, accompanied his C-in-C nearly everywhere; his account of a memorable air trip which follows demonstrates that coolness, and Auchinleck's concern for those serving under him.

Early in 1941, or maybe before that, it was thought possible that the Germans might advance through the Caucasus and threaten India, and so it was decided to set up a defensive position west of Chaman in Baluchistan at the Kojak Pass. In June 1941 the C-in-C told me that he wanted to go to the Kojak to see how this project was proceeding and so I made the necessary arrangements. We were in Simla at the time and so had to go by train – to Ambala – and fly from there to Quetta.

Our party consisted of the C-in-C and General Francis Tuker who was Director of Military Training at that time and wanted to visit units in Quetta – also Captain Francis Stuart, ADC to the Chief, and myself.

We flew in a Lockheed aircraft which had been presented to the Govt of India by HH the Maharaja of Jodhpur, and the pilot was Flt-Lieut McMillan, a New Zealander who had represented that country in skiing, also a Flight Engineer.

The flight from Ambala to Quetta:

We took off from Ambala at 0700 hrs and were due to touch down at Quetta at 0900 hrs. It was very hot, there was considerable turbulence and a layer of ground haze.

We flew over the Punjab and northern Sind desert and then the western end of the NW Frontier hills, without incident.

I had brought a thermos flask with iced barley water and I handed this round at about 0800 hrs – it was particularly appreciated by Francis Stuart who was very upset by the turbulence and was very sick.

At about 0845 hrs the C-in-C who was sitting in the seat behind me leant forward and asked me if I could recognise any of the ground below us as he could not and he knew that area well. I also knew the area round Quetta and was unable to spot any of the features such as the mountain known as Murdah which should have been in sight by then. He then told me to go forward and ask McMillan where we were.

I suggested that McMillan might think that he was worried and that I should wait a few minutes – and he agreed.

After about five minutes I went in to the cockpit carrying my map and asked McMillan to show me where we were – and he said, 'I haven't the foggiest idea!' I went back and repeated this to the Chief who simply said, 'Oh hasn't he?' and settled back in his seat and appeared to go to sleep. General Tuker just laughed and my impression was that Francis Stuart was not interested.

I sat down and examined my own thoughts. There we were, about 12,000 feet up, over mountainous country and completely lost, HE the Commander-in-Chief, India and party. The maze seemed to increase. We would suddenly head straight in to a mountain-side and the unhappy pilot would pull us round in a steep bank – only to confront another mountain – and so it went on.

I pictured headlines in the papers in about a week's time. 'C-in-C's aircraft found at last by shepherds on such-and-such a mountain. All the party must have died instantly except the Military Assistant who had had a lingering death' and so on – would my wife be able to get a passage home?

I looked round – the C-in-C still appeared to be asleep, the Director of Military Training was still smiling and Francis the ADC was still clutching his unsavoury paper bag. I felt better and had another go at trying to recognise the ground beneath.

Time and evasive action went on. I had a rather hollow little chat with the pilot and then at about 1100 hrs we ran out of the mountains and over a desert. I shall always remember the relief, though it was short-lived, when I remembered that we had drunk the only liquid we had and so would now probably die of thirst.

I went forward to McMillan and together we peered down and almost together we spotted a railway line, and he shouted, 'I believe it is the Sind desert and we must be near Jacobadad.'

He was right and soon we were circling round over the railway station and a minute landing ground used almost solely by a civil plane flying once a week between Karachi and Lahore.

We touched down . . . with ten minutes' flying time of fuel left in the tanks. It was the the middle of June and the temperature was close on 120°.

From the Station Master's office I telephoned Quetta and got through to General Norton – of Everest fame – who was understandably very worried about us. I told him our story and said we hoped to be with him at 1500 hrs.

I sent for the clerk in charge of the fuel depot and asked him to supply petrol. He naturally questioned my authority and said the civil plane was the only aircraft he could refuel. However, with the temperature at 120°, and our recent experience, and the fact that the Jangi Lat Sahib was aboard, he soon gave up the struggle. The petrol was sent along in 2 gallon tins and it took a long time under those conditions to do the job but in the end it was done.

In the meantime the C-in-C was utterly unmoved. We took over the waiting room on the station and a Khitmutgar produced cold drinks. One bottle burst as the poor chap was opening it and cut his hand badly and we all had to buckle to to do first aid.

Soon after 1400 hrs I telephoned Quetta again that we were starting, and we then flew up the Bulan Pass and came in to land at about 1500 hrs. The landing ground there was a wretched little place on a slight slope, and we came in much too fast, poor McMillan must have been overcome with relief at seeing the end. He touched his brakes and one jammed and we spun round like a top – I landed on General Tuker's lap – he still laughed!

We were a rather untidy party that finally disembarked.

The C-in-C and I went with General Norton to his house and were taken up to our rooms. I sponged my face and felt better and then went in to see how my Chief was. He said, 'Do you think that McMillan is worried?' I replied that it was very probable, so he said, 'Get a car and go down and tell him from me that I think he did a damn fine job in getting us here and in such very bad conditions.'

I set off and arrived to find an utterly miserable McMillan standing looked at his aircraft. I told him why I had come and he gazed at me and said, 'Did he *really* say that?' and I said, 'Yes, he did, Mac. Cheer up.'

We stayed in Quetta for several days and then flew to the Zhob valley where we stayed a night, and from there flew back to Ambala. This too was a turbulent flight with some incidents, but as Kipling said, 'That's another story.'

I hope that what I have written will convey a little of what 'The Auk' is like and why we all loved him.

Lt-Col. E. W. Robinson-Horley, who was Comptroller of Auchinleck's Household in India from 1945–7, said: 'In all the time I knew him, and we had many long talks together, I never knew him say anything nasty about anyone in speech or in writing. We loved him. Admittedly he seemed to have lost interest at the end [after Partition] when the die was cast.' (The British officers and their families with the Indian Army made this comment too; they might have agreed with Montgomery that Auchinleck's main interest was with the Indians and not with the British still serving there. He was never unmindful of his British troops, however, as his comments at the time of the closure of Supreme HQ show.) Robinson-Horley describes Auchinleck as 'a shy and lonely man. If you talked to him he listened and he had that knack of being able to understand the unsaid word'; but he shared the view that Auchinleck did not choose subordinates wisely and, when people made mistakes, 'he covered up for them'. Auchinleck could converse freely with soldiers, with Indians as well as British, since he spoke Pushtu, Punjabi and Urdu fluently, among other languages. But he hated devious politicians and self-seekers, and was plainly ill at ease in his dealings with them.

As long as Auchinleck had work to do which interested him he did not need to relax, Robinson-Horley remembered. His tastes were spartan, but he would enjoy a drink with friends, would smoke a pipe (later changed for snuff), and would take a delight in childish games, like those played on Mess Dinner nights. ('Mess games' are a dangerous pastime sometimes indulged in after formal dinners, and expensive clothes are often damaged in rugger scrums, High Cockalorum, and other simple but strenuous activities. Sometimes a human pyramid is formed to enable members to write their names on the ceiling, while broken legs and arms are by no means unknown. Nobody would deny that Mess games are both childish and dangerous, but they are immensely amusing at the time and have the added virtue that pompous and strait-laced people, almost regardless of rank, have to prove they can be human, or suffer being sat upon more thoroughly than is the lot of their fellows. The following day dignity is reassumed, but tensions may have been relaxed, and there is perhaps a hint of better understanding all round.) Mrs Georgina Scott has memories of Auchinleck enjoying slightly less strenuous activities when she recalls the friendship between him and her husband in the early 1930s: 'Both men very ambitious and both very keen on squash.'

Auchinleck slept on a hospital bed – not a comfortable one – and would get up each day at 5.30, swim many lengths of his pool immediately after rising, and would often work till after midnight. Although he had ridden in earlier life, he seemed later to have lost any interest in horses he may have had. As C-in-C, India he was allotted two Cadillacs, but never used either: 'Far too ostentatious', he said, a view he held of many supposed benefits. On the floor of his office was a leopard-skin carpet, left by a predecessor. 'I must get rid of this,' he said to Robinson-Horley. 'It simply is not my sort of thing at all.'

Auchinleck was quick to see real needs. Lt-Col. Patrick Emerson wrote:

I came across the Auk a number of times in India but being very junior stood afar and looked on in awe. However, when he came down to the Indian Grenadiers Centre one time I was commanding the Boys' Company. This had been started as an experiment to try and concentrate on educating younger Indians from the villages so that when they moved on to be ordinary recruits they would be literate enough to handle the more sophisticated weapons that were being introduced. After he had had a good look around mine he asked if there was anything which would help to improve matters. I brashly said, 'Money', as I wished to equip a proper club for them. My Colonel gave me a horrified look and said, 'Of course not – a cup for boxing would be quite adequate.' The Auk said nothing and left. A couple of weeks later, a fine cup for boxing turned up in the Colonel's office with a note for me enclosed. In this was a personal cheque from the Auk for 1000 rupees with best wishes for the Boys' Club. Since then he has of course been one of my favourites.

Nothing was too much trouble, then or later. Kenneth Lewis, MP, wrote:

In 1962–3 Sir Claude came to Stamford, Lincs because an ordinary soldier called Conner asked him to do so. I think at some time during the war Conner was probably a batman to him.

He put on full dress uniform, sword, the lot, and reviewed the very small Armistice Day Parade in Stamford and went to the British Legion afterwards.

I thought that this gesture, his friendly willingness to talk to everybody and all the trouble taken by the Field-Marshal was greatly to his credit. And, of course, everyone in Stamford was delighted.

All his life Auchinleck had been sensitive to other people's feelings. Mrs Elizabeth Rogers wrote, with delightful frankness:

I met Field-Marshal Sir Claude Auchinleck in 1936 on board the SS *Mongolia* en route for India.

I had been sent to join the Fishing Fleet before being considered permanently on the shelf and was placed at the Captain's table so that he could keep a fatherly eye on me. [The 'Fishing Fleet' was the name given to the young women who were sent to India to visit relatives – and, more importantly, perhaps to meet a future husband.] The Field-Marshal, at that time the youngest General in the Indian Army, and his friend Colonel Vickers were seated next to me.

I have never forgotten how kind they were to someone so shy and inarticulate as I. They spent their evenings after dinner playing chess, insisting on my having a Guinness with them before I went to bed, as being good for me.

336

Another story comes from Mrs Anne Naylor:

During the winter of 1943–4 my greatest friend and I decided to do some carol singing for charity. We were then eleven and twelve and my father was an Engineer and hers Commander of the Viceroy's bodyguard. We gathered up about six other friends and determinedly plodded our way from house to house in New Delhi. We ended up at the tented officer's quarters outside the Commander-in-Chief's residence where we had a tolerable reception and were given suitable refreshment. Spurred on by this success, I boldly suggested we might go and sing to the Auk, as I had been told to call him. Everyone else was a bit apprehensive but, fired with lemonade, I marched them up the gravel drive to the imposing front door. It was opened by a servant. 'Fetch the Commander-in-Chief,' I ordered imperiously. The servant looked about fearfully and disappeared to come back with a young ADC. 'I say, you can't have the C-in-C,' he said. 'He's in his bath.'

'But he would love to hear us sing!'

'No, he wouldn't.'

'Yes, he would,' said another voice and with that the splendid figure of Field-Marshal [in fact, General] Sir Claude Auchinleck appeared, clad only in a bath towel.

'All right, sing,' he said. So we gave him the different carols.

'*Very* nice,' he said. 'What's it for?'

So we told him it was for Christmas for British soldiers and he gave us the then princely sum of ten rupees. 'Thank you very much,' he said politely. 'I think I had better go back to my bath.'

So we retreated rejoicing.

In the charitable spirit of modern times, which defines almost every disinterested activity as having dubious underlying motivation, it has been suggested that Auchinleck's interest in Boys' Companies and Boys' Clubs must represent homosexual tendencies, even if only repressed ones. It is impossible, and pointless, to argue with those who believe that all schoolmasters, scoutmasters, soldiers, sailors, airmen or clerics possess such tendencies – the pseudo-psychologists will merely point to the few homosexuals who have moved adroitly in these fields and instance them as proof that everyone must be the same. If a man claims to be wholly heterosexual, and to have his thoughts totally occupied with carnal desire for the opposite sex, this carries no conviction: clearly he is either 'ambidextrous' or is trying to sublimate his homosexuality.

Some of Auchinleck's friends, particularly in the artistic world, were homosexual, and one acquaintance used openly to boast about it – to Auchinleck's embarrassment. But no one, man or woman, who knew Auchinleck well regarded the suggestion that he might be homosexual as anything but ludicrous nonsense. Ambitious, fond of his own appearance perhaps, but definitely not homosexual.

However, although he was greatly admired by women, and very much enjoyed their company, sex did not enter into this either; he regarded them as pretty decoration. While married he had eyes for no one but his wife, and no scandal was ever attached to him; subsequently, in his sixties, he settled back quietly into a bachelor existence.

They had no children; Auchinleck used to say that the memory of the hard struggle his mother had had to bring up her family made him decide not to have children for at least ten years after he married. His own parents had not had a child for ten years and then, when his mother had been widowed eight years later, it had been difficult enough; to have had children earlier and to have left a widow to bring them up on what would have been an even more meagre pension would have been an unwarrantable risk. But eventually, for Auchinleck himself, there were to be no children, and in those days there could be no doubt as to where the blame for that must lie; it could not possibly be with the male.

Of the three hammer blows Auchinleck received, the loss of his wife to a friend was the most shattering. The marriage had always been happy, and Jessie had always stood by her husband, but for Auchinleck it had never been a passion. When he had been dismissed from Middle East Command in 1942 and returned to India he had little to do for some ten months, and – although he did not show it – was depressed; but his wife helped him to appear indifferent to the great setback his career had sustained.

Three years later, however, his marriage ended when, in a blaze of unexpected publicity, Jessie went off with Air Chief Marshal Sir Richard Peirse, Allied Air C-in-C for SE Asia Command in 1943-4. Peirse was sixty-two, almost the same age as Auchinleck, and had been C-in-C Bomber Command in 1940-2 and AOC-in-C, India in 1942-3. He had won a DSO and AFC in the First World War when he served with the RNAS and RFC on fronts from France to the Dardanelles, and had gained the nickname 'Lucky Peirse', though some said it should have been 'Plucky Peirse' from his skill in dog-fights. As C-in-C, Bomber Command, he had been criticised, however, for the raid against Berlin in November 1941, when the RAF lost thirty-seven aircraft. He too had his clashes with Churchill, and indeed protested to the Prime Minister when he heard that Auchinleck was about to lose the Middle Eastern Command. He and Jessie were married after Auchinleck's divorce was granted in 1946.

When the marriage broke up there was sympathy for both but little surprise. For years their friends had noted that Auchinleck's overriding interest was in the Army, and principally the Indian Army. He was a dedicated soldier, and when it was suggested that life might be easier for him if he had Jessie with him in the Middle East he brushed off the suggestion. He had not the time then for a social life, something which in any case he found rather irritating. He enjoyed his home life, but considered it to come second to his job, and there can be little doubt that he took stability at home, and his wife's presence, rather for granted.

In retrospect, it seems that the outcome was inevitable. There was that attractive Richard Peirse with an eye for a lively, beautiful woman (and Jessie was very beautiful), and there was the wife left to her own devices, without children and with no duties to speak of. Earlier in the war she had fried eggs for the troops in the canteen in Delhi, driven in convoys, and stripped down engines, as a sergeant in the Woman's Auxiliary Corps of India; she refused a commission. She enjoyed the society of men but had never slept with anyone except Auchinleck; she remained equally faithful to Peirse (who died in 1970), although the same could not be said of him.

Auchinleck and Jessie never met again, but she retains a very great affection for him. When she met Peirse she fell in love with him, and that was that, though she hated the idea of hurting her husband. But, for Auchinleck, his wife's departure came at a difficult time, and was further complicated by the publicity, by his friendship with Peirse, and by the fact that he almost certainly had no inkling of its imminence. The blow to his pride must have been considerable; his sister, Cherry, said he was never the same after Jessie left him. In later years Auchinleck would never speak of the break-up of his marriage, but Lt-Col. Robinson-Horley believed he had been deeply hurt, and even after the divorce he always carried a photograph of Jessie in his wallet. When the time came for his departure from India, and he went round the house deciding what to take and what to leave, he noted among some of his choicest possessions gifts to him from world leaders or maharajahs. Those which his wife had particularly liked he arranged should be sent on to her.

When a man reaches the top of his profession the question is usually asked: 'How did he do it?' Sometimes the factors contributing to success are all too obvious: ruthlessness, influence, a taste for intrigue, luck, and driving ambition. Auchinleck does not seem to have possessed any of these, apart from ambition, but without doubt he had recognisable merit. For his performance in the field he was awarded a DSO and received six Mentions in Despatches 'for gallant and distinguished service'. He placed no value on the certificates of these honours, most of which he burnt when he left England.

In 1977 Major Alex Greenwood, who had been Auchinleck's longest-serving ADC, and who had later done much to help him with financial activities, after the Field-Marshal retired, felt very strongly that Auchinleck's enormous contribution to victory in the Second World War merited further recognition. He therefore wrote to Mountbatten, and received the following reply:

Dear Greenwood,

Thank you for your letter of the 26th October with the interesting suggestion that a further honour should be given Field-Marshal Sir Claude Auchinleck.

I think the situation has been terribly complicated by his absolute refusal to receive either a Peerage or any other honour which I offered him at the end of my time as Viceroy. We remain very good friends but he has explained to me that he would be grateful if I would not try and get him any further honour which he would certainly have to reject.

In some ways therefore I am the last person in the world who could resurrect the idea of an honour.

However, I shall be attending the Service and luncheon for the members of the Order of Merit with the Queen on the 17th November and I will make some very discreet inquiries as to whether there is any possibility of backtracking to get him an OM. If there is any sign that this is feasible I will certainly follow it up but if there is any difficulty about it I know that 'The Auk' himself would hate me to do anything further about it.

Will you please therefore leave it with me and if it looks at all possible I will get in touch with you again. But if clearly I can't help any further I am sure you will forgive me for not bothering you again.

Yours sincerely
Mountbatten of Burma

The question of further awards was never raised again, and the man who had held four vital posts during the Second World War received less public recognition than might have been expected. He did, of course, refuse a peerage. Had that peerage been offered to him directly by King George VI or Queen Elizabeth II he would have accepted, whatever his feelings about India. But to receive the offer from a go-between such as Attlee or Mountbatten made it unacceptable, for in his mind it was linked with the premature partition of India. He did not see it as an acknowledgement of his services in Norway, in Southern Command, in the Middle East or as the driving force behind the Indian war effort. For those he felt he was adequately rewarded by the rank of Field-Marshal, which he had earned in the service.

At the age of ninety-six, when this book was finished, Auchinleck had outlived friends and enemies – Montgomery, Mountbatten, Churchill, Seago, Peirse – and even his own memory of them. He was still, in January 1981, very well, though deaf; he still enjoyed a walk to his favourite café, a look at a newspaper, some friends to talk to. Although extremely old, he was still dignified and distinguished.

There is no doubt that this was a great man, not entirely without faults, but worthier of fame than many better-known soldiers. He could have won Waterloo, or Blenheim, or Naseby; he could have won the Italian and Normandy battles in 1943 and 1944. But he won his share of the vital battles of his war, of his time. The only battle he lost was for his own fulfilment.

I have done the state some Service and they know't.
                    (*Othello* Act V, Scene ii)

APPENDIX A

LESSONS OF
THE TIRAH CAMPAIGN

In the Tirah campaign of 1897 many lessons were learnt by the Indian Army. Tirah is the mountainous area to the south-west of the Peshawar valley. The region was peopled by two Pathan tribes, the Afridis and the Orakzais, who boasted that their region had never been penetrated by an invader; together, they numbered about 60,000 tribesmen, In 1897 they began raiding outside their own area and captured a number of frontier posts. It was clear that these raids would continue, penetrate more deeply into India and destroy more and more property. In 1897 Colonel C. E. Callwell published this appreciation of them (and others' in his *Lesson from the Tirah Campaign*:

All tribesmen of the North-West Frontier can be classed as exceptionally fine mountaineers but the Afridis are pre-eminent in this respect. Their grass shoes and their agility enable them to move with astonishing rapidity over the most rugged ground and they enjoy the advantage of being acquainted with every goat-track leading through their territory. Like most savages they can see far better in the dark than Europeans can, which renders them particularly formidable at night. The Pathans in general are admirable marksmen even when depending on indifferent firearms: but the Afridis in 1897 owned large numbers of modern rifles, their wealth enabling them to purchase these weapons in the bazaars of Afghanistan and the Punjab and they had an abundance of ammunition in their possession. Moreover, many of the Afridis and Orakzais had served in the Indian Army and fully understood its tactical methods. A great advantage which these hillmen furthermore enjoy in combat is that quite apart from the aptitude which they invariably display for concealing themselves their presence is difficult to detect owing to the colour of their dirty garments being industinguishable from that of the crags and boulders amongst which they lurk. Capable of living for several days on the grain which he is able to carry with him, the Pathan is less encumbered than the regular soldier is with impediments to his movements. And there is also another respect in which disciplined troops are always severely handicapped during struggles with these marauding cut-throats.

In civilised warfare the dead and wounded can be left on the field of battle. But in Indian frontier campaigns, as in most cases of contest with irregular warriors, the wounded may not be abandoned to the tender mercies of the foe; and as it is the practice of these ferocious adversaries to dishonour the dead those who have fallen have to be carried off if it be possible. It takes four men to carry a wounded comrade and another man to carry the weapons of the party so that a single badly wounded soldier may mean the loss of six rifles out of the firing line, and that a heavy casualty list in some detachment speedily deprives it of its fighting power. The knot of men carrying an injured comrade, moreover, offers an easy mark to the hostile marksmen of which they are apt to take full advantage, so that one casualty tends to beget others.

Callwell further described the tribesmen as 'endowed with that cunning which no amount of training will instil into the soldier recruited in a civilised country.'

Contrary to general belief, the region was not hot but 'the climate is very severe in the winter time when the whole region is generally covered with snow for some weeks.' Many of the Indian Army's successes on the Frontier and elsewhere were owed to the valuable, if hard, experience gained in campaigns such as this. The rules learned were applied for many years to come; even with the advent of aircraft, tanks and wireless Auchinleck's actions in 1933 and 1935, and arguably in Norway, would have been based upon the rules laid down for warfare against the tribesmen Callwell depicted.

APPENDIX B

WELLINGTON COLLEGE

Auchinleck, his brother Leslie, and his future brother-in-law, Chenevix Baldwin, were all on the Foundation (i.e. educated for £10 a year) at Wellington, as were eighty-five other Foundationers at the time. He was always very proud of his connection with Wellington, and frequently wore the Old Wellingtonian tie in Marrakech. (He did not wear a tie in the hot weather, but at other times of the year he wore either the school tie or the tie of his former regiment.)

In 1962 a classroom at Wellington was converted into an exhibition room and named the Auchinleck Room. There is one picture in the room, the portrait by James Gunn, showing Auchinleck seated, full face, wearing battledress and medal ribbons.

Among the books which Auchinleck presented to Wellington is *The Call to Honour* by Charles de Gaulle. It is inscribed in de Gaulle's own handwriting: 'Au Field Marshal Sir Claude Auchinleck en souvenir et avec les meilleurs voeux de C. de Gaulle – 9 novembre 1955.'

THE IMPERIAL
DEFENCE COLLEGE

At the time of the fiftieth anniversary of the founding of the IDC, in 1977, Maj.-Gen. A. E. Younger, DSO was the Army Instructor. Auchinleck, as one of the first-termers, visited the College, and General Younger asked him: 'What was it like in those days?' 'It was all Dill,' answered the Field-Marshal. 'How do you mean – all Dill?' 'Well, Dill was the Chief Instructor and with his tremendous energy and drive dominated and directed the course which made it a great success.' Dill later became Chief of the Imperial General Staff.

For the anniversary a medal was struck with Churchill's head on it. This recognised that the College owed its formation to Churchill's inspiration. He felt that the students, who were all people likely to achieve very high rank and therefore to take decisions affecting the lives of many outside the Services, must be given a full understanding of the implications of all the decisions they took. The course emphasised the fact that the Services were part of the general community, not something apart.

THE EL ALAMEIN POSITION

From Mr Norman Clark to the author, June 1980:

I cannot claim to have had any close or personal contact with Auchinleck, but as the *News Chronicle*'s war correspondent in the Desert during the Gazala battle I had longish conversations with him on two occasions – the first, and the more significant, being on the 'black day' of Saturday, June 13.

I write to you because I feel this, the 'watershed' of The Auk's career, deserves fuller expatiation than it got in Connell's book. Perhaps the release you mention in your letter to the 'Telegraph' of more official papers now make this possible.

The fact of the matter is that I have never been able to reconcile what Connell wrote in his 'Battle of the Cauldron' chapter with what The Auk told me at Gambut that June day.

With another correspondent I had gone back to Army HQ to hand in our day's dispatches for the liaison flight to Cairo. When The Auk heard we were about – we were unaware he had come up to the Desert – he asked to see us. There, on a barren waste of sand away from the small collection of ACVs that were Ritchie's HQ and with only his ADC in attendance he told us the full implications of the tank debacle of the previous day. It was clear from what he said that he had already weighed up the contingencies. In brief he said he had two options:

1. If (which he explained he did not expect to happen) Rommel, as in April, 1941, split his army into two groups – one to attack Tobruk and the other to pursue us back to the frontier wire running South from Sollum – we would allow Tobruk to be invested and re-group on the frontier with the main part of Eighth Army. Since it was self-evident the Navy no longer had the strength to maintain a supply line to the

garrison from Alex, Tobruk would have to withstand a siege for a month or so when we would advance again from the frontier to its relief.

2. But the Auk said he did not expect Rommel to make the same mistake twice, he would undoubtedly attack Tobruk with his full resources and so reduce it that the garrison had to surrender. Rommel would in any case need Tobruk as his main supply port for the invasion of Egypt. Tobruk taken, Rommel would then advance on the Delta.

All this seemed to us the acme of clear-mindedness.

We asked: If Rommel did develop his advantage this way presumably we could hold him on the frontier. Oh no, said Auchinleck, our armour had been so badly 'savaged' in The Cauldron battle of the day before that we had fewer than 50 'runners' and Rommel would have the upper hand for some time to come. No, The Auk explained, if things turned out the way he had outlined we had no option but to fight a rearguard action to Alamein. Alamein? We had never heard of it. Somewhere around Mersa Matruh perhaps? No, the C-in-C said, at this point asking his ADC to go back to his car for his map-case. And there, amid the desolation of the windless desert, the map was unfolded on the sand at our feet. The Auk's finger showed the line of retreat ... back ... back ... into Egypt ... to Alamein.

We were aghast at the import of this plan. Then, with the Auk's help, we recalled the concrete bunkers North of the Desert road that we had passed so often without giving them a thought on our way to the front from the Delta.

It was obvious to us then that, in the circumstances The Auk had detailed, Tobruk could not hold out. But, if the Eighth Army was not to be overwhelmed and the Delta fall into Axis hands, the fall-back to Alamein made consummate good sense – Rommel's supply line would be inordinately stretched and our own l. of c. shortened to some 60 miles or so from the Delta dumps and workshops. We could clearly reinforce our line at many times the rate Rommel could strengthen his.

In the Delta were the Grants and the 17-pounder anti-tank guns Churchill had told the Commons were already involved in the Gazala fighting – but which we, as correspondents, knew had amounted to only a token few.

After this briefing we felt buoyed up – this was the way Libya would be won. Stretch Rommel and break him on ground of our own choosing, bring him on to our anvil and use the sledge-hammer. The Desert where the campaign for Africa had been fought so far was neutral ground and gave little military advantage to whichever side held it – unless it could be crossed, Tripoli taken, Malta sustained, and the Mediterranean opened.

With the plan outlined to us it can be said that The Auk saved Africa, lost a battle to win a campaign.

Here, however, comes my difficulty. The Auk's written signals to Churchill and Ritchie nowhere seem to conform to the thinking he had vouchsafed to us and which, as things developed, was so clearly the intended course he had then already decided to follow. This begs the question whether The Auk deliberately kept Churchill in the dark as to his full intentions. I believe there is good evidence that he did.

Relations between Auchinleck and Churchill were never good; the PM at this time seems to have withdrawn any confidence that The Auk was the man to beat Rommel, and The Auk for his part resented Winnie's attempts to dictate the way the Desert Campaign should be fought. As The Auk told David Dimbleby in the BBC's 'The Auk at 90' interview in June, 1974: 'Churchill didn't know how things were on the ground; I did.'

Only by concluding that The Auk kept his full intentions from Churchill, fearing perhaps that he would have command of the Middle East forces taken from him at a critical time, does Churchill's 'astonishment' make sense when Roosevelt handed him in Washington the telegram that Tobruk had surrendered with 25,000 men. 'This was so surprising,' Churchill says in 'The Second World War', 'that I could not believe it.' If the Prime Minister had been in the picture as much as two war correspondents had been for a week he would have expected the news – though perhaps not so soon.

Rommel had attacked Tobruk with his full forces but the garrison, before surrender, destroyed the supplies that had been built up there for use in the advance into Tripolitania should the Gazala battle have gone our way.

In the same Dimbleby interview The Auk answers with great candour three questions about Tobruk:

Dimbleby: Was it really necessary to make such a fuss about the holding of Tobruk? The Auk: Not in my opinion, no.

Dimbleby: Why was it made then? The Auk: I don't know.

Dimbleby: It was Churchill who wanted Tobruk held? The Auk: Yes. As far as I was concerned it had no strategic value at all.

All along, it seems to me, The Auk did not have the holding of Tobruk in any of his plans. His Operation Instruction 110 ... says: 'It is not my intention to try to hold, permanently, Tobruk or any other locality West of the frontier.' Was this Instruction ever brought to Churchill's attention by the CIGS? Yet on June 15 Churchill writes to The Auk '... glad to have your assurances that you have no intention of giving up Tobruk.'

There are numerous other references in Connell's book to double-think between The Auk and Churchill, particularly at the time of Gazala and Tobruk, and I think the subject should be gone into more deeply in the light of later official releases.

It may be that Churchill was feigning his 'astonishment' in Washington in order to wring more supplies for the Middle East from Roosevelt, though I am inclined to think not. I have such a clear recollection of my June 13 encounter with Auchinleck that I feel my interpretation that The Auk deliberately deceived Churchill is the more likely one.

I hope these few notes may help you to render a more complete account of The Auk during those days.

A CORRESPONDENCE
IN *THE TIMES*

After the publication of *The Times* obituary of Auchinleck (25 March 1981), which was unsigned, Field-Marshal Lord Carver wrote a letter commenting on its account of General Ritchie's conduct of the Gazala battle. In particular, he objected to the phrase 'General Ritchie disregarded Auchinleck's advice to hold back the armour and concentrate it in a counter-attack against Rommel and instead dissipated his armour in penny packets, enabling Rommel to destroy it'. Lord Carver felt that this was unfair to Ritchie, and said: 'The fact that Norrie's armoured brigades were not concentrated in time to meet it [the main thrust] was no fault of Ritchie's. The blame for it must be shared between Generals Norrie, Messervy and Lumsden.' He added, 'Ritchie faced many handicaps, not the least of which was having his Commander-in-Chief constantly breathing down his neck both before and during the battle'.

The letter was answered by Mr Correlli Barnett, from the Faculty of History at Cambridge, who drew attention to the account in the official history.

Lord Carver responded by suggesting that 'instead of relying on the summary in the official history', Mr Barnett should 're-read the full correspondence between the two generals'.

Mr Barnett, who was probably familiar with this correspondence, did not reply, and the last word was spoken by Colonel Lord Clifford:

> As at the time a mere major and commanding, due to deaths and wounds, the remnants of the support group to 22nd Armoured Brigade at the battle of the 'Devil's Cauldron' (June 5/6, 1942), I make bold to say that the consensus of opinion, discussed *ad nauseam* as PoWs, was that the generals inviting criticism were Ritchie and Messervy. Auchinleck and Lumsden were never faulted.
>
> In an earlier prewar existence as a subaltern in northern India I recollect the awe in which Auchinleck was then held as the only general who could give a complete divisional commander's orders without using a note.

THE AUCHINLECK–EADON
CORRESPONDENCE

Between 1967 and 1977 Auchinleck corresponded with Nicholas Piers Eadon, who was a friend of the family. Mr Eadon asked Auchinleck who had been the greatest influence on the Field-Marshal's life. The mention of Liddell Hart is particularly interesting, since Rommel would have been familiar with the Liddell Hart theories of tank warfare.

But Auchinleck refused to be drawn about Montgomery. All he would say of him was 'he was a very fine soldier and leader, as all the world knows'.

[Beccles, Suffolk]   15th May 1967

Dear Sir
    Your letter of May 13th. You ask two quite distinct questions! Both are almost unanswerable! But in my days as a young officer in India sixty and more years ago and then between the two World Wars, I should say that Colonel Henderson author of 'Stonewall Jackson, a Confederate general in the American Civil War', and Captain Sir Basil Liddell Hart did more than any one else to form my outlook on my profession as a soldier. Your other question as to influences on my life is really too complex! First of all, of course my mother who I think did much to form my character, for better or for worse! But, really at the age of nearly 83, so many people have come into and gone out of my life that I can not give any reasonable answer to this one!
                            Sorry to be so unhelpful
                                Your sincerely
                                C. J. Auchinleck

[Beccles, Suffolk]   18th May 1967

Dear Mr Eadon
    Thank you for your letter of the 16th – *Basil Liddell Hart*. Because he, after the First World War, really gave a tremen-

dous impetus to the study of tactics and especially to the training of infantry. His influence was most remarkable and affected, in my opinion, the whole outlook and training of the Army. I should have added Clausewitz to my list of mentors. His writings and 'dicta' had a great influence on my thinking fifty years ago and I had a notebook full of quotations from his writings! As to July 2nd 1942, I am an interested party and it is not for me to say! Sorry!!

Yours sincerely
C. J. Auchinleck

3 Villa Rikichou   6.6.79
Rue Hafid Ibrahim
Marrakech
Morocco

Dear Nicholas

Thank you your note of 28th May, received to-day.

I am very well thank you and still active in spite of my approaching 93rd birthday – on June 21st!

I am sorry but I am now too [sic] old to have accurate memories of meetings with Winston Churchill or any else [sic]! Of course, I have a personal view of Montgomery but it remains personal. He was a very fine soldier & leader as all the world knows. I really can not tell you what important decisions I had to make about the 8th Army. You will have to decide for yourself!! These questions which you so kindly put to me are for people like *you* to answer, not for me. So please forgive me . . . I hope all is well with you.

Yours sincerely
C. J. Auchinleck

SOURCES AND BIBLIOGRAPHY

In a biography such as this there seemed little virtue in breaking up the flow of the narrative by annotating the sources. Quoted extracts, other than those from the books listed in the bibliography below and from the individuals acknowledged in the Introduction, are from the Auchinleck Papers, held in the John Rylands Library, University of Manchester, and from the following documents in the Public Record Office, London: CAB 65, CAB 66, CAB 69, CAB 79, CAB 80, CAB 88, CAB 105, WO 106, WO 199, FO 921, AIR 16, AIR 22, PREM 3.

PUBLISHED SOURCES

Agar-Hamilton, J. A. I. and L. C. F. Turner, *The Sidi Rezeg Battles 1941* (London, 1952)

Alexander, Field-Marshal Lord, *The Alexander Memoirs 1940–1945* (London, 1962)

Ash, Bernard, *Norway 1940* (London, 1964)

Bailey, Lt-Col. F. M., *No Passport to Tibet* (London, 1937)

Barker, A. J., *Townshend of Kut* (London, 1967)

Barnett, Correlli, *The Desert Generals* (London, 1960)

Bryant, Arthur, *The Alanbrooke War Diaries:* Vol I, *The Turn of the Tide, 1939–1943* and Vol II, *Triumph in the West, 1943–1945* (London 1957 and 1959)

Callwell, Colonel C. E., *Lesson from the Tirah Campaign* (London, 1897)

—— *Tirah, 1897* (London, 1911)

Calvocoressi, Peter, *Top Secret Ultra* (London, 1980)

Carver, Field-Marshal Sir Michael (Ed.), *The War Lords* (London, 1976)

Chalfont, Lord, *Montgomery of Alamein* (London, 1976)

Churchill, Winston S., *The Second World War*, Vols I, II, III, IV (London, 1948–51)

Collier, Basil, *The Defence of the United Kingdom* (London, 1957)

Connell, John, *Auchinleck: A Critical Biography* (London, 1959)

Crimp, R. L., *The Diary of a Desert Rat* (London, 1971)

Dean, Sir Maurice, *The Royal Air Force and Two World Wars* (London, 1979)

De Guingand, Maj.-Gen. Sir Francis, *Generals at War* (London, 1964)

—— *Operation Victory* (London, 1947)

Derry, T. K., *The Campaign in Norway* (London, 1950)

Elliott, Maj.-Gen. J. G., *A Roll of Honour: The Story of the Indian Army 1939–1945* (London, 1965)

Fergusson, Bernard, *Beyond the Chindwin* (London, 1945)

Golant, William, *The Long Afternoon: British India 1601–1947* (London, 1965)

Hamilton, Nigel, *Monty: The Making of a General 1887–1942* (London, 1981)

Harrer, Heinrich, *Seven Years in Tibet* (London, 1953)

Hunt, Sir David, *A Don at War* (London, 1966)

Irving, David, *The Trail of the Fox: The Life of Field-Marshal Erwin Rommel* (London, 1977)

Lewin, Ronald, *Churchill as Warlord* (London, 1973)

—— *Montgomery as Military Commander* (London, 1971)

—— *Slim the Standardbearer* (London, 1976)

—— *Ultra Goes to War* (London, 1978)

Liddell Hart, Sir Basil H., *The History of the First World War* (London, 1970)

—— *The History of the Second World War* (London, 1970)

—— (Ed.) *The Rommel Papers* (London, 1953)

Lucas Phillips, Brigadier C. E., *Alamein* (London, 1962)

Mason, Philip, *A Matter of Honour: An Account of the Indian Army, its Officers and Men* (London, 1974)

McMunn, Lt-Gen. Sir G. and Captain Cyril Falls, *Military Operations in Egypt and Palestine to 1917* (London, 1928)

Mehta, Ved, *Mahatma Gandhi and his Apostles* (London, 1977)

Mellenthin, Maj.-Gen. Friedrich W. von, *Panzer Battles 1939–45* (London, 1955)

Moberley, Brig.-Gen. F. J., *The Campaign in Mesopotamia*, Vols I and II (London, 1924)

Montgomery, Bernard L., *The Memoirs of Field-Marshal the Viscount Montgomery of Alamein* (London, 1958)

Montgomery, Brian, *A Field-Marshal in the Family* (London, 1973)

Moulton, J. L., *The Norwegian Campaign of 1940* (London, 1960)

Official History of Operations on the North-West Frontier of India 1936–7 (New Delhi, 1943)

Parkinson, Roger, *The Auk: Auchinleck, Victor at Alamein* (London, 1977)

Pitt, Barrie, *The Crucible of War: Western Desert 1941* (London, 1980)

Playfair, Maj.-Gen. I. S. O. and others, *The Mediterranean and Middle East*, Vols II and III (London, 1960)

Prendergast, John, *Prender's Progress: A Soldier in India 1931–1947* (London, 1979)

Qureshi, Major Mohammed Ibrahim, *The First Punjabis* (Aldershot, 1958)

Rhodes James, Richard, *Chindit* (London, 1980)

Slim, Field-Marshal Sir William, *Defeat Into Victory* (London, 1956)

Spear, Percival, *The Oxford History of Modern India 1740–1975* (Oxford, 1978 edn)

Taylor, A. J. P., *English History 1914–1945* (London, 1965)

—— *The Second World War: an Illustrated History* (London, 1975)

Terraine, John, *The Life and Times of Lord Mountbatten* (London, 1968)

—— *The Smoke and the Fire: Myths and Anti-Myths of War 1861–1945* (London, 1980)

Woodburn Kirby, Maj.-Gen. S., *The War Against Japan*, Vol II (London, 1958)

Young, Brigadier Desmond, *Rommel* (London, 1950)

Young, Brigadier Peter, *World War 1939–1945* (London, 1966)

—— and Brigadier Michael Calvert (Eds), *A Dictionary of Battles 1816–1976* (London, 1977)

INDEX

357

363

Barbara Riefe

SO WICKED THE HEART

Snatched from safety and her husband's harbouring
arms by the lawless corsairs of Algiers, fiery but tender
Lorna Singleton is forced to obey a pirate captain's
bold lusts. But Ahmed's animal passion does not lack
barbaric splendour. As a Christian slave in brutal
Muslim hands, Lorna must find a protector to save her
from the torment and degradation that awaits her in
the casbah . . . even if the price of salvation is her
virtue.

SO WICKED THE HEART is a gale-force story of
surging passion and turbulent love, an unabashed tale
of a woman's struggle to defend the storm-wracked
fortress of her heart against an onslaught of
unparalleled savagery and betrayal.

HISTORICAL ROMANCE   0 7221 7363 6   £1.95

WILL

The remarkable autobiography of

G. GORDON LIDDY

WHAT MADE LIDDY KEEP SILENCE WHEN HIS
FELLOW WATERGATE CONSPIRATORS WERE
PREPARED TO TALK? WHAT MADE LIDDY
PREPARED TO KILL E. HOWARD HUNT AND
NEWSPAPER COLUMNIST JACK ANDERSON?
WHAT MADE LIDDY OFFER TO BE
ASSASSINATED? WHAT MAKES HIM SUCH AN
EXTRAORDINARY MAN?
READ *WILL* AND YOU'LL FIND OUT . . .

G. Gordon Liddy's refusal to talk about his role
in Watergate resulted in a prison sentence of
twenty years. After serving nearly five years,
President Carter reduced Liddy's sentence. Now
Liddy is a free man. And now he is prepared to
reveal the truth.

'What is most striking about WILL is what it
reveals about the kind of man who will do
anything to stop those he sees as his country's
enemies' *Time*

AUTOBIOGRAPHY   0 7221 5550 6   £1.75

A selection of bestsellers from SPHERE

FICTION

PALOMINO	Danielle Steel	£1.75 □
CALIFORNIA DREAMERS	Norman Bogner	£1.75 □
NELLA	John Godey	£1.75 □
RAILROAD	Graham Masterton	£2.75 □
HAND-ME-DOWNS	Rhea Kohan	£1.75 □

FILM & TV TIE-INS

WHOSE LIFE IS IT ANYWAY?	David Benedictus	£1.25 □
FORT APACHE, THE BRONX	Heywood Gould	£1.75 □
ON THE LINE	Anthony Minghella	£1.25 □
SHARKY'S MACHINE	William Diehl	£1.75 □
FIREFOX	Craig Thomas	£1.75 □

NON-FICTION

YOUR CHILD AND THE ZODIAC	Teri King	£1.50 □
THE PAPAL VISIT	Timothy O'Sullivan	£2.50 □
THE SURVIVOR	Jack Eisner	£1.75 □
THE COUNTRY DIARY OF AN EDWARDIAN LADY	Edith Holden	£4.50 □
OPENING UP	Geoff Boycott	£1.75 □

All Sphere books are available at your local bookshop or newsagent, or can be ordered direct from the publisher. Just tick the titles you want and fill in the form below.

Name _____

Address _____

_____

Write to Sphere Books, Cash Sales Department, P.O. Box 11, Falmouth, Cornwall TR10 9EN

Please enclose a cheque or postal order to the value of the cover price plus:

UK: 45p for the first book, 20p for the second book and 14p for each additional book ordered to a maximum charge of £1.63.

OVERSEAS: 75p for the first book plus 21p per copy for each additional book.

BFPO & EIRE: 45p for the first book, 20p for the second book plus 14p per copy for the next 7 books, thereafter 8p per book.

Sphere Books reserve the right to show new retail prices on covers which may differ from those previously advertised in the text or elsewhere, and to increase postal rates in accordance with the PO.